AQA English Language and Literature A

AS

Exclusively endorsed by AQA

Marilyn Banks
Lizzie Bell

Series editor
Chris Purple

 Nelson Thornes

Published in 2008 by:
Nelson Thornes Ltd
Delta Place
27 Bath Road
CHELTENHAM
GL53 7TH
United Kingdom

08 09 10 11 12 / 10 9 8 7 6 5 4 3 2 1

A catalogue record for this book is available from the British Library

ISBN 978 0 7487 9960 2

Cover photograph/illustration: Photolibrary/Photodisc
Page make-up by Pantek Arts Ltd, Maidstone
Printed and bound in Slovenia by Korotan-Ljubljana Ltd

Contents

AQA introduction

Nelson Thornes and AQA

Nelson Thornes has worked in collaboration with AQA to ensure that this book offers you the best support for your AS or A level course and helps you to prepare for your exams. The partnership means that you can be confident that the range of learning, teaching and assessment practice materials has been checked by the senior examining team at AQA before formal approval, and is closely matched to the requirements of your specification.

Blended learning

Printed and electronic resources are blended: this means that links between topics and activities between the book and the electronic resources help you to work in the way that best suits you and enable extra support to be provided online. For example, you can test yourself online and feedback from the test will direct you back to the relevant parts of the book.

Electronic resources are available in a simple-to-use online platform called Nelson Thornes learning space. If your school or college has a licence to use the service, you will be given a password through which you can access the materials through any internet connection.

Icons in this book indicate where there is material online related to that topic. We are constantly developing new online resources for this subject so check the learning space for updates. The following icons are used:

Learning activity

These resources include a variety of interactive and non-interactive activities to support your learning.

Progress tracking

These resources enable you to analyse and understand examination questions (On your marks…).

Research support

These resources include WebQuests, in which you are assigned a task and provided with a range of web links to use as source material for research.

Study skills

These resources support you in developing a skill that is key for your course, for example planning essays.

Analysis tool

These resources help you to analyse key texts and images by providing questions and prompts to focus your response.

When you see an icon, go to Nelson Thornes learning space at **www.nelsonthornes.com/aqagce**, enter your access details and select your course. The materials are arranged in the same order as the topics in the book, so you can easily find the resources you need.

How to use this book

This book covers the specification for your course and is arranged in a sequence approved by AQA. The introduction to the book explains what will be required of you as an English Language and Literature student. The book is divided into two units and each unit into two sections. Each section will prepare you for a certain type of question in your examination. Unit 1 covers integrated analysis and text production: Section A will guide you in developing analytical and critical approaches to the set texts; Section B is designed to help you with creative writing inspired by stimulus texts. Unit 2 is about analysing speech and its representation: Section A covers varieties of spoken English to prepare you for writing about unseen speech extracts in the exam; Section B relates these features to the speech and style in the set texts. At the end of each section there is support on preparing for the type of examination questions discussed.

The features in this book include:

Learning objectives

At the beginning of each chapter you will find a list of learning objectives that contain targets linked to the requirements of the specification.

Key terms

Terms that you will need to be able to define and understand. These terms are coloured blue in the textbook and their definitions also appear in the glossary at the end of this book.

Research point

Suggestions for further research to enhance your studies and develop the kind of thinking that will help you achieve the highest grades in your English Language and Literature A course.

Link

Links to other areas in the textbook, or in your experience from GCSE, which are relevant to what you are reading.

Think about it

Short activities that encourage reflection.

Practical activity

Activities to develop skills, knowledge and understanding that will prepare you for assessment in English Language and Literature A.

Critical response activity

Activities that focus on a specific extract to develop skills relevant to your assessment in the examination.

AQA Examiner's tip

Hints from AQA examiners to help you with your study and to prepare you for your exam.

Examiner's comments

Examples of ways in which examiners evaluate work using the assessment objectives and mark scheme.

Sample responses

Examples of answers from students. These do not necessarily represent responses that would gain the highest grades, so you will need to look at them alongside the examiner's comments.

Commentary

Examples of answers you might give to the activities. These are designed to help you to understand what type of response the examiner is looking for, not to tell you the answer. There are many equally valid responses, so you will find this book most helpful if you try the activity yourself first and then look at the commentary to read another opinion. Not all activities have a commentary.

Learning outcomes

These describe the knowledge, understanding and skills that should be gained through the study of each unit.

AQA examination questions are reproduced by permission of the Assessment and Qualifications Alliance.

Web links for this book

Nelson Thornes is not responsible for third party content online, there may be some changes to this material that are beyond our control. In order for us to ensure that the links referred to are as up-to-date and stable as possible, please let us know at webadmin@nelsonthornes.com if you find a link that doesn't work and we will do our best to redirect these, or to list an alternative site.

Introduction to this book

Integrated study of language and literature

The books in this series are designed to support you in your AS and A2 English Language and Literature studies. What is special about this subject is that it brings together aspects of two other kinds of A-level English course – the separate English Literature and English Language specifications – and there are real advantages in continuing your studies of English Language and Literature in an integrated course of this sort.

English at every level up to GCSE requires both language and literature to be studied as essential parts of the course. How can you study literature properly without being keenly interested in the medium of that literature – the ways in which words, sentences, paragraphs and chapters interrelate to create texts of various kinds? These texts may be novels, short stories, plays, documentary scripts, poems and non-fiction texts of a whole range of types and forms.

Being inquisitive about language in all of its forms and habitats is probably the most important quality that you can bring to your studies. We are immersed in language – it is our medium of communication with other people, it is the medium of entertainment (radio, television, comedy clubs, etc.) and a medium of instruction and information (how to … books, labels on medicines). More than that, my language and your language form essential parts of our identities, our individual personalities.

If you go on to study English at university, you will also encounter a subject which has largely abandoned sharp distinctions between 'literature' and 'language' study as unhelpful oversimplifications. You will inevitably be looking at how writers use language when you study a work of literature, and your knowledge about language and how it is used can help you to appreciate and understand how writers and speakers, readers and listeners can be creative and responsive in their experiences of language.

It is important not to think of A-level English Language and Literature as a mix-and-match course in which you 'do language' in one section of a unit and 'do literature' in another section. The point is that language study and literature study are integrated and you need to think about how your interest in language can extend and enhance your appreciation of literary texts. You also need to think about literary texts as examples of language being used in ways that repay close scrutiny, analysis and reflection. There are four main skills you need to develop during your AS and A2 course:

- You need to show that you are capable of reading texts closely and thoughtfully and writing about those texts in ways that show intelligent engagement and control.
- You need to show that you understand the characteristics of various kinds of spoken language, ranging from spontaneous exchanges between friends or strangers to carefully prepared speeches that are designed to persuade large numbers of people in live events or via television and radio.

Think about it

'Language most shows a man: speak that I may see thee.' *Ben Jonson*

- What do you think Jonson meant?
- Do you form an impression of a person from the way he speaks?
- Did Jonson intend his comment to apply to women, do you think? If so, why did he not refer to women as well as men?
- Does Jonson's comment also apply to the way men and women write?

■ You need to show that you are capable of producing writing that is appropriate to the purpose and audience specified in the task, showing conscious control of your choices of vocabulary, grammar and structure.

■ You need to show that you are capable of writing in a focused and analytical way about your own writing – the processes you apply, the choices you make and the evaluation of whether the text works as well as you intended.

All of these activities build directly on the skills you have developed during your GCSE course and in your earlier secondary years, as well as in your primary school and during the pre-school years when you learned language skills by imitating adults and children with whom you grew up. These are skills that many of us continue to develop as the range of our experiences as readers, writers, speakers and listeners expands.

■ The units

This course focuses on a number of literary texts and on particular language topics. Here is a preview of each of the four units that make up the AS and A2 course.

■ **Unit 1 (ELLA1): Integrated analysis and text production**
(Examination: one hour and 30 minutes)

Two texts are studied from a list of 10 prose and drama texts. You will answer one question on each text. For each text, one question requires an analytical response about aspects of language and style; the second question on each text is a production task based on a thorough knowledge of the text. You must answer two questions, one analytical response and one production response. This is an **open book examination**.

This unit introduces you to the integrated literary and linguistic study of texts. You will study two texts chosen from a set list which includes prose fiction and drama and you will be required to answer an analytical question on one of them and a creative question on the other. This is an open book examination but your texts must not be annotated.

For each text in the examination, there are two questions. The first question for each text is labelled A. For the A questions, you will be asked to write an analytical essay in response to one of your set texts, focusing on language and style, as well as such aspects as character, theme and narrative technique. The second question for each text is labelled B. For the B questions, you will be asked to produce a creative response to the second of your chosen texts, such as a letter, article or speech, which is based on a thorough knowledge of the text. Remember that you must answer one analytical (A) question and one creative (B) question. Your answers must be on different texts and you will be able to choose which text you want to use for each task in the examination.

■ **Unit 2 (ELLA2): Analysing speech and its representation**
(Examination: one hour and 30 minutes)

In the first question of the examination you will study two **unseen spoken texts** and answer a question that requires analytical comparison. The second question in this unit is based on your study of one text selected from a list of eight prose and drama texts. The focus for this question is the representation of speech and other stylistic features, with an extract from the text provided as a focus for your response. This is a **closed book examination**.

■ Think about it

Think about how much of your ability in the subject we call English is derived from your experiences in school and how much is derived from ordinary everyday contacts within your network of friends and family.

For example, if you focus on spoken language for the moment, have you considered how you acquired your accent? Have you ever consciously modified the way you speak or been told to by someone else? If so, what does this suggest about the range of attitudes to spoken language?

■ Key terms

Open book examination: an examination in which you are allowed to take unmarked copies of the books you have studied into the examination room and refer to them if you wish as you write your answers.

Unseen spoken texts: transcripts of spoken language that have not been studied prior to the examination.

Closed book examinaton: an exam in which you are not allowed to take your set text into the examination room.

Unit 3 (ELLA3): Comparative Analysis and Text Adaptation
(Examination: two hours and 30 minutes)

The Section A question requires you to compare the language of unseen texts, drawn from speech, non-fiction texts and fiction texts, building on what you have learned in your AS studies. The Section B question requires you to rework a printed extract from the collection of women's journalism, Cupcakes and Kalshnikovs or the collection of tales of life abroad, A House Somewhere. This reworked text will be non-fiction and will demonstrate your skills of adaptation and production. It will differ from the printed extract in form, audience and purpose. In addition you will be required to write a commentary which draws attention to the choices you made in creating your new non-fiction text.

Unit 4 (ELLA 4): Comparative Analysis through Independent Study
(Coursework)

This coursework unit requires you to produce a response of 2,000 to 2,500 words in which you analyse and compare aspects of one text selected from List A (Poetry) and a second text selected either from List A or List B (Other Genres). The question must be approved by your tutor before you embark on this task, and this should help to ensure that you focus on challenging comparative issues that link your chosen texts.

Units 3 and 4 comprise the second year of the A2 course.

Preparation

How should you prepare for approaching your studies in this way? The essential points are that you need to:

- approach your reading and writing in an integrated way, building on both linguistic and literary understanding and methods
- develop your creativity and independence as you encounter both spoken and written language
- think about texts and the relationships between texts, which also requires that you think about the social, cultural and historical contexts of these texts
- develop independent ways of working so that your individual skills as a producer of spoken and written language are extended, and you also become increasingly thoughtful and responsive in your judgements and evaluations of the language you encounter as reader and as listener.

Assessment Objectives

You also need to be clear about the Assessment Objectives (AOs) that underpin all of your studies within this subject. Although the term Assessment Objective may sound a little remote and forbidding, you do need to understand their importance in order to study effectively and give yourself the best possible chance of achieving high grades. The AOs are set by the Qualifications and Curriculum Authority (QCA), the agency responsible for overseeing the examination system, and they apply to all specifications in this subject (Table 1).

Table 1 *Assessment Objectives*

Assessment Objectives	Questions to ask yourself
AO1 Select and apply relevant concepts and approaches from integrated linguistic and literary study, using appropriate terminology and accurate, coherent written expression	Can I write accurately and coherently about a range of texts of various sorts, using specialist linguistic and literary terms and concepts that will help me to be clear and precise?
AO2 Demonstrate detailed critical understanding in analysing the ways in which structure, form and language shape meanings in a range of spoken and written texts	Can I discuss and write about structure, form and language of spoken and written texts in ways that reveal my critical and analytical understanding?
AO3 Use integrated approaches to explore relationships between texts, analysing the significance of contextual factors in their production and reception	Can I use my linguistic and literary understanding to interpret and evaluate texts and to compare different texts and their social, cultural and historical contexts?
AO4 Demonstrate expertise and creativity in using language appropriately for a variety of purposes and audiences, drawing on insights from literary and linguistic studies	Can I use my linguistic and literary understanding to produce written and spoken language appropriately to communicate effectively with a range of audiences and for a range of purposes?

You will have noticed that running through the questions in Table 1 is an insistence on the need to apply your knowledge and understanding of both language and literature, and this is the key to success on this course of study.

■ How to read

In 2007 John Sutherland, a professor of English, published *How to Read a Novel*, which is subtitled 'A User's Guide'. This book, which is accessible and well worth reading, raises many issues relevant to your studies at AS and A2 level in its 28 short chapters. Sutherland shows us the importance of developing autonomy as a reader – that is, approaching our reading thoughtfully and evaluating what we encounter for ourselves, and not uncritically accepting the opinions of others. In his final chapter, for example, Sutherland explains why, for him, Thackeray's *Vanity Fair*, is one of the greatest English novels. He also quotes the philosopher, Alain de Botton, who describes the book as 'the most over-rated ever'. There could hardly be a sharper contrast between their opinions, yet each man is capable of developing a cogent and persuasive case in support of his judgement. You as a reader need to work towards developing your critical and thinking skills so that you can form judgements, advance them and defend them in discussion and writing. It is also important to take your time and hold back from making judgements about texts that you might find unusual or difficult to get to grips with. As far as your examination texts are concerned, you need to persevere especially with works that you find difficult on a first reading, and you need to be receptive to a range of critical and explanatory comment from your teachers, books or web sources. If you eventually judge a book to be flawed in some way and you can establish a clearly argued and well supported case, you will be demonstrating exactly the kinds of skills and understanding that will entitle you to high marks in the examinations or in your coursework. Look again at AO3 and corresponding third question in Table 1.

Before you begin to think in detail about how to read a novel (or a play, poem or non-fiction text), you need to ask an even more fundamental question: Why am I reading this book? More specifically, what exactly is my purpose as a reader? At different times in your reading life you will doubtless have a wide range of justifications or reasons for reading. Because you are following a course in English Language and Literature, it is a safe bet that you enjoy reading as a leisure activity and you value the contacts you have via the printed page with the thoughts, ideas, stories and experiences of others. However, for the reading you do as part of the English Language and Literature course, you will almost certainly have an additional reason, a pragmatic or utilitarian one: to achieve the highest possible grades as a passport to a university place or a career.

Different kinds of reading can fit into three main categories:

- **Reading the lines**: reading for surface meanings. Much of our day-to-day reading takes place at this level: skimming a newspaper for details of what is on television, checking how long the ready meal needs in the microwave or reading a gossip column in a magazine, for example.

- **Reading between the lines**: this requires the reader to be alert to what a text hints at or implies, as well as what is stated explicitly. This is the kind of careful 'reading in low gear' that you must engage in as you study your examination texts; they have been selected for study because they offer richness and complexity of various sorts. They are not so much puzzles to be solved as creations of the writers' imaginations and they offer language and ideas which you, as a reader, need to interpret and enjoy on a number of levels, including the intellectual and the imaginative. You cannot study them adequately if you simply skim-read them and students who do not apply their skills of inference, evaluation and judgement will not be working in the ways necessary for success at AS, let alone A2, level.

- **Reading beyond the lines**: this refers to the ability of readers to extend their thinking so that their understanding of a particular book is related to their experience of life, their knowledge of other books, their attitudes to moral issues, their judgements about artistic values – indeed, the whole of a reader's awareness of his or her world. Some books can affect us so much that we are forced to take stock of what we really believe and what we really feel; reading beyond the lines enables us to develop as individuals. We engage so closely with a book that we allow it to expand our awareness, our understanding, our values: it can help to make us, in some small way, a different person after we have read the book than we were before.

Developing your skills

How can you best develop the skills and understanding necessary for success in your English Language and Literature A course? This book will give you a practical guide through the course and supplement the work you do at school or college. You will get the most out of it if you try the practical activities, follow the research hints and use the associated e-resources. You need to study your set texts and language topics carefully, and to develop your ability to talk and write about books effectively. That takes practice and a willingness to learn from others.

An excellent starting point is to listen to radio or TV programmes about books and reading. here are some suggestions of programmes that will widen your knowledge:

■ *Bookclub* (Radio 4) shows the discussion of a chosen book by its writer and a small panel of readers. It's available in the BBC Radio website using the 'Listen Again' feature and gives an excellent insight into different readers' responses to the novel and the writer's approaches to writing.

■ *A Good Read* (also Radio 4) involves discussion between three readers of a chosen book. Sometimes they agree about the merits of a particular book, but often they disagree. Listening to a discussion in which three intelligent readers express different views about the same book conveys a powerful message: what matters most is your personal response to books and your ability to explain and, where necessary, defend your position.

■ The Richard and Judy Bookclub has been an annual feature of their show on their Channel 4 programme. As of 2008, Richard and Judy will feature on the pay-TV channel UKTV, along with their book club feature, so keep your eyes open for them. There is also a useful Richard and Judy Bookclub website that includes reviews and other features on books and authors.

■ *World Book Club* and *The Word* is a radio show on the BBC Radio World Service, in which well-known authors discuss their work with a studio audience. Past programmes can be accessed via the World Service website at www.bbc.co.uk/worldservice

■ *Emagazine* is a subscription magazine aimed specifically at English A level students, with contributions from both teachers and students on a wide variety of topics. Your college may already subscribe to this, or you can take out an individual subscription. Information is available on their website www.emagazine.org.uk

■ Try reading book reviews in the Saturday editions of newspapers such as *The Guardian*, *The Independent*, *The Times* and the *Daily Telegraph* and their Sunday editions. These reviews will help to familiarise you with the process of evaluating and conveying to others your judgements and responses to your reading.

Remember, though, that the AS and A2 course is designed to develop your personal responses, and not to turn you into an obedient mouthpiece for the views of this critic or that critic. If you enter the examination room having acquired detailed knowledge of your set texts and topics, as well as independent judgement, you are well prepared for success in the exam, and the benefits that come from a lifetime experience of being a good reader and a thoughtful writer.

A Analytical and critical approaches to reading texts

This unit covers:

- ■ **AO1** Select and apply relevant concepts and approaches from integrated linguistic study, using appropriate terminology and accurate, coherent written expression.

- ■ **AO2** Demonstrate detailed critical understanding in analysing ways in which structure, form and language shape meanings in a range of spoken and written texts.

- ■ **AO4** Demonstrate expertise and creativity in using language appropriately for a variety of purposes and audiences, drawing on insights from linguistic and literary studies.

Section A introduces you to a range of literary and linguistic ideas. You will be looking at the issue of narrative viewpoint and narrative voice in novels, as well as focusing on aspects of language and style including features of genre, syntax and imagery. You will consider how novelists create characters through descriptions of their physical appearance and their actions and behaviour, as well as through their dialogue. You will also look at a range of dramatic techniques, such as features of genre, structure and style, and consider how dramatists create character through dialogue. You will have the opportunity to consider extracts from a number of the set texts for this unit, focusing on how their writers use language to develop characters and explore issues and themes.

In the examination, you will need to write an essay that gives an informed personal response to one of your two set texts, making close reference to the language and style the writer has used. You will also be assessed for the technical accuracy of your writing so you will need to pay attention to your spelling, punctuation and grammar. This will be an open book examination, which means you may take copies of your set texts into the exam with you, but they must be 'clean copies' (that is, free from annotations and notes).

Your answers to the analytical questions (labelled A on the exam papers) will be assessed for Assessment Objectives AO1 and AO2:

- ■ For AO1, you will need to show that you can choose relevant linguistic and literary concepts and terminology to analyse your set text. The accuracy of your own written expression will also be assessed. *(15 marks)*
- ■ For AO2, you will need to show in detail that you understand and can analyse the ways in which structure, form and language shape your chosen writer's meaning. *(15 marks)*

B | Approaching creative writing through stimulus texts

Section B will introduce you to the ways in which you can use your analytical studies of your set texts to produce a piece of your own creative writing. For the creative task in the examination, the question will give detailed requirements for your answer such as writing in a particular narrative voice or style or using a specific form or genre. Whatever task you are given, your writing must be clearly related to your source text.

In this part of the unit, you will be looking at some of the techniques writers use and how you can apply them to your own work. The first consideration for any writer in the production of a text is the purpose of the piece of writing and its intended audience. An understanding of these two terms is central both to the analysis of texts and to the creation of your own. You will explore some of the forms and genres which you could be expected to use in your answers and how to use an appropriate style and register for the tasks in the examination.

The set texts include a range of writing from two different genres: prose and drama. You will look first at making creative responses based on novels and then at the additional features which you will need to take into account when you are considering a drama text. Even if you are studying only drama texts, you should work through the novel-based topics first as many of the same considerations apply.

Your answers to the creative response 'production' questions (labelled B on the exam papers) will be assessed for Assessment Objectives AO4, and part of AO1:

- For AO4 you will need to show creativity in using language appropriately for a variety of purposes and audiences, and show an understanding of different types of writing. *(30 marks)*
- For AO1 you will need to show accuracy and coherence in your written expression. *(15 marks)*

1 Narrative methods

Key terms

Narrative viewpoint: the perspective or point of view adopted by a writer in order to tell a story.

First person narrative: a story that is narrated by a character from within the story itself using the pronoun 'I'.

Third person narrative: a story that is told from a less personal point of view than a first person narrative, such as from the author's own perspective.

First person pronoun: these are 'I', 'me' and 'myself'. We use these words to stand in place of our name.

Irony: a mismatch or discrepancy between what is written or said and what is actually meant. It can be described as the difference between appearance and reality.

Ironic: the adjective used to describe something that contains irony.

i Research point

Irony is a complex concept; try searching for more information on the internet to help your understanding.

Narrative viewpoint

The **narrative viewpoint** of a novel is the perspective or point of view adopted by the writer in order to tell the story. The two most common narrative viewpoints are those of a **first person narrative** and a **third person narrative**.

First person narrative

In a first person narrative the story is seen from the perspective of a character in the story, who becomes the narrator and describes events from a single point of view using the **first person pronoun** 'I' throughout. This narrator may be central to the action, like Amir in *The Kite Runner*, or more of an observer, such as Mr Lockwood in *Wuthering Heights*, who merely records the story he is told rather than actively participating in it. A first person narrative may seem to address the reader directly in some way; for example, when Jane Eyre famously announces 'Reader, I married him' at the end of Charlotte Brontë's novel, the narrator Jane is conscious of our presence as readers. Alternatively, the narrative may seem to take the form of a more personal account for the narrator's own benefit. Mr Lockwood, for example, includes notes to himself ('NB – I dine between twelve and one o'clock'), which perhaps suggests the narrative is at times similar to a diary in form.

A first person narrative allows us to see right into the heart and mind of a character. However, it may also give us a biased, single-sided and perhaps unreliable account. Novelists may use a first person narrative to encourage us to sympathise with the narrator, or they may wish to create **irony** by making their narrator present views and attitudes that we cannot share. For example, in *Property* by Valerie Martin the narrator Manon Gaudet describes her father's treatment of the slaves on his plantation: 'Father was strict and fair. None of our people could marry off the farm, indeed they could never leave it unless they had some compelling reason, and visits by negroes from the neighbouring farms and plantations were strictly forbidden.' Clearly, Manon is unconscious of the fact that the reader is unlikely to share her attitudes towards slavery and will view her father's behaviour as far from 'fair'. This discrepancy between the words used and the meaning we draw from them is therefore heavily **ironic**.

Third person narrative

In a third person narrative the story is seen from a less personal viewpoint, usually that of the author, rather than through the eyes of a character. The narrator seems more distant, referring to the characters by name or with the **third person pronouns** 'he' and 'she'. In many novels the narrator can be described as an **omniscient narrator**; in other words, the narrator knows everything that is happening and can move freely between different characters and scenes. Alternatively, a writer may choose to use a **restricted narrator**, focusing on only one character's experiences. For example, in the *Harry Potter* novels the third person narrative follows

Harry's thoughts and experiences closely. As readers, we are rarely given access to any information that Harry does not have, only discovering the secrets of the wizarding world as Harry does himself. In this way, a third person narrative can sometimes allow us the same insights into a character's thoughts and feelings as a first person narrative.

Although a third person narrative often gives us a more remote, possibly less biased viewpoint, many writers cannot resist the temptation of occasionally stepping into the narrative themselves to give their opinions. Jane Austen is this sort of **intrusive narrator**, as we can see in the following extract from *Persuasion* in which Austen describes the two sisters, Elizabeth and Anne Elliot, entering a concert room in Bath.

> Very, very happy were both Elizabeth and Anne Elliot as they walked in. Elizabeth arm-in-arm with Miss Carteret, and looking on the broad back of the Dowager Viscountess Dalrymple before her, had nothing to wish for which did not seem within her reach; and Anne – but it would be an insult to the nature of Anne's felicity to draw any comparison between it and her sister's; the origin of one all selfish vanity, of the other all generous attachment.

Here, by giving up on writing her sentence 'and Anne – ', Austen draws attention to herself as the author and inserts her own opinions of her characters instead, thus intruding into the story.

Narrative voice

When considering the narrative viewpoint of a text, we also need to think about the **narrative voice**, or the tone and style of the narrator's language. We can identify the character and attitudes of the narrator by analysing the writer's **lexical choices**.

In the extract from Valerie Martin's *Property*, you may have noticed and reacted to Manon Gaudet's lexical choice 'negroes'. Although we would consider this an offensive and derogatory term nowadays, Manon's unselfconscious and unashamed use of the word creates, for most modern readers, the impression of an arrogant, self-satisfied narrative voice. Equally, when Manon is considering Mr Roget's proposal to buy her servant Sarah in the following extract, her lexical choices of 'ugly and dark' and 'mad yellow dog' create a narrative voice that conveys her callousness and sense of superiority.

> What possessed the man? He had already gone to the expense of financing Sarah's escape. He was probably paying someone to hide her as we sat there. If I agreed, he would have to pay to bring her back, then take on two children not his own, one ugly and dark, the other no better than a mad yellow dog.

Critical response activity

In *Wuthering Heights*, Emily Brontë interestingly gives us a narrative voice within a narrative voice, when the initial narrator, Mr Lockwood, starts to recount the story Nelly Dean tells him. Read the following extract from the beginning of the novel, using these questions to guide your reading.

- What differences can you see between the narrative voice of Mr Lockwood, and that of Nelly Dean?
- What lexical choices help to create these differences?

Key terms

Third person pronouns: these are 'he', 'him', 'she', 'her' and 'it' in the singular form, and 'they' or 'them' in the plural. They stand in place of nouns and names. They are referred to as third person as they follow the first person 'I/we', and the second person 'you'.

Omniscient narrator: a narrator who has a complete overview of the story and can move freely between different characters and scenes, with full knowledge of everything that happens.

Restricted narrator: a narrator who gives only a limited view of the story, usually focusing on the experiences of a single character.

Intrusive narrator: an author who inserts his or her own opinions into the story.

Practical activity

Read the opening paragraphs of 10 different novels from a variety of genres and consider how the narrative viewpoint is established in each case.

Key terms

Narrative voice: the tone or style of a narrator's language, which gives us an impression of the narrator's character.

Lexical choices: the vocabulary consciously selected by a writer to create a specific tone or effect.

'Well, Mrs Dean, it will be a charitable deed to tell me something of my neighbours: I feel I shall not rest, if I go to bed; so be good enough to sit and chat an hour.'

'Oh, certainly, sir! I'll just fetch a little sewing, and then I'll sit as long as you please. But you've caught cold: I saw you shivering, and you must have some gruel to drive it out.'

The worthy woman bustled off, and I crouched nearer the fire; my head felt hot, and the rest of me chill: moreover I was excited, almost to a pitch of foolishness, through my nerves and brain. This caused me to feel, not uncomfortable, but rather fearful (as I am still) of serious effects from the incidents of today and yesterday. She returned presently, bringing a smoking basin and a basket of work; and, having placed the former on the hob, drew in her seat, evidently pleased to find me so companionable.

Before I came to live here, she commenced – waiting no further invitation to her story – I was almost always at Wuthering Heights; because my mother had nursed Mr Hindley Earnshaw, that was Hareton's father, and I got used to playing with the children: I ran errands too, and helped to make hay, and hung about the farm ready for anything that anybody would set me to. One fine summer morning – it was the beginning of harvest, I remember – Mr Earnshaw, the old master, came down stairs, dressed for a journey; and after he had told Joseph what was to be done during the day, he turned to Hindley, and Cathy, and me – for I sat eating my porridge with them – and he said, speaking to his son, 'Now, my bonny man, I'm going to Liverpool today, what shall I bring you? You may choose what you like: only let it be little, for I shall walk there and back: sixty miles each way, that is a long spell!' Hindley named a fiddle, and then he asked Miss Cathy; she was hardly six years old, but she could ride any horse in the stable, and she chose a whip. He did not forget me; for he had a kind heart, though he was rather severe sometimes. He promised to bring me a pocketful of apples and pears, and then he kissed his children, goodbye, and set off.

Commentary

In the extract above, you may well have noticed that Lockwood's narrative voice is much more inward-looking than Nelly Dean's. He focuses on himself, his health and feelings, seen in lines such as 'I was excited, almost to a pitch of foolishness, through my nerves and brain.' As a narrator, he seems rather pompous and patronising, both in his description of Nelly as 'the worthy woman' who 'bustled off' and in his view that she was 'evidently pleased to find me so companionable'. His expression and vocabulary are relatively sophisticated here, and his narrative voice suggests a sense of his self-importance. On the other hand, Nelly's narrative voice is much less sophisticated, suggested in straightforward phrasing and language such as 'I ran errands too, and helped to make hay, and hung about the farm ready for anything that anybody would set me to.' She often goes into a great deal of detail, even remembering that they were eating 'porridge' at the time, or that Cathy 'was hardly six years old, but could ride any horse in the stable'. This, combined with the way she includes the words of the people involved, such as 'Now, my bonny man, I'm going to Liverpool today', creates a lively and vivid narrative. The impression you may have formed of Nelly's narrative voice is that of a simple, talkative, cheerful woman.

Critical response activity

In the following extract from *The Kite Runner*, the narrator, Amir, who has grown up in an affluent home in Afghanistan but now lives in America and has finished his education there, is describing his first success as a writer. Read the extract carefully, using the following questions to guide your reading.

- Which lexical choices indicate that this is the narrative voice of an educated writer?
- Which lexical choices best reveal the personality of the narrator?
- Which lexical choices convey a sense of conflict between the narrator's Afghani origins and his current life?

In the summer of 1988, about six months before the Soviets withdrew from Afghanistan, I finished my first novel, a father-son story set in Kabul, written mostly with the typewriter the general had given me. I sent query letters to a dozen agencies and was stunned one August day when I opened our mailbox and found a request from a New York agency for the completed manuscript. I mailed it the next day. Soraya kissed the carefully wrapped manuscript and Khala Jamila insisted we pass it under the Koran. She told me that she was going to do *nazr* for me, a vow to have a sheep slaughtered and the meat given to the poor if my book was accepted.

'Please, no *nazr*, Khala jan,' I said, kissing her face. 'Just do *zakat*, give the money to someone in need, okay? No sheep killing.'

Six weeks later, a man named Martin Greenwalt called from New York and offered to represent me. I only told Soraya about it. 'But just because I have an agent doesn't mean I'll get published. If Martin sells the novel, then we'll celebrate.'

A month later, Martin called and informed me I was going to be a published novelist. When I told Soraya, she screamed.

We had a celebration dinner with Soraya's parents that night. Khala Jamila made *kofta* – meatballs and white rice – and white *ferni*. The general, a sheen of moisture in his eyes, said that he was proud of me. After General Taheri and his wife left, Soraya and I celebrated with an expensive bottle of Merlot I had bought on the way home – the general did not approve of women drinking alcohol, and Soraya didn't drink in his presence.

'I am so proud of you,' she said, raising her glass to mine. 'Kaka would have been proud too.'

'I know,' I said, thinking of Baba, wishing he could have seen me.

Later that night, after Soraya fell asleep – wine always made her sleepy – I stood on the balcony and breathed in the cool summer air. I thought of Rahim Khan and the little note of support he had written me after he'd read my first story. And I thought of Hassan. *Some day, Inshallah, you will be a great writer,* he had said once, *and people all over the world will read your stories.* There was so much goodness in my life. So much happiness. I wondered whether I deserved any of it.

Language and style

This chapter covers:

- introduction to genre, register, titles, syntax and imagery
- explanation of how these features contribute to the writer's style.

Key terms

Genre: a class or category of text, with its particular conventions of language, form and structure, for example, short story, science fiction novel, Shakespearean comedy.

Link

Use your prior knowledge about genres from GCSE to help you with this activity.

Genre

Drama, poetry and prose are the three main literary **genres** you are likely to come across in your studies. However, there are many more genres which can be identified within these three basic categories: drama may be subdivided into tragedy or comedy, for example, and the broad genre of poetry includes different types of writing such as epic poetry, romantic poetry or free verse. The prose genre encompasses many styles of writing such as science fiction, horror and autobiography. Each genre has its own characteristics and features of style, although within any genre individual writers retain distinctive features that attentive readers who are familiar with those writers' works will be able to identify.

Practical activity

1 Identify as closely as you can the genre for each of the following prose extracts.

a I descended, minding carefully where I went, for the stairs were dark, being only lit by loopholes in the heavy masonry. At the bottom there was a dark, tunnel-like passage, through which came a deathly, sickly odour, the odour of old earth newly turned. As I went through the passage the smell grew closer and heavier. At last I pulled open a heavy door which stood ajar, and found myself in an old, ruined chapel, which had evidently been used as a graveyard.

b 'Papers are going to have a field day with this,' someone was muttering. There were a dozen figures shuffling around in the covered walkway between two of the high-rise blocks. The place smelled faintly of urine, human or otherwise. Plenty of dogs in the vicinity, one or two even wearing collars. They would come sniffing at the entrance to the walkway, until chased off by one of the uniforms. Crime-scene tape now blocked both ends of the passage. Kids on bikes were craning their necks for a look. Police photographers were gathering evidence, vying for space with the forensic team. They were dressed in white overalls, heads covered.

c 'Next stop, planet Aggadon!' cried Captain Teggs Stegosaur as he bundled aboard his space shuttle. A new adventure was beginning, and he could hardly wait.

d All afternoon I followed the Great Wall into the mountains. Cracked open by farmers' tracks or half buried under the shelving earth, it crossed the plain in broken chunks then hoisted itself through the foothills. At first it went squat and straight as a causeway. I strode in its shadow over a river of debris, dotted with dead animals scarcely seen in life – rabbits, snakes, cats – and on through fields rustling with sugar-cane into a scrub-covered waste. Then the Wall rose into quiet.

2 In identifying the different genres of these extracts, you may have been helped to make your decision by noticing a pattern of words relating to the same topic in each passage. For example, in Extract C the words 'planet' and 'space shuttle' may have led you to assume that this text is taken from a science-fiction novel. Groups of topic-related words such as this are members of **semantic fields**.

Look again at each extract and decide which semantic fields enabled you to identify the genre of each text.

Key terms

Semantic field: a group of words within a text relating to the same topic, e.g. tyre, brake pedal, starter motor and exhaust are all from the semantic field of cars.

In Extract A, which is taken from Bram Stoker's *Dracula*, you were probably able to identify the gothic horror genre from the repeated references to darkness and the selection of words from the semantic field of death, such as 'deathly sickly odour', 'old ruined chapel' and 'graveyard'. Extract B is from a detective novel, *Fleshmarket Close* by Ian Rankin, evident from the semantic field of police procedure: 'uniforms', 'crime-scene tape', 'evidence', 'forensic team'. We've already seen that Extract C is from the science-fiction genre, although it is also clearly aimed at children – it is from a book called *Astrosaurs: the Planet of Peril* by children's writer Steve Cole. Extract D comes from Colin Thubron's travel book about China *Behind the Wall* and you may well have identified the genre of travel writing here from Thubron's use of words from the semantic field of landscape, such as 'mountains', 'plain', 'causeway' and 'scrub-covered waste'. However, there is also an autobiographical feel to the extract – remember, a book need not be confined to only one genre and may contain elements of several different types of writing.

🔍 Register

The genre of a text will affect the **register** in which it is written or indeed spoken. Different situations or contexts require different styles and approaches, as well as different levels of formality, in the language chosen, and these different types of language are known as registers. Writers (and speakers) aim to select an appropriate register to suit the audience for their work, taking into account their relationship with the audience and the level of formality or informality they consider acceptable given the nature of the relationship. They also take into account the purpose of their work; the register of, for example, a witty story intended to entertain its audience will be very different to the register of a set of instructions for a new gadget. Context will also play an important part in the choice of register. For example, a solicitor writing a letter to a client in a professional context will almost certainly choose a highly formal register using a vocabulary of legal terms appropriate to the situation, whereas the same solicitor would be likely to use a much more informal register and simpler vocabulary when sending postcards while on holiday.

▪ Key terms

Register: a type of language defined in terms of its appropriateness for the type of activity or context in which the language is used, including the purpose, audience and situation of a piece of speech or writing.

▪ Link

Refer to Section B for more information on register, as well as more ideas about choosing language appropriate for different audiences and purposes.

▪ Practical activity

1. Read the following extracts and identify the register in each case. Rate each extract on a scale of 1 to 10, where 1 is very informal and 10 is very formal.

   a. It was only a tiff, but it could easily have escalated into something much more serious. Let me explain. In this prison we live on 'spurs': dark, warren-like corridors, flanked on either side by a row of cells. On a spur, there are twelve single cells and one double. There are usually two spurs to a landing. The occupants are serving terms of anything from a couple of years to life. Not surprisingly, with so many men forced to live together in such close proximity for such long periods of time, tensions can sometimes run high.

   b. We'd like to help you avoid slipping into the red. It may not be something you'd expect to hear from your bank but we've come up with some new ideas which make it easier for you to avoid slipping into the red and paying any overdraft fees.

c Jose M-m-m-m-Mourinho!?!! Don'tchaluvhim?!? Every gal in Great Britain is reaching for her Kleenex to dry her tears. And for why?!? Because the sultry sex bomb from the Land of the Sardine has been given the red card and told 'Adios amigo!' by the Stalin of Stamford Bridge – that's Roman Abramovich to you Mister!?!! Will us gals ever forget you a-smoulderin' on the touchline in your Gucci overcoat with your stubbly chin?!? 'No way Jose!' Geddit?! All together now –Boo-hoo-hoo! I've got the Chelsea Blues!?! (Geddit?!)

d President Hoover, Mr Chief Justice, my friends: This is a day of national consecration. And I am certain that on this day my fellow Americans expect that on my induction into the presidency, I will address them with a candour and a decision which the present situation of our people impels.

Sources: a *A Life Inside* by Erwin James (Atlantic, 2003); b Letter to a customer rom Lloyds TSB; c *Private Eye* (October 2007); d Opening lines from a speech by Franklin D. Roosevelt (1933)

2 Which lexical choices and features of language enabled you to make these judgements about the register of each extract?

■ Titles

Within any genre, it is the title of the book, poem or play that we are likely to notice and be drawn to first. A title may give us some obvious clues about the genre or nature of the text – the title of Agatha Christie's novel *Dial M for Murder* suggests quite clearly that the book belongs to the genre of crime fiction. Alternatively, a title may seek to intrigue us through its lack of obvious clues to the text's content or may provide an ironic contrast between title and content. For example, the title of Philip Larkin's poem 'A Study of Reading Habits' has a formal register and style typical of an academic genre while the poem itself contains informal lines such as 'books are a load of crap'. Writers choose the language of their titles carefully to intrigue and encourage their readers into reading the rest of the text. For example, in Alan Bennett's *The History Boys* it is the juxtaposition of the **abstract noun** 'History' with its connotations of age with the youthful-sounding **concrete noun** 'boys' which stimulates our interest.

Practical activity

1 For each of the following titles, think about your expectations of the text and its likely genre:

■ *Fleshmarket Close*

■ *A Streetcar Named Desire*

■ *Things Fall Apart*

■ *The Kite Runner*

■ *A Short History of Tractors in Ukrainian*

■ *Wuthering Heights*

■ *Power, Corruption and Pies*

■ *Close Range.*

2 Analyse closely the precise effect each writer has created through his or her choice of language.

3 After you have analysed all the titles, use the internet or a library to find out a little more about each book and see if your initial expectations are fulfilled.

▮ Syntax

A key aspect of the writing in any text you may well notice is the **syntax**, or the type and structure of sentences used.

Sentences can be constructed in different ways and can perform different functions. The three main types of sentence are known as simple, compound and complex sentences.

▮ A **simple sentence** has only one main **clause**; for example, in the simple sentence 'The dog ran' there is only one subject (the dog) and only one verb or action happening (ran). Simple sentences are often short. However, the words 'short' and 'simple' are not interchangeable here. For example, the sentence 'The flea-bitten grey dog with the long bandy legs ran quickly into his moss-covered kennel with fear in his eyes' is still grammatically a simple sentence, despite its length, because it contains only one subject (the dog) and one verb ('ran'). Simple sentences may be used to create a straightforward, accessible style. They may also be used selectively to achieve impact, particularly if they occur in close proximity to complex and compound sentences.

▮ A **compound sentence** has two or more clauses, which are linked by **coordinating conjunctions** such as 'and' or 'but'. For example, when Mr Lockwood encounters Cathy's ghost in *Wuthering Heights*, he describes his reaction using the compound sentence 'I tried to jump up, but could not stir a limb; and so yelled aloud, in a frenzy of fright.' The compound sentence structure here helps to build up a sense of urgency and tension in the scene.

▮ A **complex sentence** also contains two or more clauses, but unlike a compound sentence in this case the clauses are linked with **subordinating conjunctions** such as 'after', 'although', 'when', 'because' and 'if'. Remember, complex does not necessarily mean the same as complicated – a sentence such as Lockwood's cry to the ghost 'let me go, if you want me to let you in!' is not particularly complicated to understand, but is grammatically complex in structure because it contains one main clause ('Let me go') and one subordinate clause ('if you want me to let you in!').

When analysing the syntax of a text, there are some generalisations that can be made, such as the idea that a large number of simple and compound sentences may suggest a young audience or a need to explain points simply and clearly, while a text made up of predominantly complex sentences may be intended for a more sophisticated audience and explore more difficult ideas and relationships. However, it is important to look at examples of syntax on their own merit and in relation to the context in which they appear, as even simple story books for children can make use of a variety of sentence types.

▮ Sentences can perform four main functions:

▮ a **declarative sentence**, or statement, conveys information

▮ an **interrogative sentence** asks a question

▮ an **imperative sentence** gives a command

▮ an **exclamatory sentence** contains an exclamation of some sort to convey heightened feelings such as shock, surprise, excitement or indignation.

Look again at the complete description of Lockwood's encounter with Cathy's ghost in *Wuthering Heights*:

▮ Key terms

Syntax: the study of the way words are combined to form sentences.

Simple sentence: a sentence with only one clause.

Clause: a part of a sentence that contains both a subject and a verb. It can stand alone as a sentence as in 'I bought a book' (main or independent clause) but it need not do so as in 'when I went out' (subordinate or dependent clause).

Compound sentence: a sentence with two or more clauses linked by coordinating conjunctions.

Coordinating conjunction: words such as 'and', 'but' and 'or', which are used to link together independent clauses, e.g. in the sentence 'he likes swimming but he hates shopping' each clause could stand independently.

Complex sentence: a sentence with two or more clauses linked by subordinating conjunctions.

Subordinating conjunction: words such as 'although', 'because' or 'unless', which are used to link a main clause to a subsidiary or dependent one, e.g. in the sentence 'Although it was raining, the party was a success', the phrase 'Although it was raining' is secondary in importance to the main point of the sentence ('the party was a success').

As it spoke, I discerned, obscurely, a child's face looking through the window – terror made me cruel; and, finding it useless to attempt shaking the creature off, I pulled its wrist on to the broken pane, and rubbed it to and fro till the blood ran down and soaked the bedclothes: still it wailed, 'Let me in!' and maintained its tenacious gripe, almost maddening me with fear.

'How can I!' I said at length. 'Let me go, if you want me to let you in!'

The fingers relaxed, I snatched mine through the hole, hurriedly piled the books up in a pyramid against it, and stopped my ears to exclude the lamentable prayer.

I seemed to keep them closed above a quarter of an hour, yet, the instant I listened, again, there was the doleful cry moaning on!

'Be gone!' I shouted, 'I'll never let you in, not if you beg for twenty years.'

'It's twenty years,' mourned the voice, 'twenty years, I've been a waif for twenty years!'

Thereat began a feeble scratching outside, and the pile of books moved as if thrust forward.

I tried to jump up, but could not stir a limb; and so yelled aloud, in a frenzy of fright.

To my confusion, I discovered the yell was not ideal. Hasty footsteps approached my chamber door: somebody pushed it open, with a vigorous hand, and a light glimmered through the squares at the top of the bed. I sat shuddering yet, and wiping the perspiration from my forehead: the intruder appeared to hesitate, and muttered to himself.

At last, he said in a half-whisper, plainly not expecting an answer,

'Is any one here?'

Here we can see Emily Brontë using a variety of declarative sentences in order to convey information about the scene and provide descriptive detail such as 'I pulled its wrist on to the broken pane.' There are also a number of imperative sentences such as Cathy's 'Let me in!', which conveys her sense of desperation, and Lockwood's 'Be gone!', which suggests he wishes to sound authoritative and take control of a terrifying situation. The extract is peppered with exclamatory sentences, such as '… there was the doleful cry moaning on!', which serve to heighten the tension and drama of the scene, conveying Lockwood's feelings of terror and Cathy's despair. The extract ends with Heathcliff's tentative interrogative sentence 'Is any one here?', which conveys his sense of uncertainty and his desire to be answered.

■ Critical response activity

Compare the following opening passages from *Things Fall Apart* and *The Kite Runner*, focusing on issues of syntax.

■ What effects have Chinua Achebe and Khaled Hosseini achieved through their choice of syntax?

■ What other techniques have the writers used to appeal to and intrigue their audiences in these important opening words?

Extract A: *Things Fall Apart*

Okonkwo was well known throughout the nine villages and even beyond. His fame rested on solid personal achievements. As a young man of eighteen he had brought honour to his village by throwing Amalinze the Cat. Amalinze was the great wrestler who for seven years was unbeaten, from Umuofia to Mbaino. He was called the Cat because his back would never touch the earth. It was this man that Okonkwo threw in a fight which the old men agreed was one of the fiercest since the founder of their town engaged a spirit of the wild for seven days and seven nights.

The drums beat and the flutes sang and the spectators held their breath. Amalinze was a wily craftsman, but Okonkwo was as slippery as a fish in water. Every nerve and every muscle stood out on their arms, on their backs and their thighs, and one almost heard them stretching to breaking point. In the end Okonkwo threw the Cat.

Extract B: *The Kite Runner*

December 2001

I became what I am today at the age of twelve, on a frigid overcast day in the winter of 1975. I remember the precise moment, crouching behind a crumbling mud wall, peeking into the alley near the frozen creek. That was a long time ago, but it's wrong what they say about the past, I've learned, about how you can bury it. Because the past claws its way out. Looking back now, I realize I have been peeking into that deserted alley for the last twenty-six years.

One day last summer, my friend Rahim Khan called from Pakistan. He asked me to come see him. Standing in the kitchen with the receiver to my ear, I knew it wasn't just Rahim Khan on the line. It was my past of unatoned sins. After I hung up, I went for a walk along Spreckels Lake on the northern edge of Golden Gate Park. The early-afternoon sun sparkled on the water where dozens of miniature boats sailed, propelled by a crisp breeze. Then I glanced up and saw a pair of kites, red with long blue tails, soaring in the sky. They danced high above the trees on the west end of the park, over the windmills, floating side by side like a pair of eyes looking down on San Francisco, the city I now call home. And suddenly Hassan's voice whispered in my head: *For you, a thousand times over*. Hassan the harelipped kite runner.

Imagery

When analysing the style of a particular writer, an important feature to consider is the writer's use of **imagery**. This term refers to the way in which a writer creates pictures or images in words, although these images may not only be visual but draw on our other senses, such as touch and hearing, as well. The language of imagery can be either **literal** or **figurative**. Direct description using literal language provides us with a straightforward realistic description of a character, scene or event, and is of course essential to enable any story to unfold. However, although a realistic image may be created, some of the details described may also have a more symbolic value, as we will see below. Figurative language creates a more imaginative picture for the reader – one that is not intended to be taken literally. At GCSE level you almost certainly used

Key terms

Imagery: in literary terms, imagery refers to the pictures created by a writer's choice of language, e.g. their use of metaphor or personification.

Literal language: language that conveys meaning according to the explicit, non-figurative sense of words or phrases

Figurative language: language that draws an imaginative comparison between what is described and something else, resulting in an image which cannot literally be true but that may enable us to perceive something more vividly or allow us greater insight into the story or character.

■ Key terms

Simile: an imaginative comparison drawn between two different things, linked with the words 'like' or 'as', e.g. 'her hands were as cold as ice' or 'the man was like a bear'.

Metaphor: a direct comparison drawn between two different things, as if the subject really is the thing it is being compared to, e.g. 'her hands were ice blocks' or 'he was a bear of a man'.

Personification: a form of metaphor where something that is not human is endowed with human characteristics, e.g. 'the windows stared blankly'.

Symbolism: a writer's deliberate use of an object or action to represent an idea or concept beyond its basic meaning. For example, a white dove is just a bird on a literal level but is often used to signify the idea of peace.

AQA Examiner's tip

When you are writing about a text, it is important not to engage in mere 'feature spotting'. In other words, avoid simply pointing out examples of features such as similes and metaphors without any further comment, and make sure you actually analyse the language and explore in detail the *effects* of particular images the writer has created. For example, in chapter two of *The Kite Runner*, Amir describes his friend Hassan's face as 'like a Chinese doll chiseled from hardwood'. You could point out here that the simile of the 'doll' gives us more idea of Amir's attitude towards Hassan, seeing him as a plaything and possession rather than a friend, while the word 'hardwood' suggests Hassan's toughness. Even a short quotation such as this can offer opportunities for detailed analysis. Remember, it is often better to write 'a lot about a little', than the other way round!

---

the terms **simile**, **metaphor** and **personification**, and these techniques are all good examples of figurative language. By responding to these techniques in action we can often gain more imaginative and vivid insights into a character or scene.

Look again at the opening extract from *The Kite Runner*.

> After I hung up, I went for a walk along Spreckels Lake on the northern edge of Golden Gate Park. The early-afternoon sun sparkled on the water where dozens of miniature boats sailed, propelled by a crisp breeze. Then I glanced up and saw a pair of kites, red with long blue tails, soaring in the sky.

Here Khaled Hosseini gives us a realistic direct description of what Amir did and saw, thus enabling us to gain a sense of the story's setting. Although the picture created is literal, you may also uncover some **symbolism** in the images chosen. For example, the image of the 'miniature boats … propelled by a crisp breeze' could perhaps symbolise the idea that we are all being pushed around by some sort of powerful controlling destiny. Equally, the two kites could appear to symbolise friendship and freedom at this point in the story. If you are studying *The Kite Runner* as one of your set texts, you will no doubt explore the changing symbolism of the kite as it develops throughout the novel.

Khaled Hosseini then continues the description, changing to a more figurative style.

> They danced high above the trees on the west end of the park, over the windmills, floating side by side like a pair of eyes looking down on San Francisco, the city I now call home.

Here the writer personifies the kites with the metaphor 'danced', which intensifies the feeling of freedom and excitement at this point. He then uses a simile to describe the kites, 'like a pair of eyes looking down'. This slightly sinister comparison perhaps suggests Amir's sense of guilt about the past and the feeling that he is always being watched. It might also allude to some sort of divinity looking down on Amir and guiding his destiny.

💡 Critical response activity

Read the following extract which is a description of Okonkwo from *Things Fall Apart*.

■ Analyse and explore in detail the figurative language and imagery used.

> Okonkwo did not taste any food for two days after the death of Ikemefuna. He drank palm-wine from morning till night, and his eyes were red and fierce like the eyes of a rat when it was caught by the tail and dashed against the floor. He called his son, Nwoye, to sit with him in his obi. But the boy was afraid of him and slipped out of the hut as soon as he noticed him dozing.
>
> He did not sleep at night. He tried not to think about Ikemefuna, but the more he tried the more he thought about him. Once he got up from bed and walked about his compound. But he was so weak that his legs could hardly carry him. He felt like a drunken giant walking with the limbs of a mosquito. Now and then a cold shiver descended on his head and spread down his body.

3   Character

When exploring a character within a novel, short story or play, it is important to go beyond just describing *what* your character is like and instead move on to analysing *how* that person has been created through the use of literary techniques and choices of language. You have already looked at some of the techniques a writer might use when developing a character, such as Valerie Martin's use of irony in the characterisation of Manon Gaudet in *Property* (see p4 and p5) or Chinua Achebe's use of similes in the description of Okonkwo (see p14). Other aspects of characterisation to explore are how characters are described physically, how characters are made to behave and how they are presented through their dialogue and speech. It is also worth considering smaller details such as the relevance of the name a character has been given or how characters are connected to the settings in which they are placed.

🔍 Names

One of the first things you may want to find out as you start to build up an impression of any character is their name. There is a long tradition in literature of writers giving their characters names that imply something about their personalities or give the character a symbolic significance. For example, in the late 17th century, John Bunyan gave the hero of his book *The Pilgrim's Progress* the name Christian – an apt choice for a character whose travels are presented as an allegory for our spiritual journey through life. On his way, Christian encounters other characters with names such as Worldly Wiseman, Hopeful and Faithful. These choices are hardly subtle but allow us to understand their symbolic meaning easily. Before and since Bunyan, there are many more examples of writers endowing the names of their characters with significance; in a more recent children's book, *The Promised One*, the writer David Alric gives a handy glossary at the end of the novel, explaining his reasoning behind his choice of names, as we can see in this extract.

Practical activity

Names can be especially symbolic in drama text. If you are studying a drama text, consider the choice of names for characters you have come across, particularly in *The Rivals*, *The Importance of Being Ernest* and *A Streetcar Named Desire*.

Enganador *Chapter 7* Don Juan Enganador is Chopper's 'inside man' who tricked Lucy into a trip to the Brazilian embassy and arranged her kidnap. *Enganador* is a Portuguese word for deceiver.

Fairfax *Chapter 7* Miss Fairfax works in an office and undoubtedly sends extremely good *faxes*.

Fetterson *Chapter 11* Inspector Fetterson is a policeman who might have to restrain criminals. *Fetters* are chains or ankle shackles similar to handcuffs.

Finnegan *Chapter 3* Mr *Finn*egan is the director of the dolphinarium.

Fossfinder *Chapter 22* Helen and Julian Fossfinder are palaeontologists who look for *fossils*.

Icares *Chapter 6* Domingos Icares was the pilot who crashed to his death while flying Richard across the jungle. Icarus was someone in Greek mythology who had wings made of wax. He flew too near to the sun, the wax melted, and he fell to his death.

■ **Think about it**

In your own wider reading, have you come across any characters whose names appear to have a particular significance or tell us something more about the character?

💡 Key terms

Allusion: a reference to another work of literature or other source by a writer. The writer may well assume that the reader has some knowledge of the work referred to and will understand the allusion. For example, in the list above, David Alric makes an allusion to the story of Icarus when he names his unfortunate pilot Icares.

Asyndetic list: a form of list in which there is no conjunction (such as 'and' or 'but') separating the final two items. This can be used for rhetorical effect, as in the famous line 'I came, I saw, I conquered', or it can give an open-ended feel to the list, perhaps suggesting that there is more which could be added. The opposite to this is a syndetic list such as 'At the market I bought apples, oranges, pears and bananas.'

Modifier: a word or phrase which, when added to another word, provides readers with additional detail or greater precision about the sense of that word. Adjectives are typical examples of modifiers. In the phrases 'the happy boy' and 'the blue boy', the adjectives 'happy' and 'blue' give us an entirely different impression of the boy. Adverbs are also a form of modifier; if we say 'he walked slowly' or 'he walked quickly', the meaning has been modified by the choice of adverbs. However, many words, not just adjectives and adverbs, can perform the function of modifier in the right context. For example, in the phrase 'London Underground' the name London takes on the job of modifier here, even though it is usually a proper noun.

Although you are unlikely to find the names of the characters in your set books spelt out in such detail, it is worth noting from this example that a character's name may be created from relevant everyday words, it may perhaps draw on words from a different language or it may make an **allusion** to other stories or sources. However, there may not always be a hidden meaning to a name – in Jane Austen's *Persuasion*, for example, the plain, simple elegance of the name Anne Elliot suits the character perfectly, without any obvious significance to the words themselves.

🔍 Physical appearance

In order to provide a physical description of a character, a writer will use a variety of language choices and grammatical features to give us an impression of the person being presented. Read this extract from 'The Half-skinned Steer', a short story from the collection *Close Range* by Annie Proulx. The story is in the form of a third person narrative, but is seen from the viewpoint of Mero, now an old man, who is remembering his father's girlfriend.

> He had pulled away at the sudden point when it seemed the old man's girlfriend – now he couldn't remember her name – had jumped the track, Rollo goggling at her bloody bitten fingers, nails chewed to the quick, neck veins like wires, the outer forearms shaded with hairs, and the cigarette glowing, smoke curling up, making her wink her bulged mustang eyes, a teller of tales of hard deeds and mayhem. The old man's hair was falling out, Mero was twenty-three and Rollo twenty and she played them all like a deck of cards. If you admired horses you'd go for her with her arched neck and horsy buttocks, so high and haunchy you'd want to clap her on the rear. The wind bellowed around the house, driving crystals of snow through the cracks of the warped log door and all of them in the kitchen seemed charged with some intensity of purpose. She'd balanced that broad butt on the edge of the dog food chest, looking at the old man and Rollo, now and then rolling her glossy eyes over at Mero, square teeth nipping a rim of nail, sucking the welling blood, drawing on her cigarette.

Here, Proulx uses a simile – 'neck veins like wires' – to give us a physical picture of the girlfriend, in this case an image of her steely toughness. She also uses an **asyndetic list**, beginning with 'her bloody bitten fingers', to build up a sketch of the character quickly and dynamically. There is a certain symbolic value to some of the details chosen in this physical description; for example, the fact she is smoking and has 'forearms shaded with hairs' could signify a masculine edge to her character and the image of her 'sucking the welling blood' from her bitten fingers might suggest that she will have a destructive impact on the family, in a vampire-like or parasitic manner.

However, one of the most interesting features of the writing here is Proulx's use of **modifiers** to enhance and extend the description of the girlfriend and to guide us as we form our opinions of her. Many of the modifiers chosen here seem to compare the girlfriend to a horse – 'her *bulged mustang* eyes', 'her *arched* neck and *horsy* buttocks', 'her *glossy* eyes' and '*square* teeth'. Bearing in mind that Proulx's stories are set in America and feature cowboys and ranch workers, these choices might imply that the men struggle to relate to her as a woman and view her as just another piece of livestock.

Critical response activity

Read this description of Leeland Lee from the short story 'Job History', also from *Close Range* by Annie Proulx.

- What use does Proulx make of modifiers and other language features to create an impression of the character?

> Leeland Lee's face shows heavy bone from his mother's side. His neck is thick and his red-gold hair plastered down in bangs. Even as a child his eyes are as pouchy as those of a middle-aged alcoholic, the brows rod-straight above wandering, out-of-line eyes. His nose lies broad and close to his face, his mouth seems to have been cut with a single chisel blow into easy flesh. In the fifth grade, horsing around with friends, he falls off the school's fire escape and breaks his pelvis. He is in a body cast for three months. On the news an announcer says that the average American eats 8.6 pounds of margarine a year but only 8.3 pounds of butter. He never forgets this statistic.

Remember, the narrative form of a novel, or even a short story, allows it to cover a long period of time – perhaps years – so the presentation of a character is likely to change and develop as the story unfolds and the character ages. Occasionally writers may choose to focus on a much more limited time-span, such as Ian McEwan in the novel *Saturday* or Anne Tyler in *Breathing Lessons*, both of which focus on the events of a single day. However, even in such tight time frames a character may well be portrayed differently in different parts of the novel and our sympathies may well change. When you make notes on the characters in your set texts, remember to gather evidence from throughout the novel, so that you build up a complete picture of your character.

Link

See p49 for more information on character development through a novel.

Critical response activity

Compare and contrast how the character of Heathcliff is presented in the following two extracts from *Wuthering Heights*, one from early in the novel and one from later on.

In Extract A, a teenage Heathcliff and the servant Nelly Dean are discussing Heathcliff's appearance, in comparison to that of his rival, Edgar Linton.

In Extract B, Heathcliff has returned after an absence of several years. The narrator is again Nelly Dean and she describes Heathcliff's meeting with Edgar Linton.

- What use does Emily Brontë make of modifiers in both extracts?
- What other literary or linguistic techniques are used to create a physical impression of Heathcliff?
- What differences and similarities are there between the two descriptions?
- How does Brontë contrast Heathcliff with Edgar Linton?

Extract A

Heathcliff's face brightened a moment; then it was overcast afresh, and he sighed.

'But, Nelly, if I knocked him down twenty times, that wouldn't make him less handsome, or me more so. I wish I had light hair and a fair skin, and was dressed, and behaved as well, and had a chance of being as rich as he will be!'

'And cried for mamma at every turn' – I added, 'and trembled if a county lad heaved his fist against you, and sat at home all day for a shower of rain. – Oh, Heathcliff, you are showing a poor spirit! Come to the glass, and I'll let you see what you should wish. Do you mark those two lines between your eyes, and those thick brows, that instead of rising arched, sink in the middle, and that couple of black fiends, so deeply buried, who never open their windows boldly, but lurk glinting under them, like devil's spies? Wish and learn to smooth away the surly wrinkles, to raise your lids frankly, and change the fiends to confident, innocent angels, suspecting and doubting nothing, and always seeing friends where they are not sure of foes – Don't get the expression of a vicious cur that appears to know the kicks it gets are its desert, and yet, hates all the world, as well as the kicker, for what it suffers.'

Extract B

Now fully revealed by the fire and candlelight, I was amazed, more than ever, to behold the transformation of Heathcliff. He had grown a tall, athletic, well-formed man; beside whom, my master seemed quite slender and youth-like. His upright carriage suggested the idea of his having been in the army. His countenance was much older in expression and decision of feature than Mr Linton's; it looked intelligent, and retained no marks of former degradation. A half-civilised ferocity lurked yet in the depressed brows and eyes full of black fire, but it was subdued; and his manner was even dignified: quite divested of roughness, though too stern for grace. My master's surprise equaled or exceeded mine: he remained for a minute at a loss how to address the ploughboy, as he had called him. Heathcliff dropped his slight hand and stood looking at him coolly till he chose to speak.

🔍 Actions and behaviour

How characters act and behave has a huge influence on our opinions and understanding of them and is a key aspect of characterisation. For example, when in *Wuthering Heights* Heathcliff instinctively catches the baby Hareton, who has been dropped over the banisters by his own father, you may detect an innate goodness in his behaviour and character which you can here admire. However, elsewhere, when he hangs Isabella's dog from a tree as they elope, you are likely to react with shock at such dramatic cruelty and may well despise Heathcliff at this point in the novel. Thus your sympathies can change according to how a character acts. Many literary characters, including Heathcliff, are portrayed as outsiders and rebels who ignore or undermine the social conventions of their society through their behaviour. Others, such as Jane Austen's heroines, are constrained by the expectations of behaviour imposed on them by their society and can act only according to these social rules.

■ **Practical activity**

Choose a character from one of your set books and find two extracts from different parts of the novel which give a physical description of him or her.

Analyse the language choices and techniques used to create an impression of your character.

Manon Gaudet, the narrator of Valerie Martin's novel *Property* is a good example of a character whose actions are constrained by the social conventions of the time during which the novel is set. She is trapped in a marriage with a man she despises but cannot leave because of social expectation and custom and as a woman her freedom is limited – as she wistfully remarks to her aunt when Sarah, her slave who has escaped disguised as an elderly white gentleman, is captured, 'she has tasted a freedom you and I will never know … she has traveled about the country as a free white man'. However, earlier in the novel Manon is obliged to abandon all sense of social convention when she is forced to escape from a gang of runaway rebel slaves invading her home. In the following extract, how do Manon's actions and behaviour influence our view of her as a character?

> My skirt caught on every bramble. I paused long enough to pull it up between my legs and knot it above my knees. Insects swarmed around my head; my hand closed on something sinuous and leathery. I recoiled, losing my balance, and sat down hard on a tree root. I could hear the men's voices, not as close, but not far enough. Keep going, I told myself, and got to my feet. Something skittered across the ground; a bat whirred overhead. I took a few steps, holding my hands out before me. I was standing in a few inches of water. Wrong way, I thought, and changed direction, but the next steps only brought the icy water to my knees. Wrong way, I told myself again, turning once more. This time my feet found less water, more mud; mud to my shins. I slogged through it. My shoulder had turned into a throbbing mass; the pain made me groan with every step. Insects flew into my mouth and eyes, buzzing louder and louder until I couldn't hear anything else. They will eat me alive, I thought.
>
> I would die where I stood. Then miraculously a solution occurred to me, one I'd seen the negroes use, to my disgust. I bent down and plunged my hands into the cool mud, then smeared it over my face, my arms, and into my hair. Put it on thick, I told myself, squatting to get another handful. The buzzing subsided. I went on, feeling my way. I was out of the mud on soft ground, then my feet found a patch of cool ferns that felt like a carpet laid beneath my feet. I stopped, listened, heard a variety of noises, but none of them voices. They wouldn't waste what little time they had left in this world to search the swamp for a wounded woman, I thought. A powerful lethargy swept over me. My legs were leaden; I could not lift my head. A little farther, I told myself. I could make out the trunk of a big oak just ahead, as wide around as a cabin. I staggered to it, stumbling in the maze of its roots, which sprawled out in every direction, making various moss-covered nests. I sat down in one of these, close to the trunk. It seemed a perfect resting spot. When I moved my arm, the pain made me cry out. My dress was stuck to my back from my shoulder to my waist. How much blood have I lost? I wondered.

In this extract, the reader is likely to admire the unusual strength, courage and resourcefulness of Manon's behaviour. One of the most noticeable features of this extract is Martin's choice of **verbs**. There are many powerful choices here, such as 'recoiled', 'slogged', 'staggered' and 'stumbling'. All of these are **dynamic verbs**, or verbs that describe physical actions, and here they serve to create a very physical and dramatic sense of Manon's escape. Occasionally a **stative verb**, or a verb that describes a state of being or thought process rather than an action, is used, such as 'I thought' and 'I wondered'. These give us a glimpse of

Key terms

Verbs: words that describe actions, e.g. 'to run' or 'to walk'.

Dynamic verbs: verbs that describe physical actions, e.g. 'to jump'.

Stative verbs: verbs that describe states of being and thought processes, e.g. 'to be', 'to think' or 'to seem'.

Manon's inner turmoil, but on the whole the focus here is on physical action, which gives the reader a strong impression of Manon's new-found sense of purpose and physical courage.

In addition, Valerie Martin makes use of several of the language features and techniques you have already looked at elsewhere in this chapter to describe Manon's actions in this extract. For example, Martin uses a range of syntax, including simple sentences such as 'I slogged through it' for dramatic impact, and imperatives such as 'keep going' to give us a sense of Manon's determination and strength of character. She also uses an asyndetic list – 'I stopped, listened, heard a variety of noises' – to create a fast-paced description with a sense of continuous, unfinished action. There are many words and phrases from the semantic field of pain and violence to heighten the drama of the scene. There is also great irony in the description of Manon, the white slave-owner, blackening her face with mud. Another feature to note here is Martin's use of long **paragraphs**, which help to convey the action in a breathless, unbroken manner. The pause between the two long paragraphs here perhaps reflects Manon's momentary indecision as she pauses to think what to do.

> ### 💡 Key terms
>
> **Paragraphs:** sub-sections of a written text, usually devoted to one main idea or stage in a narrative, comprising at lease one sentence.

◼ Critical response activity

Read the following extract from *The Kite Runner*, which describes Amir's escape from Afghanistan, and analyse the language used to describe his actions and behaviour.

- How does Khaled Hosseini's choice of verbs help to create a vivid impression of Amir?
- What other language features and techniques are used to add to the sense of drama and tension?

PANIC.

You open your mouth. Open it so wide your jaws creak. You order your lungs to draw air, NOW, you need air, need it NOW. But your airways ignore you. They collapse, tighten, squeeze, and suddenly you're breathing through a drinking straw. Your mouth closes and your lips purse and all you can manage is a strangled croak. Your hands wriggle and shake. Somewhere a dam has cracked open and a flood of cold sweat spills, drenches your body. You want to scream. You would if you could. But you have to breathe to scream.

Panic.

The basement had been dark. The fuel tank was pitch-black. I looked right, left, up, down, waved my hands before my eyes, didn't see so much as a hint of movement. I blinked, blinked again. Nothing at all. The air wasn't right, it was too thick, almost solid. Air wasn't supposed to be solid. I wanted to reach out with my hands, crush the air into little pieces, stuff them down my windpipe. And the stench of gasoline. My eyes stung from the fumes, like someone had peeled my lids back and rubbed a lemon on them. My nose caught fire with each breath. You could die in a place like this, I thought. A scream was coming. Coming, coming …

And then a small miracle. Baba tugged at my sleeve and something glowed green in the dark. Light! Baba's wristwatch. I kept my eyes glued to those fluorescent green hands. I was so afraid I'd lose them, I didn't dare blink.

> Slowly I became aware of my surroundings. I heard groans and muttered prayers. I heard a baby cry, its mother's muted soothing. Someone retched. Someone else cursed the *Shorawi*. The truck bounced side to side, up and down. Heads banged against metal.
>
> 'Think of something good,' Baba said in my ear. 'Something happy.'
>
> Something good. Something happy. I let my mind wander. I let it come.

A writer will include descriptions of a character's actions and behaviour in order to give us an insight into the personal qualities and values of that character, as we can see in both of the extracts above. Such descriptions may have no further significance than this; for example, the incident mentioned previously when Heathcliff hangs Isabella's dog as they elope has no significance or importance to the development of the plot of *Wuthering Heights*; it merely serves to demonstrate Heathcliff's ruthless cruelty at this point. However, some actions will do more than just give us an insight into that character, also acting as pivotal moments in the development of the plot, with subsequent actions contingent on what has been done.

Dialogue

A good deal of our opinions about characters will be formed from reading their dialogue, or what they say, and the manner in which they say it. Some aspects of how speech is represented in literary texts will be covered in more detail in Unit 2, including issues such as the presentation of accent and use of dialect terms. In that chapter you will develop a vocabulary of linguistic terms to enable you to analyse the spoken language of the characters from your set texts more closely. In this chapter, we will simply focus on characters' language choices and what these say about them, as well as the way their speech is described by the author.

The following extract from *Wuthering Heights* tells us a great deal about the characters of Heathcliff, his son Linton and the young Catherine. As you read, look for aspects of the characters' speech which tells you something about their character.

Link

See Unit 2 for more details on speech and its representation in literary texts.

> 'Now,' said he, with curbed ferocity, 'I'm getting angry – and if you don't command that paltry spirit of yours – Damn you! Get up, directly!'
>
> 'I will father!' he panted. 'Only let me alone, or I shall faint! I've done as you wished – I'm sure. Catherine will tell you that I – that I – have been cheerful. Ah! Keep by me, Catherine; give me your hand.'
>
> 'Take mine,' said his father, 'stand on your feet! There now – she'll lend you her arm … that's right, look at her. You should imagine I was the devil himself, Miss Linton, to excite such horror. Be so kind as to walk home with him, will you? He shudders, if I touch him.'
>
> 'Linton, dear!' whispered Catherine, 'I can't go to Wuthering Heights … papa has forbidden me … He'll not harm you, why are you so afraid?'
>
> 'I can never re-enter that house,' he answered. 'I'm not to re-enter it without you!'
>
> 'Stop … ' cried his father. 'We'll respect Catherine's filial scruples. Nelly, take him in, and I'll follow your advice concerning the doctor, without delay.'

'You'll do well,' replied I, 'but I must remain with my mistress. To mind your son is not my business.'

'You are very stiff!' said Heathcliff. 'I know that – but you'll force me to pinch the baby, and make it scream, before it moves your charity. Come then, my hero. Are you willing to return, escorted by me?'

Here, the modifying phrase 'with curbed ferocity' gives Heathcliff's speech an animal-like brutality, linking to the animal imagery which surrounds him throughout the novel. In contrast, the verb choice 'panted', used to describe Linton, conveys his weakness, while the verb 'whispered' suggests Catherine's growing anxiety as the scene unfolds. Both Linton and Heathcliff use imperative sentences in their dialogue, although while Heathcliff's convey his authority and dominance ('Get up, directly!'; 'stand on your feet!'), Linton's suggest his neediness and vulnerability ('keep by me, Catherine'). Heathcliff chooses several expressions to convey his contempt of Linton – 'that paltry spirit', 'baby', 'it' and the sarcastic 'my hero'. Meanwhile Linton's pauses, represented by a dash, and the repetition in 'that I – that I – ' show his sense of panic as he struggles to find the right words. In Catherine's dialogue, the childish phrase 'papa has forbidden me' gives us a sense of her youth and naivety. Her use of **ellipsis**, represented by the three dots (…), suggests that her utterances are incomplete – there are many things she doesn't have the time or the courage to say here.

Key terms

Ellipsis: the omission of part of a sentence. 'Hope you get well soon' is an example of ellipsis, as the pronoun 'I' has been left out. Ellipsis can also be represented by three dots (…) to indicate the missing part of the sentence.

■ Critical response activity

Analyse the presentation of dialogue in the following extract from *Things Fall Apart*. This exchange takes place when Okonkwo and the medicine-man Okagbue are forcing Okonkwo's daughter Ezinma to reveal where she has buried her *iyi-uwa* – a sort of talisman which supposedly signifies that Ezinma is an *ogbanje*, or 'one of those wicked children who, when they died, entered their mother's wombs to be born again'.

■ What do the language choices of each character tell us about them?

■ What do you notice about Chinua Achebe's choice of verbs and modifying phrases to describe how the dialogue is spoken?

'If you bring us all this way for nothing I shall beat sense into you,' Okonkwo threatened.

'I have told you to let her alone. I know how to deal with them,' said Okagbue.

Ezinma led the way back to the road, looked left and right and turned right. And so they arrived home again.

'Where did you bury your *iyi-uwa*?' asked Okagbue when Ezinma finally stopped outside her father's *obi*. Okagbue's voice was unchanged. It was quiet and confident.

'It is near that orange tree,' Ezinma said.

'And why did you not say so, you wicked daughter of Akalogoli?' Okonkwo swore furiously. The medicine-man ignored him.

'Come and show me the exact spot,' he said quietly to Ezinma.

'It is here,' she said when they got to the tree.

'Point at the spot with your finger,' said Okagbue.

'It is here,' said Ezinma touching the ground with her finger. Okonkwo stood by, rumbling like thunder in the rainy season.

'Bring me a hoe,' said Okagbue.

Setting and character

The setting of a novel might seem to be a separate issue to that of characterisation. However, writers often choose the details of their settings and backgrounds carefully to reflect internal aspects of their characters. Physical details of a particular location may be used to represent ideas about characters; for example, the wild, exposed, isolated location of the house Wuthering Heights reflects the wild unrestricted passions felt by some of its inhabitants, whereas the more sheltered gentle climate of Thrushcross Grange reflects its owner's calmer nature. Equally, details about the weather may be used in a similar way: the famous storm scene in Shakespeare's *King Lear* is usually considered to physically represent Lear's inner mental turmoil or 'this tempest in my mind' as Lear himself describes it, whereas in the following extract from the end of Annie Proulx's short story 'The Half-skinned Steer' the bleak snowy setting ominously seems to reflect Mero's sense of his impending death.

> He walked against the wind, his shoes filled with snow, feeling as easy to tear as a man cut from paper. As he walked he noticed one from the herd inside the fence was keeping pace with him. He walked more slowly and the animal lagged. He stopped and turned. It stopped as well, huffing vapor, regarding him, a strip of snow on its back like a linen runner. It tossed its head and in the howling wintry light he saw he'd been wrong again, that the half-skinned steer's red eye had been watching for him all this time.

This technique of creating a sympathetic background to reflect the human feelings and emotions of a story is often referred to as the **pathetic fallacy** and you will probably be familiar with this concept from films – it is always raining when there is a funeral and always dark or foggy as soon as someone has to go to the spooky house or into the woods.

Critical response activity

Read the following extract from *Wuthering Heights*, which follows the moment when Heathcliff has run off after overhearing Cathy telling the narrator Nelly Dean she could never marry him. Comment on the effect of Emily Brontë's use of pathetic fallacy at this point.

> It was a very dark evening for summer: the clouds appeared inclined to thunder, and I said we had better all sit down; the approaching rain would be certain to bring him home without further trouble.
>
> However, Catherine would not be persuaded into tranquillity. She kept wandering to and fro, from the gate to the door, in a state of agitation which permitted no repose: and, at length, took up a permanent position on one side of the wall, near the road; where, heedless of my expostulations, and the growling thunder, and the great drops that began to plash around her, she remained calling, at intervals, and then listening, and then crying out right. She beat Hareton, or any child, at a good passionate fit of crying.
>
> About midnight, while we still sat up, the storm came rattling over the Heights in full fury. There was a violent wind, as well as thunder, and either one or the other split a tree off at the corner of the building; a huge bough fell across the roof, and knocked down a portion of the east chimney-stack, sending a clatter of stones and soot into the kitchen fire.

Think about it

If you are studying a drama text, consider the choice of setting or settings the playwright has made. What does each setting add to characterisation, plot or the meaning of the play?

Key terms

Pathetic fallacy: the literary technique of representing internal human states and emotions through the description of external details such as landscape and weather. In this sense 'pathetic' means arousing sympathy, in other words, the term 'pathetic' suggests that the landscape is reflecting a character's feelings. The word 'fallacy' reminds us that this relationship is a deception: inanimate objects cannot truly echo the feelings and emotions of people, even though writers may have us believe otherwise.

4   Dramatic techniques

This chapter covers:

- dramatic genres and dramatic structure
- aspects of style and characterisation that are specific to drama texts.

Link

You will find it useful to refer to Unit 2 for more information on how to analyse spoken and rhetorical language and the representation of speech in a literary text.

Key terms

Tragedy: a serious play, often portraying the fortunes and misfortunes of the main character. The central character, or tragic hero, is often of high status; their downfall may result from a particular character flaw, such as Othello's jealousy or Macbeth's ambition.

Comedy: a play intended to entertain and amuse the audience, in which the problems encountered by the characters are resolved happily at the end.

Comic relief: a humorous episode included in a tragedy to relieve the emotional tension of the drama, which may also heighten the tension through the shock of the contrast.

Juxtapose: to place side by side. In literature, writers often juxtapose ideas to create interesting or surprising effects.

In this chapter we will look at the plays from the list of set texts for this unit. Although many features of language and style of prose fiction covered in previous chapters will be equally relevant to the study of a play, there are a number of aspects of structure, style and characterisation that are specific to drama. One of the main differences between the language of a novel or short story and that of a play is that the language of a play is intended to be spoken and heard rather than read.

Tragedy or comedy?

Drama is one of the three main genres of literary text, but there are many different genres of drama which can be included under that broad heading. Two of the main genres of play are **tragedies** (plays that portray the fortunes and misfortunes of a central character in a serious manner, ending with their downfall) and **comedies** (plays in which the twists and turns of the plot are resolved happily at the end). However, plays do not always fall neatly into such categories; a tragedy may contain elements of **comic relief**; for example, the famous gravediggers' scene in Shakespeare's *Hamlet* in which humour and serious reflection are **juxtaposed** in relation to the sombre topic of death. Equally, a comedy may include some darker moments; for example, despite its light humour and happy ending, Shakespeare's *Much Ado About Nothing* includes accusations of unfaithfulness, a fake death and the character of Beatrice demanding that her lover Benedick should kill his best friend.

Critical response activity

Compare the following extracts from two of the set plays for this unit.

In Extract A from *The Importance of Being Earnest* by Oscar Wilde, two friends, Algernon and Jack, are discussing Jack's cigarette case.

In Extract B from *A Streetcar Named Desire* by Tennessee Williams, Stella challenges her husband Stanley after he throws their radio out of the window for disturbing his poker game.

- What do you consider the genre of each play to be, based only on the extract given and without considering the outcome of the play as a whole text?
- What features of the language, style and content of each extract give you this impression?

Extract A: *The Importance of Being Earnest*

Algernon: Yes; but this isn't your cigarette case. This cigarette case is a present from someone of the name of Cecily, and you said you didn't know anyone of that name.

Jack: Well, if you want to know, Cecily happens to be my aunt.

Algernon: Your aunt!

Jack: Yes. Charming old lady she is, too. Lives at Tunbridge Wells. Just give it back to me, Algy.

Algernon (*retreating to back of sofa*): But why does she call herself little Cecily if she is your aunt and lives at Tunbridge Wells? (*Reading*) 'From little Cecily with her fondest love.'

Jack (*moving to sofa and kneeling upon it*): My dear fellow, what on earth is there in that? Some aunts are tall, some aunts are not tall. That is a matter that surely an aunt may be allowed to decide for herself. You seem to think that every aunt should be exactly like your aunt! That is absurd. For Heaven's sake give me back my cigarette case. (*Follows Algernon round the room*)

Algernon: Yes. But why does your aunt call you her uncle? 'From little Cecily, with her fondest love to her dear Uncle Jack.' There is no objection, I admit to an aunt being a small aunt, but why an aunt, no matter what her size may be, should call her own nephew her uncle, I can't quite make out. Besides, your name isn't Jack at all; it is Ernest.

Jack: It isn't Ernest; it's Jack.

Extract B: *A Streetcar Named Desire*

Stella: Drunk – drunk – animal thing, you! [*She rushes through to the poker table*] All of you – please go home! If any of you have one spark of decency in you –

Blanche (*wildly*): Stella, watch out, he's –

(*Stanley charges after Stella*)

Men (*feebly*): Take it easy, Stanley. Easy, fellow. – Let's all –

Stella: You lay your hands on me and I'll –

(*She backs out of sight. He advances and disappears. There is the sound of a blow. Stella cries out. Blanche screams and runs into the kitchen. The men rush forward and there is a grappling and cursing. Something is overturned with a crash.*)

Blanche (*shrilly*): My sister is going to have a baby!

Mitch: This is terrible.

Blanche: Lunacy, absolute lunacy!

Mitch: Get him in here, men.

(*Stanley is forced, pinioned by the two men, into the bedroom. He nearly throws them off. Then all at once he subsides and is limp in their grasp. They speak quietly and lovingly to him and he leans his face on one of their shoulders.*)

Stella (*in a high, unnatural voice, out of sight*): I want to go away, I want to go away!

Mitch: Poker shouldn't be played in a house with women.

(*Blanche rushes into the bedroom*)

Blanche: I want my sister's clothes! We'll go to that woman's upstairs!

Mitch: Where is the clothes?

Blanche (*opening the closet*): I've got them! (*She rushes through to Stella*) Stella, Stella, precious! Dear, dear little sister, don't be afraid!

(*With her arms around Stella, Blanche guides her to the outside door and upstairs*)

Research point

Use the internet or a library to find out more about these dramatic genres: history play, mystery play, kitchen-sink drama, farce, Theatre of the Absurd.

Subplot: a set of events that is secondary to the main story of a play but which may enhance our understanding of the main plot, e.g. by mirroring or contrasting with the main events.

Climax: the most dramatic moment of a play, also referred to as the crisis.

Exposition: the opening part of a play, which introduces the main characters and explains the background to the story.

Inciting moment: an event that occurs early on in a play and triggers the rest of the action.

Rising action: the part of the plot of a play in which the action develops towards the climax of the drama.

Complication: the problems, dilemmas and conflict encountered by the characters in a play during the rising action of the plot.

Conflict: the struggle or tension that is central to a drama and leads to the development of the action.

Falling action: the part of the plot of a play that follows on from the climax, leading to the close of the play.

Resolution: the part of a play where all the complications of the plot are worked out and a conclusion reached.

Denouement: the final resolution of the plot in a play or novel.

■ Dramatic structure

In classical times, the Greek writer Aristotle noted that plays of the time tended to be structured following the three 'unities' of action, time and place: the 'unity of action' requires a play to have only one plot, and no **subplot**; the 'unity of time' means that the action of the play should cover a period of no more than one day; and the 'unity of place' confines the action of the play to only one location. Of course, most playwrights, both past and present, disregard these conventions and restrictions; for example, in *The Winter's Tale*, Shakespeare ranges across two countries and a time-span of 17 years, and in many of his plays he makes great use of a subplot to enhance our understanding of the main events and action. However, it is worth noting that, in comparison to many novels, plays are generally more limited in scope, tending to focus on a smaller number of characters and events taking place over a shorter period of time.

In the 19th century the German novelist and critic Gustav Freytag used a diagram in the shape of a pyramid to represent the structure of plays, to suggest how the action rises to a **climax** (the peak of the pyramid) and then falls away as the story is resolved. This distinctive structure of a typical play is often described using the terms shown in Figure 1.

- The play begins with some sort of **exposition**, introducing the main characters and explaining the background to the story. There is likely to be an **inciting moment** or event which sets the ball rolling for the rest of the action.
- As the play develops, the **rising action** leads the story towards its climax. This section is often referred to as the **complication**, as the characters encounter problems, dilemmas and **conflict**.
- The **climax** of the play is the most dramatic moment in the story and can also be referred to as the **crisis**.
- The **falling action** describes the part of the plot that follows on from the climax, leading us back down to the close of the play. This part of the play is also referred to as the **resolution**, where all the complications of the plot are worked out and a conclusion reached, whether happy or tragic. The term **denouement**, which means 'unknotting', can also be used here.

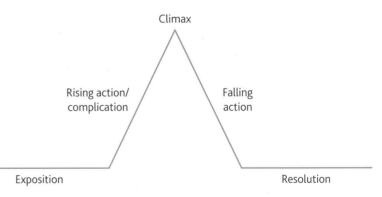

Fig. 1 *A pyramid diagram*

Practical activity

Read the following brief plot summary *of A Streetcar Named Desire* by Tennessee Williams, and see how it follows the structure outlined in Fig. 1 by dividing the story into sections using the terms given in bold. If you are studying a different play as one of your set texts, you could repeat this activity using a summary of your own text.

Blanche Dubois arrives to stay at her sister Stella's home in New Orleans and is shocked at how small and shabby it is. The large plantation home owned by Blanche and Stella has been lost through debt. Blanche cannot get on with Stella's rough, arrogant husband Stanley, who is angry at the loss of the sisters' land. Stella and Blanche go out to avoid Stanley's poker game, but when they return Stanley and his friends are still playing. Blanche talks to Stanley's friend Mitch. After a row about the women putting on the radio, Stanley hits Stella and she and Blanche take refuge with a neighbour, but to Blanche's shock Stella almost immediately returns to him. The next day, without realising Stanley is listening, Blanche tells Stella what she thinks of him. Tensions grow in the household. Stanley reveals to Blanche what he has found out about her past exploits with men in the town she has left behind. Blanche starts going out with Mitch and tells him about the suicide of her young husband years ago. On Blanche's birthday, a party is prepared but Mitch fails to turn up, as Stanley has now told him about Blanche's past. Stanley gives Blanche a bus ticket home, which upsets her. Stella, who is pregnant, goes into labour. Stanley comes home from the hospital in high spirits, but starts to argue with Blanche. Afraid, she threatens him with a smashed bottle. Stanley overpowers her and, we assume, rapes her. Some weeks later, Stella tells her neighbour that she could not believe Blanche's story and continue to live with Stanley. Stella therefore refuses to believe Blanche and needs to get rid of her. A doctor and nurse arrive to take Blanche away, as she has lost her mind. Stella cries and is comforted by Stanley.

One final aspect of the structure of a play to consider is the order in which events unfold. You have probably noticed in the summary in the Practical activity that the scenes are presented in **chronological order** – that is, in the order in which they happen. Many novels, such as *The Kite Runner* and *Wuthering Heights*, are not structured chronologically but make use of techniques such as **flashbacks** and reminiscences to explore events from the past. These techniques are less likely to be found in plays, which are written to be performed, often to give the audience the illusion that they are watching a story developing before their eyes. However, this is not necessarily true of all dramas; for example, in *The History Boys* Alan Bennett plays with the chronological sequence of the story to intriguing effect: the opening scene, showing the teacher Irwin as an MP in a wheelchair, seems not to make much sense or bear any relation to the schoolboy scenes that follow, until we learn much later that this is an episode from Irwin's future and the main part of the story becomes a sort of flashback from this point. Bennett also occasionally allows some of the characters to step out of the action and reflect on the present events on stage as if from the perspective of looking back on the past, thus disrupting the illusion that you are watching a scene from 'real life'. For example, in the following extract, Scripps almost seems to act as a narrator as he remembers the arrival of Irwin from an adult point of view, as the scene of Irwin's arrival is actually presented simultaneously before us.

Key terms

Chronological order: the sequencing of events in the order in which they occur in time.

Flashback: the technique of shifting from the present to a scene in the past in order to show something of significance that has happened previously.

Scripps: I'd been on playground duty, so I saw him on what must have been his first morning waiting outside the study. I thought he was a new boy, which of course he was, so I smiled. Then Felix turned up.

(*Irwin is a young man, aged about twenty-five or so*)

Headmaster: You are?

Irwin: Irwin.

Headmaster: Irwin?

Irwin: The supply teacher.

Headmaster: Quite so.

(*He beckons Irwin cagily into the study*)

Scripps: Hector said that if I wanted to write I should keep a notebook, and there must have been something furtive about Irwin's arrival because I wrote it down. I called it clandestine, a word I'd just learnt and wasn't sure how to pronounce.

Style

Alan Bennett's technique of allowing characters to step out of the action and address the audience directly, moving seamlessly between past and present, as seen in the extract above, is a key aspect of the individual style of this play. Although Alan Bennett notes in the Faber edition of *The History Boys* that he has 'not included many stage directions or even noted changes of scene; the more fluid the action the better', many playwrights use stage directions to convey their ideas about the style and presentation of their work.

Many playwrights aim to create a sense of **realism** or real life in their work, such as the truthful portrayal of domestic life in Tennessee Williams's *A Streetcar Named Desire* or Gerard's experiences in prison in David Hare's *Murmuring Judges*, often to make a comment about the society and attitudes of the time. In *A Streetcar Named Desire*, Tennessee Williams creates a powerful, hard-hitting drama by presenting realistic dialogue and real-life scenes that unfold naturally in chronological order. However, many dramatists, particularly in contemporary theatre, use devices and techniques that have moved a long way from this sort of naturalistic presentation to create a distinctive style of their own.

Look carefully at the style of presentation of the following extracts and consider the impact each will make on the audience.

In Extract A from *Murmuring Judges*, Jimmy and Barry are two policemen, Beckett is a warden at the prison where Gerard McKinnon is an inmate, and Irina and Sir Peter are McKinnon's lawyers spending the evening at the opera.

In Extract B from *The History Boys*, the teachers Irwin and Mrs Lintott are discussing one of the boys, Posner.

Extract A: *Murmuring Judges*

Sir Peter: McKinnon? Did you? Well, if you wish.

(*At this point, Gerard returns to his cell. He sits down on the edge of his bed, a thoughtful expression on his face. The stage is now divided into three: the opera house, the police station and the cell. Sir Peter smiles and leans in towards Irina, pointing to some of the crowd in the Crush Bar.*)

■ **Practical activity**

Create a diagram or timeline to represent the order in which events are presented in one or both of your set texts, highlighting any flashback sequences.

■ Link

Section B covers the use of stage directions in detail (see p54).

■ Key terms

Realism: a style of writing in which life is portrayed in an accurate, realistic manner.

Do you know Sir Hamish Tyrone over there?

Irina: No.

Sir Peter: He's the Cabinet Secretary. That's the Lord Chief. You know him, of course.

Irina: Tell me, if you run the country, is it compulsory to go to the opera in the evening?

(*Sir Peter smiles, enjoying himself*)

Sir Peter: You tell me. I have no idea.

(*Gerard turns a moment, as if hearing something. In the other part of the stage, Jimmy stirs, trying to reach Barry, who is staring gloomily into space.*)

Jimmy: You're always saying it's impossible. You say it's all a lost art. But we did it last week.

Barry: Just. By the skin of our teeth.

(*Sir Peter and Irina, carrying their programmes, move on down towards us*)

Irina: Well, what's your answer?

(*Sir Peter thinks a moment, serious*)

Sir Peter: You know as well as I do, the young man did everything wrong. He told a complete pack of lies. He persisted in them long after he should. I don't have to tell you the Appeal Court will be starkly prejudiced against him. (*He pauses. Then he's quiet*) But if you want me to, I'll take it on.

(*They stand a moment. Irina smiles. They arrive at the auditorium and opposite them now are the huge red curtains of the Royal Opera House. Meanwhile, the other areas come to life. Beckett and two other screws patrol down the corridor outside the cells.*)

Barry: Shall we get a drink?

Sir Peter: Is there time for a drink?

Beckett: Lights out! Lights out!

Extract B: *The History Boys*

Irwin: Posner came to see me yesterday. He has a problem.

Mrs Lintott: No nickname, but at least you get their problems. I seldom do.

Posner: Sir, I think I may be homosexual.

Irwin: Posner, I wanted to say, you are not yet in a position to be anything.

Mrs Lintott: You're young, of course. I never had that advantage.

Posner: I love Dakin.

Irwin: Does Dakin know?

Posner: Yes. He doesn't think it's surprising. Though Dakin likes girls basically.

Irwin: I sympathised, though not so much as to suggest I might be in the same boat.

Mrs Lintott: With Dakin?

Irwin: With anybody.

Mrs Lintott: That's sensible. One of the hardest things for boys to learn is that a teacher is human. One of the hardest things for a teacher to learn is not to try and tell them.

Posner: Is it a phase, sir?

Irwin: Do you think it's a phase?

Posner: Some of the literature says it will pass.

Irwin: I wanted to say that the literature may say that, but that literature doesn't.

Commentary

In both extracts you probably noticed that you are unusually able to watch more than one scene at the same time: in Extract A you are watching three scenes taking place simultaneously, whereas in Extract B you see a blending of a scene from the present with one from the past. In Extract A the presentation of the three scenes simultaneously has the effect of reinforcing for us the interconnections between the three sets of people, and these links are further emphasised by the way in which some lines seem to cross over from one scene to another. For example, Sir Peter's line 'Is there time for a drink?' seems to answer Barry's 'Shall we get a drink?' even though they are in separate locations, while the warder's 'Lights out!' seems to refer to the opera house as well as the prison, which emphasises the difference between the two places or perhaps even suggests an ironic similarity between them. Gerard's sense of loneliness and isolation in prison is heightened through the visual contrast with the pairs of characters chatting in the other scenes. In Extract B you may have found it quite surprising and entertaining that Irwin could appear to be in two scenes at once, talking to both Mrs Lintott in the present, and Posner in the past. Recreating the scene with Posner, rather than having Irwin relate it to Mrs Lintott, does make it more vivid and merging the scenes in this way makes the action more 'fluid', to use Alan Bennett's own word. It is a very economical way of conveying ideas in a fast-paced manner. Remember, you may also have other ideas about the impact and effect of these stylistic features.

🔍 Character

You may have noticed in the extract from *Murmuring Judges* that David Hare's stage directions give us some impression of character; for example, when Sir Peter 'smiles, enjoying himself' you are given a glimpse of his self-satisfaction and arrogance. However, on the whole, in contrast to a novel with its scope for narrative description, characters in a play are revealed almost entirely through spoken language. For example, the following speech from early on in *The History Boys* immediately gives us a strong impression of Hector's character.

Now fades the thunder of the youth of England clearing summer's obligatory hurdles.

Felicitations to you all. Well done, Scripps! Bravo, Dakin! Crowther, congratulations. And Rudge, too. Remarkable. All, all deserve prizes. All, all have done that noble and necessary thing, you have satisfied the examiners of the Joint Matriculation Board, and now, proudly jingling your A Levels, those longed-for emblems of your conformity, you come before me once again to resume your education.

Here, the **hyperbole** in Hector's metaphor of 'the thunder of the youth of England clearing summer's obligatory hurdles' to describe the examination system suggests his mocking attitude towards the process,

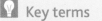

Think about it

If you are studying a drama text that is not one of the two covered in detail here, consider aspects of style that are specific to your playwright or play. One of the possible aspects is given below for each of the texts, how many more can you think of for your text?

The Importance of Being Ernest – word play

The Rivals – malapropisms

A Streetcar Named Desire – use of music

💡 Key terms

Hyperbole: an extravagant exaggeration in writing.

as well as his love of poetry, perhaps. His use of a variety of **synonyms** to congratulate the boys – 'Felicitations', 'Well done', 'Bravo' – reflect his love of language and word-play, as does the rhetorical repetition of 'All, all'. His line 'you come before me once again … ' suggests his opinion of himself as a powerful figure, admired and almost worshipped by the boys.

Paying close attention to his language choices, what impression do you get of the character of Stanley Kowalsky from *A Streetcar Named Desire* from the following extract?

> *Stanley*: Compliments to women about their looks. I never met a woman that didn't know if she was good-looking or not without being told, and some of them give themselves credit for more than they've got. I once went out with a doll who said to me, 'I am the glamorous type, I am the glamorous type!' I said, 'So what?'
>
> *Blanche*: And what did she say then?
>
> *Stanley*: She didn't say nothing. That shut her up like a clam.
>
> *Blanche*: Did it end the romance?
>
> *Stanley*: It ended the conversation – that was all. Some men are took in by this Hollywood glamour stuff and some men are not.

Aspects of character may be revealed in a play when a character is alone through the use of dramatic techniques such as **soliloquies**, **monologues** and **asides**, or when a character is talking with others in the form of **dialogue**.

Soliloquies

A soliloquy is a speech delivered by a character who is alone on stage. It is a useful device for giving the audience an insight into the innermost or secret thoughts and feelings of that character which could not easily be conveyed through dialogue. One very famous soliloquy is Hamlet's 'To be or not to be' speech, which has led to much discussion and debate about Hamlet's inner feelings on life and death. Shakespeare is renowned for his soliloquies; however, many other playwrights have also used this technique to give greater depth to their characters. Read this short soliloquy given by Mrs Lintott in *The History Boys*, when Bennett temporarily places her alone on stage, and consider what the soliloquy adds to Mrs Lintott's character.

> *Mrs Lintott*: I have not hitherto been allotted an inner voice, my role a patient and not unamused sufferance of the predilections and preoccupations of men. They kick their particular stone along the street and I watch.
>
> I am, it is true, confided in by all parties, my gender some sort of safeguard against the onward transmission of information … though that I should be assumed to be so discreet is in itself condescending. I'm what men would call a safe pair of hands.

As the only woman in a play dominated by male characters, Mrs Lintott here gives us a glimpse of her sense of isolation in her choice of the metaphor 'they kick their particular stone along the street and I watch', where the contrast between the pronouns 'I' and 'they' serves to mark her apart. Through the use of the soliloquy we learn of her private sense of frustration at being trapped in the role of the long-suffering woman that everyone confides in. Her choice of vocabulary, such as 'predilections and preoccupations', shows us an articulate and intelligent woman. However, in her opening line 'I have not hitherto been allotted an inner voice' Mrs

Key terms

Synonym: a word that has the same or a similar meaning to another word, e.g. 'smile' and 'grin' are synonyms, as they mean more or less the same thing but carry different **connotations**.

Connotation: the associations and feelings we attach to words on top of their basic meanings, e.g. although 'smile' and 'grin' mean more or less the same thing, the word 'smile' has connotations of warmth and friendship whereas the word 'grin' may have connotations of falseness or stupidity about it.

Soliloquy: a speech delivered by a character who is alone on stage, in which they reveal inner thoughts and feelings aloud to the audience.

Monologue: an extended speech delivered by a single character.

Aside: a brief line or speech spoken by a character to the audience and unheard by the other characters on stage, in which the speaker reveals their inner thoughts and intentions.

Dialogue: conversation between two or more characters presented in writing.

Lintott makes a witty allusion to the fact that she is not actually real but the fictional creation of the writer.

■ **Critical response activity**

Read the following soliloquy from Sheridan's *The Rivals*, in which Faulkland describes his feelings for Julia.

■ What attitudes towards love does Faulkland reveal?

■ How do his language choices help to convey these attitudes?

Faulkland: They told me Julia would return directly; I wonder she is not yet come! How mean does this captious, unsatisfied temper of mine appear to my cooler judgment! Yet I know not that I indulge it in any other point; but on this one subject, and to this one subject, whom I think I love beyond my life, I am ever ungenerously fretful, and madly capricious! I am conscious of it, yet I cannot correct myself! What tender, honest joy sparkled in her eyes when we met! How delicate was the warmth of her expressions! I was ashamed to appear less happy, though I had come resolved to wear a face of coolness and upbraiding. Sir Anthony's presence prevented my proposed expostulations: yet I must be satisfied that she has not been so very happy in my absence. She is coming! Yes! I know the nimbleness of her tread, when she thinks her impatient Faulkland counts the moments of her stay.

Monologues

A monologue is similar to a soliloquy in that it is an extended speech delivered by one character. However, the main difference is that there are likely to be other characters on stage during a monologue, who hear what is said. Therefore a monologue does not necessarily reveal a character's honest, inner thoughts, but may have a different purpose or motive. In the following example, from Sheridan's *The Rivals*, Julia Melville's purpose here is not just to reveal her thoughts about the 'many unhappy hours' she has suffered as a result of the delay in her marriage to Faulkland, but to loyally defend Faulkland against Lydia Languish's criticisms, which she does by counterbalancing his faults with more positive features and by drawing on the semantic field of love and affection. Were Julia to present her true feelings in the form of a soliloquy at this point, she might not be so charitable towards Faulkland!

Julia: Nay, you are wrong entirely. We were contracted before my father's death. That, and some consequent embarrassments, have delayed what I know to be my Faulkland's most ardent wish. He is too generous to trifle on such a point. And, for his character, you wrong him there too. No, Lydia, he is too proud, too noble to be jealous; if he is captious, 'tis without dissembling; if fretful, without rudeness. Unused to the fopperies of love, he is negligent of the little duties expected from a lover – but, being unhackneyed in the passion, his affection is ardent and sincere, and, as it engrosses his whole soul, he expects every thought and emotion of his mistress to move in unison with his. Yet, though his pride calls for this full return, his humility makes him undervalue those qualities in him which would entitle him to it; and not feeling why he should be loved to the degree he wishes, he still suspects that he is not loved enough. This temper, I must own, has cost me many unhappy hours, but I have learned to think myself his debtor for those imperfections which arise from the ardour of his attachment.

■ **Practical activity**

If you are studying a play as one of your set texts, see if you can find any examples of monologues and think about the speaker's purpose in each case. Explore the language choices the character makes to achieve their purpose.

Asides

An aside is similar to a soliloquy or monologue as it is another device that can be used by a dramatist to reveal a character's secret thoughts, although it is usually only a short line rather than an extended speech. Unlike a monologue, it is intended to be heard only by the audience and not by other characters on stage. In the following example from Shakespeare's *Othello*, Iago reveals to the audience through his use of an aside his intention to control and destroy the relationship between Othello and Desdemona as he watches their romantic reunion.

> **Iago** (*aside*): O, you are well tuned now! But I'll set down the pegs that make this music, as honest as I am.

An aside may create **dramatic irony** as the audience becomes privy to information that other characters on stage do not have.

Dialogue

Although soliloquies, monologues and asides are important techniques to reveal the inner emotions of characters, the bulk of nearly all plays is made up of dialogue between characters, which is, of course, essential in the development of both plot and character. Dialogue can reveal many aspects of character; for example, the fast-paced exchanges between the boys in *The History Boys* demonstrate their wit and intelligence as well as the web of relationships between them. In *A Streetcar Named Desire* much of the dialogue reveals the conflict which is at the heart of the play, especially between Blanche and Stanley.

Key terms

Dramatic irony: a situation in a drama where the audience is aware of something that some of the characters on stage do not know about.

Critical response activity

In the following extract of dialogue between Blanche and Stanley in *A Streetcar Named Desire*, how is language used to create a sense of the conflict and tension between the two characters?

> **Stanley**: If I didn't know that you was my wife's sister I'd get ideas about you!
>
> **Blanche**: Such as what?
>
> **Stanley**: Don't play so dumb. You know what! – Where's the papers?
>
> **Blanche**: Papers?
>
> **Stanley**: Papers! That stuff people write on!
>
> **Blanche**: Oh, papers, papers! Ha-ha! The first anniversary gift, all kinds of papers!
>
> **Stanley**: I'm talking of legal papers. Connected with the plantation.
>
> **Blanche**: There were some papers.
>
> **Stanley**: You mean they're no longer existing?
>
> **Blanche**: They probably are, somewhere.
>
> **Stanley**: But not in the trunk.
>
> **Blanche**: Everything that I own is in that trunk.
>
> **Stanley**: Then why don't we have a look for them? (*He crosses to the trunk, shoves it roughly open and begins to open compartments*)
>
> **Blanche**: What in the name of heaven are you thinking of! What's in the back of that little boy's mind of yours? That I am absconding with something, attempting some kind of treachery on my sister?

– Let me do that! It will be faster and simpler … (*She crosses to the trunk and takes out a box*) I keep my papers mostly in this tin box. (*She opens it*)

Stanley: What's them underneath? (*He indicates another sheaf of paper*)

Blanche: These are love-letters, yellowing with antiquity, all from one boy. (*He snatches them up. She speaks fiercely*.) Give those back to me!

Stanley: I'll have a look at them first!

Blanche: The touch of your hands insults them!

Stanley: Don't pull that stuff!

Commentary

One of the main ways that a sense of conflict and tension is created between the two characters here is the frequent use of interrogatives. Stanley uses questions such as 'Where's the papers?' to demand authority over Blanche and to taunt her – 'Then why don't we have a look for them?' Blanche equally uses questions such as 'Papers?' and 'Such as what?' to provoke and defy Stanley. They both use imperatives such as 'Give those back to me!' and 'Don't pull that stuff!' as they struggle for control of the situation and the frequent exclamations, both in these examples and elsewhere, show their heightened passions and the tension between them at this point. Blanche's exclamation 'Oh, papers, papers! Ha-ha!' has a deliberately mocking tone to it, designed to annoy and infuriate Stanley. Both characters choose language to insult the other – Stanley calls Blanche 'dumb' while Blanche attempts to belittle him by referring to 'that little boy's mind of yours'. Stanley's language seems basic and unsophisticated, seen in lines such as 'What's them underneath?' In contrast, Blanche uses more sophisticated lexical choices, such as 'absconding' and 'treachery', and poetic expressions such as 'yellowing with antiquity', in an attempt to assert her intellectual superiority over Stanley and make him look stupid.

Character types

In plays, the central character, such as Blanche in *A Streetcar Named Desire*, is often referred to as the **protagonist** and the main character who is in opposition or conflict with them, such as Stanley, is known as the **antagonist**. A character such as Stanley, who is in conflict with the world around him and lacks the traditional qualities we might expect of a hero while still having some attractive features (especially as portrayed by Marlon Brando in the original film version of the play), can also be described as an **antihero**. Another type of character you may well come across in your study of plays is the **stock character**. This sort of character will not be portrayed in as much depth or developed in the same way as the main characters are likely to be; rather, they are likely to be one-dimensional stereotypes. They are often included to represent a theme or idea, or to make a point, rather than to present us with a realistic portrait of a human being. For example, the police officer Lester in *Murmuring Judges*, with his banter and innuendo, could be described as a stock character: he is a stereotype, included to represent a particular image of the police force and to dramatise and convey a certain set of attitudes, rather than because he is personally important to the unfolding of the action and relationships in the play.

💡 Key terms

Protagonist: the central character in a play.

Antagonist: a character who is in opposition to the protagonist, who creates conflict with the main character.

Antihero: the main character of a text who lacks the conventional heroic qualities.

Stock character: a one-dimensional stereotypical character, often included to make a point or represent an idea rather than as a realistic portrayal of a person.

5 Preparing for the examination

This chapter covers:

- preparation for the analytical questions in your examination

- selecting references from your set text

- sample questions, answer and examiner's comments.

For the Unit 1 analytical question in the examination, the questions will focus on 'the ways in which language and style help the writer to develop and explore issues within the text (such as theme and character). Candidates will be expected to produce an informed response underpinned by close textual reference and stylistic discussion.'

This question is worth 30 out of the 75 marks available in the examination, split between Assessment Objectives 1 and 2.

- For AO1, you will need to show that you can choose relevant linguistic and literary concepts and terminology to analyse your set text. The accuracy of your own written expression will also be assessed. *(15 marks)*

- For AO2, you will need to show in detail that you understand and can analyse the ways in which structure, form and language shape meaning. *(15 marks)*

You are advised to spend approximately 40 minutes on this question. Here are some tips to help you make the most of your time before and during the exam:

- Make sure you have a thorough knowledge of your set texts – A-level students are often advised to read their set texts at least three times.

- As your texts cannot be annotated at all, use an alternative system to keep detailed notes on different characters and themes to revise from.

- Make sure you can find key scenes and references quickly – you do not want to waste valuable time thumbing through your text to find a particular page.

- Include plenty of examples from the text in your answer. Although it is not a good idea to spend time learning lengthy quotes before the examination, you may be able to memorise a few short lines, which could save you time.

- It is essential to learn a range of different literary and linguistic terms which you can use as a framework to help you analyse your set texts. Use the glossary at the end of this book to remind yourself of the range of concepts and terminology covered in this book.

- Decide on a suitable approach for the question set; for example, if you are asked to comment on the development of a particular character, it may make sense to follow that character in a linear way through the text, whereas if you are asked about a theme, it may be better to start with a key episode and then work around that.

Selecting references from your set text

In the examination, it is important to select material from your set text which is relevant to the question and which allows you to show your understanding of the text as a whole. For example, if you choose to answer a question about the character of Heathcliff in *Wuthering Heights*, you will want to select material about him from the early parts of the novel where he is a young man, as well as choosing extracts from the second half of the novel where he returns as an adult so that you can reflect on the changes in his character. Similarly, if you choose to

■ Link

This principle is also covered in 'Selecting an appropriate episode' in Unit 2 Section B (see p151).

tackle a question on Irwin in *The History Boys*, you could look at the scenes where Irwin is presented as an MP and a television presenter and compare these episodes to some of the scenes where he is teaching the boys, thus enabling you to look at a range of aspects of his character. It is, of course, much easier to select material from a short play than from a long novel; however, if you follow the tips above and keep thorough detailed notes about a range of characters and themes, you should be able to choose relevant appropriate material to refer to in the examination, whatever text you are studying. Read the sample response to *A Streetcar Named Desire* on pages p37–38 and the examiner's comments that follow, and note how this student has managed to select material that is both relevant to the question and covers a range of scenes from throughout the play.

◤ ☑ Sample questions and answers

The kinds of question you will encounter in the examination will be similar in pattern. You can expect to be asked about the presentation of a character or the relationship between characters, or about a particular theme or issue. All questions will ask you to consider the writers' language choices. If you are tackling a question on prose fiction, you will also be asked about narrative viewpoint, whereas questions on the set plays will ask you to consider dramatic techniques.

Here are examples of the sort of analytical questions you will find in the examination. Other specimen questions for all the set texts are available on the AQA website.

Read Question 1 below and the sample response and examiner's comments that follow. Try writing a complete answer to one of the questions on your set texts.

1   *A Streetcar Named Desire*: **Tennessee Williams**

How does Williams portray the character of Stanley and his attitudes?

In your answer you should consider:

a   Williams's language choices

b   dramatic techniques.

Sample response

In the play, Stanley is portrayed as a very masculine, aggressive character, with chauvinistic attitudes to both Stella and Blanche. However, despite his thuggishness, he is also portrayed as attractive – Stella can't live without him – and he is sometimes seen to have a more naive vulnerable side to his character.

One of the first dramatic techniques Williams uses to introduce us to Stanley in Scene 1 is that of stage directions. In these, Williams describes Stanley as having 'the power and pride of a richly feathered male bird among hens', and this metaphor conveys his masculine sense of superiority and chauvinistic attitude. It is also one of many animal references associated with Stanley. Williams uses many dynamic verbs in the stage directions for Stanley, such as 'throws the screen door of the kitchen open', also reflected later on when he 'snatches' the radio and 'tosses' it out of the window. These dynamic verbs give us a strong sense of his physical presence. Williams also uses an asyndetic list – 'his heartiness with men, his appreciation of rough humour, his love of good drink and food and games, his car, his radio, everything that is his, that bears his emblem of the gaudy seed-bearer' – to build up a picture of Stanley as a typical man, with the repeated pronoun 'his' really emphasising his masculinity.

This sense of masculinity is made apparent when we first see Stanley, throwing a parcel of meat to Stella. His attitude is that he is the hunter and provider, while she must stay at home and cook for him. This is further shown at the party scene, when he says 'I am the king around here, so don't forget it.' His choice of the noun 'king' conveys his arrogance and sense of power over the women. His attitude to women is also conveyed in Scene 2, when he argues with Blanche about the loss of the plantation; he clearly believes that Stella's property belongs to him under the 'Napoleonic Code' he keeps mentioning. Williams uses a variety of syntax to convey Stanley's conflict with Blanche in this scene. For example, he uses exclamations such as 'Papers! That stuff people write on!' and 'I'll have a look at them first!', which suggest his anger and frustration with Blanche and his attempts to dominate her by shouting at her. Stanley also barks out questions at her, such as 'Where's the papers?' and also uses imperatives such as 'Don't play so dumb' and 'Don't pull that stuff!', again to control and dominate the scene. In addition, Stanley's use of non-standard English and colloquial expressions here give us an impression of an unsophisticated, insensitive man.

Stanley's aggressive character develops further in Scene 3 with the poker game, culminating in him hitting Stella. Here, as in the rape scene later on, Williams uses the dramatic technique of having the actual action off-stage – we only hear 'the sound of a blow', which makes it all the more sinister for the audience as we are not quite sure what has happened. However, Stanley is almost immediately remorseful. Williams describes him with the simile 'like a baying hound', which is another example of the animal imagery surrounding Stanley, as he calls for Stella. Stanley calls her 'my baby', 'my baby doll', 'my girl'. Here the repeated pronoun 'my' suggests his possessive feelings for Stella, whereas the noun choices show us his sentimental affection for her. When he is described as 'he falls on his knees', we perhaps see a more vulnerable side to him.

Stanley's violence towards Stella foreshadows the rape scene in Scene 10, which is the climax of the play. This scene shows Stanley's cruelty, as he is described as 'grinning'. His dominance is shown in his use of short simple imperatives such as 'Drop the bottle-top! Drop it!' When he refers to Blanche as 'tiger – tiger!' he seems to be mocking her and he describes what is happening with the noun 'date', which is cruel and sarcastic. However, just before this episode, when Stanley has arrived home from the hospital, he is shown as exuberantly happy at the thought of the baby coming. The simile of him waving his red silk pyjamas 'like a flag' to celebrate gives a rather simple, naive, child-like image of Stanley. We also see this different side when he talks to Stella about their sex life with the simple metaphor 'them coloured lights'. His non-grammatical use of 'them' shows us a simple, perhaps uneducated man.

In conclusion, Stanley is no doubt a bullying thug, some of whose actions will appal the audience. However, there are some more appealing aspects to his character, making him a complex character to analyse.

Examiner's comments

For AO1, this is a fluently written response that takes into account both language choices (such as Williams's use of non-standard and colloquial forms in Stanley's speech and the effect of different syntactical choices) and dramatic techniques (such as the use of off-stage violence and descriptive stage directions). There is clearly some close engagement with the meaning of the text and a framework of literary and linguistic terms has been used accurately, covering a range of features (including imagery such as simile and metaphor and lexical choices such as verbs, nouns and pronouns), which has allowed the candidate to give their interpretation of the character.

For AO2, there is close focus on details, with a range of examples discussed. In places, the analysis could go further; for example, the term 'asyndetic list' is used although no point really develops here. Although this response perhaps lacks any profound or illuminating comments, it provides a secure coherent analysis of the character, underpinned by good textual reference. Overall, this is a successful response to the task.

Sample questions from other texts

1 *A Streetcar Named Desire*: **Tennessee Williams**

For the sample question and response on this text, see p36.

2 *Wuthering Heights*: **Emily Brontë**

How does Brontë present the contrast between Edgar Linton and Heathcliff?

In your answer you should consider:

a Brontë's language choices

b narrative viewpoint.

3 *Property*: **Valerie Martin**

How does Valerie Martin portray the character of Manon and her attitudes up until the time of her husband's death?

In your answer you should consider:

a Martin's language choices

b narrative viewpoint.

4 *Things Fall Apart*: **Chinua Achebe**

How does Chinua Achebe use the story of Ikemefuna to influence the reader's responses to Okonkwo?

In your answer you should consider:

a Achebe's language choices

b narrative viewpoint.

5 *The Kite Runner*: **Khaled Hosseini**

How does Hosseini develop the image of the kite throughout the novel?

In your answer you should consider:

a   Hosseini's language choices

b   narrative viewpoint.

6 *Close Range*: **Annie Proulx**

How does Proulx portray the relationship between Jack and Ennis in 'Brokeback Mountain'?

In your answer you should consider:

a   Proulx's language choices

b   narrative viewpoint.

7 *The Importance of Being Earnest*: **Oscar Wilde**

How does Wilde portray the relationship between Jack Worthing and Gwendolen Fairfax?

In your answer you should consider:

a   Wilde's language choices

b   dramatic techniques.

8 *The Rivals*: **Richard Brinsley Sheridan**

How does Sheridan use the idea of deception to create comedy?

In your answer you should consider:

a   Sheridan's language choices

b   dramatic techniques.

9 *Murmuring Judges*: **David Hare**

How does Hare present the police in the play?

In your answer you should consider:

a   Hare's language choices

b   dramatic techniques.

10 *The History Boys*: **Alan Bennett**

How does Bennett present ideas about education in the play?

In your answer you should consider:

a   Bennett's language choices

b   dramatic techniques.

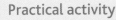
Practical activity

Look up the mark scheme for this unit on the AQA website and use the grid provided to assess your own response to one of the sample questions given above.

Learning outcomes for this section:

Knowledge, understanding and skills

Now that you have completed Section A of this unit, you should be able to:

- comment on language choices in both novels and plays

- show an understanding of the ways in which narrative viewpoint and dramatic techniques are used in texts

- use relevant linguistic and literary concepts and terminology in your analysis of texts

- show an understanding of how structure, form and language shape meaning

- apply your knowledge and understanding by selecting and commenting on appropriate aspects of your set texts in the examination.

Transferable skills

Your study of this section has provided you with a framework of terminology and concepts that you will be able to use in your preparation for Unit 2 and in your A2 studies.

Audience and purpose

This chapter covers:

- how the audience and purpose of a text affect the lexical choices, form, genre and content

- key features of texts that are written to inform, persuade, entertain or argue a case.

Link

We will be discussing in Chapter 8 (beginning on p54) some of the considerations you will need to take into account when working from a drama text.

Key terms

Voice: the distinctive manner of expression that is characteristic of a particular writer or speaker, or of a created literary character.

Audience

In any piece of writing, just as in speaking, the intention is successful communication. As the audience for a novel or other written text is not physically present, the author needs to have a clear sense of the kinds of people who will be reading the text and create a suitable text to fulfil the needs and expectations of that audience. When dramatists are writing plays or politicians are preparing speeches, they will have an intended audience clearly in mind. In many cases, it will be a live audience that eventually hears the play or listens to the speech, but often experience it via a TV or radio broadcast.

A clear awareness of the intended audience is fundamental to successful writing. Audiences can be broadly described under categories such as age, level of education, social grouping and interests. Of course, people are complex and do not fit neatly into categories, but you can walk into any bookshop or library and see the labels on the shelves: children's fiction, books for men, science fiction, historical novels. Magazines are also aimed at different audiences such as teenage girls, sports enthusiasts, weight watchers and musicians.

The kind of audience at which the text is aimed will affect the lexical choices, form, genre and content. Always ask yourself when you are writing creatively, *'Who is this text for?'*

For the creative response question you are likely to be writing for the same audience as the novelist or dramatist. For example, in *Things Fall Apart* by Chinua Achebe, you might be asked to write about Okonkwo's feelings when he accidentally kills the son of Ezueda, giving a sense of his **voice**. In doing this, you would be writing for the same readership as Achebe's novel. Later in the same text, Okonkwo kills a messenger from the white authorities and then hangs himself. The District Commissioner who is responsible for sending the messenger feels that the story of this episode would make 'interesting reading' in his book to be entitled *The Pacification of the Primitive Tribes of the Lower Niger*. The question might require you to write about the event for inclusion in this book in the voice of the District Commissioner. His language and style would be very different from Okonkwo's and he would be writing for a different audience; he would expect his readers to be sympathetic to his views about the tribes.

You might also be asked to write for a specific audience such as an individual recipient of a letter; for example, using *The Kite Runner* as the set text, a letter from Amir to his wife Soraya after he has talked to Rahim Khan in Peshawar and decided to go into Afghanistan to seek out the orphaned son of his childhood friend. In this case, the relationship between the two characters and the future development of the plot would affect both the content of your letter and the level of formality of the writing.

■ Link

A sample response to this task and a commentary on it are given on pp64–5.

Other tasks might require a more formal letter. Amir returns from Kabul with the child, who has suffered abuse in Afghanistan. He wants to adopt the boy, Sohrab, and take him back to the USA. Your task might be to imagine that Amir writes to the American Embassy seeking permission to adopt Sohrab rather than visiting the embassy in person as he actually does in the novel.

■ Purpose

This is the second fundamental consideration for a writer. Broadly speaking, an author seeks to inform, persuade, entertain or argue with the reader. However, it is necessary to go beyond these simple categories to consider purpose in more detail.

If we consider information writing, we need to think about how much detail is appropriate and precisely what the reader's purpose is in acquiring information about the chosen topic. Does the reader need a brief overview or is it essential to give a thorough and detailed account? In other words, the writer's purpose and the reader's purpose need to be considered as opposite sides of the same coin.

Persuasive writing may have as its central purpose the intention of convincing the reader to donate money to a particular cause or organisation or it may be that a campaign is seeking to alter people's attitudes towards speed limits, smoking or air travel, for example. The purpose will affect the content of the work and its style.

Writing to entertain may take a huge variety of forms and focus on any topic. The question of purpose needs to be related to your sense of the target audience and you have to think carefully about how it is likely to respond to particular forms of humour, for example. To take a specific example, some readers find mild swearing in dialogue perfectly acceptable but recoil from a more explicit taboo word that the writer might regard as simply a realistic reflection of the way some people communicate.

In writing to argue a case, texts can be used in many different ways, such as to argue that a particular idea, theory or policy is actually the case or to invite an audience to weigh up a number of possibilities. Although it is likely to have a persuasive element, the language will probably be less emotive than in a text that has the primary purpose of persuasion. Characteristically, a good argument will have a sound evidence base. Scientists engaged in research, for example, are likely to persuade through the careful amassing of evidence that supports their hypotheses rather than by the use of emotive language. The results can be far reaching, however; think of the impact of Darwin's *The Origin of Species*, which introduced the theory of evolution.

💡 Writing to inform

Writing that is primarily informative should have:

- lexical choices which are clear and not too emotive
- a structure which conveys information clearly

The following article, which is taken from the NHS Direct website *Mind and Body* magazine, is intended to inform an adult audience about healthy exercise.

www.nhsdirect.nhs.uk

Mind and body magazine

Defining exercise

It's recommended that we do at least 30 minutes of 'moderate exercise' every day. And recent studies have suggested that we need to fit more 'vigorous exercise' into our lives.

But when it comes to exercising, what exactly is the difference between light, moderate and vigorous?

Light exercise generally allows you to talk while you're doing it.

Examples of light exercise could include:

★ going for a short walk
★ light housework
★ gardening or DIY, and
★ playing with the kids in the garden.

Moderate exercise should make you feel slightly out of breath. You should feel slightly worn out, but not to the point where it's unbearable.

Examples of moderate exercise could include:

★ going for a brisk walk
★ walking up a hill, and
★ carrying heavy bags back from the shops.

Vigorous exercise should make you breathe rapidly and break into a sweat. You should feel like you are just at the point where you are pushing your boundaries (without doing your body any damage!).

Examples of vigorous exercise could include:

★ running
★ cycling
★ swimming
★ playing football
★ exercise classes, and
★ lifting weights.

Everyone is different

Don't forget that everyone is different. Factors such as weight, muscle strength and any recent exercise programs all affect what represents light, moderate or vigorous exercise for you.

If you're an adult and you haven't done any exercise since childhood, exercise that is considered moderate, such as going for a brisk walk, may feel more like vigorous exercise.

As long as you know where your boundaries are and you keep pushing them (although not too hard), then you are doing the right amount of exercise for your body's needs.

Commentary

Lexical choices such as 'muscle strength', 'pushing your boundaries' and 'brisk' are appropriate for a non-specialist adult audience. The article imparts information successfully by explaining any terms, such as 'light', 'moderate' and 'vigorous', which might be unclear to readers. The structure of the article also helps information to be absorbed easily. Subheadings and bullet points make it easy to assimilate the information. The register is informal; the reader is addressed directly using the **second person pronoun** 'you'. **Contractions** such as 'it's' and 'you're' also support this informality. Although there is an underlying element of persuasion in this article, its main purpose is to provide clear information.

💡 Writing to persuade

A text that is primarily intended to persuade will have:

▨ a clear focus on the subject matter
▨ a sustained attempt to convince the reader to accept the writer's case or message
▨ a clear structure.

💡 Key terms

Second person pronoun: the use of 'you', 'your', 'yourself' (or in older and biblical texts, 'thou', 'thy', 'thyself') in place of a name.

Contractions: words that are abbreviated using an apostrophe, e.g. 'we're' for 'we are' and 'can't' for 'cannot'. Note that the apostrophe goes in the place of the missing letter or letters.

In the example below, which is taken from a stop-smoking website, the audience would be smokers and potential smokers and the purpose to make them give up or not start smoking.

◀ ▶ ⟳ + www.gosmokefree.co.uk

Go smokefree

Imagine one of the best things you could do in your life. Making a complete break from smoking. Think about how great it would be to leave those health worries behind you. Picture yourself waking up and feeling totally fresh. Millions of people in Britain have already gone smokefree and you can too. See real life videos showing how some of those millions have achieved it.

Commentary

Here, you can see that the main emphasis is on positive features. The second person pronoun 'you' is used to create a personal appeal to the audience. The lexical choices 'think about how great' and 'totally fresh' present a picture of a completely new and rejuvenated start. Imperative verbs 'imagine' and 'picture' are used to urge the reader. Encouragement is given by suggesting that others have achieved this goal and by offering video evidence of success. The author could have used the opposite technique of choosing negative lexis, stressing the terrible health consequences of smoking, such as lung cancer, heart disease and poor circulation leading to leg amputation. In the example above, the positive message is intended to bring about action.

Writing to entertain

A text that is entertaining is one which gives pleasure but is not necessarily (or even usually) amusing. It will engage the reader's interest by:

■ making lexical choices which are interesting, unusual and appropriate for the audience

■ telling its story in a distinctive style

■ having an appropriate structure.

At last the rain came. It was sudden and tremendous. For two or three moons the sun had been gathering strength till it seemed to breathe a breath of fire on the earth. All the grass had long been scorched brown, and the sand felt like live coals to the feet. Evergreen trees wore a dusty coat of brown. The birds were silenced in the forests, and the world lay panting under the live, vibrating heat. And then came the clap of thunder. It was an angry, metallic and thirsty clap, unlike the deep and liquid rumbling of the rainy season. A mighty wind arose and filled the air with dust. Palm trees swayed as the wind combed their leaves into flying crests like strange and fantastic coiffure.

When the rain finally came, it was in large, solid drops of frozen water which the people called 'the nuts of the water of heaven'. They were hard and painful on the body as they fell, yet young people ran about happily picking up the cold nuts and throwing them into their mouths to melt.

Practical activity

Think about a storm that you have experienced for yourself but in a different environment to the one described, such as in a town or at the coast. Using a similar style, write a paragraph conveying the physical and emotional experience of this storm. Think carefully about the lexical choices, imagery and narrative voice that you need to employ in order to write in a similar way to Chinua Achebe.

Writing to argue a case

A text that argues a case will have:

- a logical structure
- points which are supported by evidence
- language which is not too emotive.

In the extract below, the philosopher Nick Bostrom explores the idea that we might be living in a computer simulation.

Are you living in a computer simulation?

Introduction

Many works of science fiction as well as some forecasts by serious technologists and futurologists predict that enormous amounts of computing power will be available in the future. Let us suppose for a moment that these predictions are correct. One thing that later generations might do with their super-powerful computers is run detailed simulations of their forebears or of people like their forebears. Because their computers would be so powerful, they could run a great many such simulations. Suppose that these simulated people are conscious (as they would be if the simulations were sufficiently fine-grained and if a certain quite widely accepted position in the philosophy of mind is correct). Then it could be the case that the vast majority of minds like ours do not belong to the original race but rather to people simulated by the advanced descendants of an original race. It is then possible to argue that, if this were the case, we would be rational to think that we are likely among the simulated minds rather than among the original biological ones. Therefore, if we don't think that we are currently living in a computer simulation, we are not entitled to believe that we will have descendants who will run lots of such simulations of their forebears. That is the basic idea. The rest of this paper will spell it out more carefully.

www.simulation-argument.com

Commentary

Unlike the overtly persuasive 'Go smokefree' extract above, there are no imperatives. Instead, more tentative expressions are used: 'suppose', 'it could be the case', 'it is then possible to argue', 'if this were the case'. The argument spells out how one set of beliefs is dependent on another. Although the text is clearly aimed at an educated audience, its purpose is the exploration of ideas rather than persuading the audience that a particular viewpoint is true.

🔍 Summary

Considerations of audience and purpose apply to all kinds of texts, including newspaper articles, advertisements and reports, as well as literary texts. Even descriptions attached to products in shops have a clear and recognisable purpose and sense of audience; think about the different effects of labels offering 'Cheddar Cheese' and 'Taste the Difference Mature West Country Farmhouse Cheddar'. You need to develop your knowledge of these techniques to prepare for the creative response in the examination.

For the creative response questions labelled B on the examination paper, your own writing will be based on your study of a set text, either prose fiction or drama. It is clearly the purpose of all of the set works to entertain readers or audiences, but some of them contain a powerfully persuasive element and also inform readers about aspects of the setting or content. For example, *The Kite Runner* could be said to inform and persuade because the reader is likely to become more informed about Afghanistan and its history as evaluated by the author and persuaded towards his views on the Taliban or international adoption, for example. By reading a variety of texts for yourself, in addition to studying your set texts, you will develop your awareness of authors' overall purposes and intentions in their writing. You will also notice the different purposes that may be shown in individual extracts. For example, in the opening of a novel the author may be intending to introduce characters, set the scene and initiate the plot, whereas later on the intention might be to explore how a character has changed in the light of experiences depicted in earlier parts of the text. In a drama, these features will be introduced and developed through speech, setting, stage directions and stage action.

7 Novels: narrative voice

This chapter covers:

- how to use the narrative voice of your set text to produce your own creative response

- how to write in the voice of a character or narrator.

Link

Re-read the section on narrative voice on pp5–7 of Unit 1.

Practical activity

Read the openings of several novels and work out for yourself the intended audience, purpose and narrative voice. Some examples are given in the Critical response activity.

In order to make a successful transition from your set text to your own answer to the creative response question in the examination, it is essential that you have carefully considered the narrative voice(s) in the text. Remember that the narrator is not necessarily reliable and objective and that as a reader you need to re-evaluate your assumptions and judgements as the text progresses.

Critical response activity

The following three examples are taken from the openings of novels. Read them carefully, using the following questions to guide your reading.

Audience

- Who are the intended audiences for each extract?

- What lexical and grammatical choices have the authors made and how do they enable you to work out the intended audience of each extract?

Purpose

- What is the author's purpose in each extract?

- What impressions do you form about the characters, setting and potential development of the plot in each case?

Narrative voice

- Identify the narrative voice in each case and consider what effect this has on your response to the characters and situations that are presented.

Extract A: *The Hobbit*

In a hole in the ground there lived a hobbit. Not a nasty, dirty, wet hole filled with the ends of worms and an oozy smell, nor yet a dry, bare sandy hole with nothing in it to sit down on or to eat: it was a hobbit-hole and that means comfort.

It had a perfectly round door like a porthole, painted green with a shiny yellow brass knob in the exact middle. The door opened on to a tube-shaped hall like a tunnel: a very comfortable tunnel without smoke, with panelled walls, and floors tiled and carpeted, provided with polished chairs and lots and lots of pegs for hats and coats – the hobbit was fond of visitors.

Extract B: *The Wasp Factory*

I had been making the rounds of the Sacrifice Poles the day we heard my brother had escaped. I already knew something was going to happen; the Factory told me.

At the North end of the island, near the tumbled remains of the slip where the handle of the rusty winch still creaks in an easterly wind, I had two Poles on the far face of the last dune. One of the Poles held a rat head with two dragonflies, the other a seagull and two mice. I was just sticking one of the mouse heads back on when the birds went up into the evening air, kaw-calling and screaming, wheeling over the path through the dunes where it went near their nests. I made sure the head was secure, then clambered to the top of the dune to watch with my binoculars.

Extract C: *Charlotte Gray*

Peter Gregory kicked the door of the dispersal hut closed behind him with the heel of his boot. He sensed the iciness of the air outside but was too well wrapped to feel it on his skin. He looked up and saw a big moon hanging still, while ragged clouds flew past and broke up like smoke in the darkness. He began to waddle across the grass, each step won from the limits of movement permitted by the parachute that hung down behind as he bucked and tossed his way forward. He heard the clank of the corporal fitter's bicycle where it juddered over the ground to his right. The chain needed oiling, he noted; the man was in the wrong gear and a metal mudguard was catching on the tyre with a rhythmic slur as the wheel turned.

Commentary

When you were thinking about the audiences for these three extracts, you may have noticed that Extract A from *The Hobbit* by J. R. R. Tolkien appears to be aimed at children. The lexical choices are simple but the use of the adjectives 'nasty, dirty' and 'wet' to describe what a hobbit hole is *not* like are contrasted with the positive adjectives 'shiny' and 'yellow' used to describe the attractiveness of the door knobs in the second paragraph in terms that children would use themselves. Expressions such as 'lots and lots' are easily identified as part of normal language usage for children. The book opens with a very clear, simple statement. The author intends to set the scene and introduce a character. Through the third person narrative we learn that this hobbit (maybe the **eponymous** Hobbit of the title) is a hole-dwelling, yet comfort-loving, individual who is sociable and proud of his house.

Extract B from *The Wasp Factory* by Iain Banks is clearly aimed at a different audience. You should have noticed straight away from the use of the personal pronoun 'I' that first person narration is used. You will also have noticed the capitalisation of the words 'Sacrifice Poles' and the 'Factory', which gives them the status of **proper nouns**. This suggests strongly that they are likely to be of significance to the plot. The idea of poles involving sacrifice is suggestive of unpleasant rituals especially when combined with the objects 'a rat head with two dragonflies, the other a seagull and two mice' which the narrator has fastened to them.

💡 Key terms

Eponymous hero: a central character who gives their name to the title of a novel, play or poem, e.g. Othello, Charlotte Gray, David Copperfield.

Proper nouns: names of particular people, places or things, e.g. London, Mr Smith.

Excitement is generated by the idea that his brother has escaped coupled with the idea that the mysterious, normally inanimate 'Factory' has 'told' him about it. The next paragraph is very descriptive, setting a desolate scene through the lexical choices: 'rusty', 'creaks' and 'easterly wind'. The semantic field of dead animals combined with the idea of sacrifice poles creates a ritualistic and sinister tone. The extract also uses a number of powerful **participles** – 'kaw-calling', 'screaming' and 'wheeling' – which suggest sound and movement. The complexity of the lexis and sentence structure and the rather sinister tone suggest a more adult audience than Tolkien aims at in *The Hobbit*. The narrator appears from his activities to be both strange and unpleasant.

Extract C is from *Charlotte Gray* by Sebastian Faulks, a novel set in the Second World War. Here, you have a third person narrative. Again, both the syntax and lexical choices are complex, indicating that the book is aimed at an adult audience. There are many verbs suggesting movement: 'kicked', 'waddle', 'bucked', 'tossed', 'juddered'. The character Peter Gregory shows an intensified awareness of his surroundings. He notices details such as the noises produced by the bicycle: 'clank', 'rhythmic slur'. These details create a sense that the character is about to embark on something dangerous that will require all his senses to be alert if he is to survive. As an audience we are disposed to admire this character as a potential hero.

▉ Writing in the voice of a character or narrator

In the examination you are likely to be asked to write in the voice of a particular character or narrator, although there are many other tasks that you might be set. To achieve this sense of voice, you need to consider your lexical choices carefully. The set text must be reflected accurately in the choices you make in relation to purpose, audience and style. You may be asked to base your writing at a particular stage of development of a play or novel so that it reflects how language is used at that point. If you are required to use an extract from the opening of a text as your springboard, your response may be very different from one you might make to a later extract. For example, in Shakespeare's *Othello*, Othello speaks in calm, measured tones in the first part of the play but he later becomes consumed by jealousy and his language becomes violent and intemperate. You need to ensure that you write in an appropriate voice for the character at the stage of the text that you are given.

▉ Critical response activity

Look back at the section on narrative methods on p4. As you have seen, in her novel *Property* Valerie Martin uses irony in the presentation of her narrator's attitudes towards slavery as the novel progresses. Read the extract below, which is the opening of this novel, and consider the following questions.

▉ What views does the narrator express towards what she is watching?

▉ What does she feel about her husband?

▉ How far do you feel sympathetic to her views and character?

▉ Is the author's presentation of the narrator's attitudes at this point in the novel ironic?

💡 Key terms

Participle: parts of verbs which indicate present or past progressive forms (-ing) such as 'she is running' or 'she was running' and past perfect forms (-ed), such as 'he shouted' or 'he was shouted at'.

▉ Practical activity

Now that you have considered Extracts A, B and C carefully, try to continue each of them in the same style as the writer. You need to think about your lexical choices, syntax and narrative voice, and use content which is consistent with the plot introduced in the opening sentences. When you have tried this, think about how successful you have been in making your own writing convincingly similar in style to the original.

It never ends. I watched him through the spyglass to see what the game would be. There were five of them. He gets them all gathered at the river's edge and they are nervous. If they haven't done this before, they've heard about it. First he reads to them from the Bible. I don't have to hear it to know what extract it is. Then they have to strip, which takes no time as they are wearing only linen pantaloons. One by one they must grasp the rope, swing over the water and drop in. It's brutally hot; the cool water encourages them to shout and slap at one another once they are in the water. Then they have to come out and do it again, only this time they hang on the rope two at a time, which means one has to hold on to the other. They had gotten this far when I looked.

Two boys were pulling the rope, one holding on while the other clutched his shoulders. They were laughing because they were slippery. The sun made their bodies glisten and steam like a horse's flanks after a long run. The boy on the ground ran down the bank and off they went, out over the water, releasing the rope at the highest point of its arc and crashing into the smooth surface below like wounded black geese. He hardly watched them. He was choosing the next two, directing one to catch the rope on its return, running his hands over the shoulders of the other which made the boy cower and study the ground. I couldn't watch any more.

They have to keep doing this, their lithe young bodies displayed to him in various positions. When he gets them up to three or four at a time, he watches closely. The boys rub against each other; they can't help it. Their limbs become entwined, they struggle to hang on, and it isn't long before one comes out of the water with his member raised. That's what the game is for. This boy tries to stay in the water, he hangs his head as he comes out, thinking every thought he can to make the tumescence subside. This is what proves they are brutes, he says and have not the power of reason. A white man, knowing he would be beaten for it, would not be able to raise his member.

He has his stick there by the tree; it is never far from him. The boys fall silent as he takes it up. Sometimes the offending boy cries out or tries to run away, but he's no match for this grown man with his stick. The servant's tumescence subsides as quickly as the master's rises, and the latter will last until he gets to the quarter. If he can find the boy's mother, and she's pretty, she will pay dearly for rearing an unnatural child.

This is only one of his games. When he comes back to the house he will be in a fine humor for the rest of the day.

Often, as I look through the glass, I hear in my head an incredulous refrain: This is my husband, this is my husband.

Commentary

We do not discover the narrator's name (Manon Gaudet) in these opening paragraphs but we learn that she is watching her husband tormenting and abusing boys. In this extract, Manon appears disgusted at what she is witnessing and we share her feelings. She describes the sun as 'brutally' hot and when a boy is made to 'cower' she cannot 'watch any more'. She quotes her husband's words 'This is what proves they are brutes' and 'have not the power of reason', apparently detaching

herself from his point of view. Her incredulous 'This is my husband' strongly suggests that she does not condone his treatment of the boys. At this point, you might feel sympathetic to her views although you might wish her to intervene actively. You might feel, however, that the brutish man she describes would react violently to any such attempt. There is, however, a hint of Manon's attitude towards the slaves in the way she uses animal imagery in her description of them. Using similes, she describes their bodies as glistening 'like a horse's flanks' and speaks of them slipping into the water 'like wounded black geese'.

Representing Manon's voice as expressed in the opening of the novel would produce a very different response from one you would make to an extract drawn from later in the text. There is only a hint of irony (created by the animal imagery) in the writing at this early stage of the novel; on the whole we feel that we can share the viewpoint of the narrator.

Practical activity

Choose an extract from the early part of one of the set texts and then select a later extract featuring the same character. Write a few sentences in the voice of the character at each stage you have chosen and look closely at the differences. Has the character changed or have you simply been allowed greater insight into their thoughts?

Critical response activity

Read the following extract from the short story 'The Mud Below', which is set in Wyoming. The story is from *Close Range* by Annie Proulx. The central character in the story, 18-year-old Diamond Felts, together with some other young men from his school, has been doing some casual work on a ranch. The ranch has three bucking bulls used in rodeo events and Diamond accepts a challenge to ride one. Read the extract and work through the following tasks.

- Consider how Annie Proulx conveys Diamond's feelings as he prepares to ride the bull and then as he actually does so. You should think about narrative voice, lexical choices and syntax.
- Choose a daunting activity that you have attempted yourself, perhaps an adventurous one such as white-water rafting or skiing or a less physical one such as speaking to an audience or performing on stage. Write a paragraph about your experience using a similar style to that of Annie Proulx.

'Atta boy, atta boy,' said Como Bewd, and handed him a rosined left glove. 'Ever been on a bull?'

'No sir,' said Diamond, no boots, no spurs, no chaps, T-shirted and hatless. Leecil's old man told him to hold his free hand up, not to touch the bull or himself with it, keep his shoulders forward and his chin down, hold on with his feet and legs and left hand, above all not to think and when he got bucked off, no matter what was broke, get up quick and run like hell for the fence. He helped him make the wrap, ease down on the animal, said, shake your face and git out there, and grinning, blood-speckled Lovis opened the chute door, waiting to see the town kid dumped and dive-bombed.

But he stayed on until someone counting eight hit the rail with a length of pipe to signal time. He flew off, landed on his feet, stumbling headlong but not falling, in a run for the rails. He hauled himself up, panting from the exertion and the intense nervy rush. He'd been shot out of the cannon. The shock of the violent motion, the lightning shifts of balance, the feeling of power as though he were the bull and not the rider, even the fright, fulfilled a physical hunger in him he hadn't known was there. The experience had been exhilarating and unbearably personal.

'You know what,' said Como Bewd. 'You might make a bullrider.'

When you have written your own paragraph in response to the Critical response activity, read the two sample responses and the commentaries that follow. Think about how successful you have been in writing about your own experience. If you feel you could improve your own response, try re-drafting it.

Sample response A

'Go for it,' said Eric, back paddling against the current. 'Ever been on a thirty-foot wave before?'

'No, Eric,' said Sal, no big muscles, no wet suit, small and helmetless. Frank told her to keep her head down, brace her knees and feet and don't lean, paddle hard and burrow through, above all not to let go of the paddle and the boat if she had to swim, then stroke like hell for the shore. He showed her the line of the wave train, helped her get the right place to break through the eddy line, said 'Go fast there' and Marty the baggage rafter watched grinning to see the girl heading to be tossed out and swimming.

But she stayed on, down the green chute of water the size of a highway, through the huge wave, paddling, not drowning in a run for the other side. She pulled herself through, panting from the adrenalin and the rush of the water, into the whirlpool on the other side, controlling it, riding it. She'd ridden the flying trapeze. The power of the water, the swift shifts of balance, the feeling of riding the river as though she were part of it, even the fear itself, fulfilled a need in her she hadn't even known had existed. It had been such an intense feeling, uniquely her own.

Commentary

In this response, you will have noticed that the student has followed the structure of Annie Proulx's writing very closely. She also mirrors the attitudes of the other characters in the scene. Como Bewd is replaced by Eric, Lovis by Marty and Leecil's old man by Frank. Like Annie Proulx, she uses an asyndetic list to show her vulnerability. Detailed instructions for riding the bull and surviving the experience are given in a syndetic list in the extract and this is matched in the student's text. As in the extract, she writes in an omniscient third person narrative using the past tense. There are some significant differences in the lexical choices, however. Annie Proulx uses a semantic field of the bull ring – 'spurs', 'chaps', 'bull', 'bucked', 'the chute door' – whereas this student chooses words such as 'wet suit', 'paddle', 'swim', 'wave train', 'eddy line', 'water', 'whirlpool', all representative of kayaking the river. Both writers use lexis representative of physical excitement, fear and exhilaration. The content and mood of both are similar; a hazardous physical activity is undertaken, mostly successfully, and the mood is of great exhilaration. This response does successfully transform the source text into a new piece of writing but the danger in using a structure that so closely resembles the source is that a less secure writer might not create a text which is sufficiently distinct from the original.

Sample response B

Andy looked down the white ribbon of slope below, crammed between tight rock walls, down at the tiny figures on the piste below. 'You're dead meat,' said Jean-Claude 'Loony', the wild French instructor they'd been with all week. Still, he'd brought them here, the challenge clear. 'Face downhill, get your edges in, jump out of the turn, get ready for the next one. Don't fall.' Andy looked down again then suddenly made his choice. A rush of fear hit him but also a charged exhilaration; he's felt nothing like it before. The first turn, jumping out of it in a great sprawl of snow and back down, muscles screaming at the effort of it, then on, feeling his power, reaching deep for the next surge. He was there, one with the snow and the hanging ice on the rocks as they flashed by, the dots on the piste growing below. The gully was opening up, spitting him out of its maw. An edge caught, just enough, spinning him wildly through the air, to land laughing and shaking in deep soft snow. The figures on the piste stared. Jean-Claude arrived in a rush of snow, perfect, controlled. 'You know what,' he said, 'you might make a real skier.'

Commentary

In this response, the structure is less closely based on Proulx's original. It opens with a description of what the main character, Andy, can see which suggests the difficulty of the challenge he faces. The instructor, Jean-Claude, takes on the roles of all three of the characters in the original. He mocks like Lovis, who is described as 'grinning' but here the character uses **direct speech** ('You're dead meat'). Jean-Claude also plays the part of Leecil's old man in giving clear advice. Here the asyndetic list that is used is slightly different to the syndetic list in the original. A short imperative sentence ('Don't fall') emphasises the danger. This syntactical form is not used in the extract but here it has a similar purpose to Leecil's instructions. The narrative voice, third person, past tense, omniscient is the same as the original. Like student A's use of the semantic field of paddling the river, this text uses lexis connected with skiing: 'white', 'piste', 'downhill', 'edges', 'jump', 'snow', 'gully', 'skier'. The figures on the piste watch as Lovis does. The last sentence mirrors the words of Como Bewd but, again, Jean-Claude takes on this role. Like student A, the content and mood of the new text closely resembles the original.

Both candidates have successfully shown their understanding of Proulx's techniques and style, despite having approached the task in different ways.

> ### Key terms
>
> **Direct speech:** the use of actual spoken words, without modification, as part of a narrative, description or explanation.

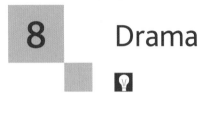

8 Drama

Like novelists, dramatists must also consider **who** they are writing for and **what** is the purpose of the writing. The script of a play is only part of its text; the final text is what is actually staged or screened. In performance, the play is influenced by the director and the actors and there may be great variations between different productions of a play. Playwrights do not have the final say about what is presented to the audience although they may seek to influence it through stage directions; the final product represents a collaboration between the playwright, the director, the actors, set designers, cameramen, etc.

Stage directions

Stage directions tended to be sparse until towards the end of the 19th century. Earlier dramatists tended to work closely with companies putting on the production. For example, Shakespeare acted in a number of his own plays. It was therefore easy for dramatists to convey their ideas about the presentation of characters. Plays were often not published until after the performance and texts might be taken from a variety of sources such as the prompt book used in early productions. Directions such as 'Thunder and lightning. Enter three witches' in *Macbeth* leave a lot of scope for a modern director's imagination. In contrast, modern dramatists usually include some detailed stage directions and these play an integral part in the representation of the writer's vision for the play. Nowadays, playwrights are not usually directly involved in productions of their work and the stage directions offer an opportunity for the dramatist to communicate their ideas to the director, set designers and actors. The novelist can comment on a character's appearance, actions and state of mind through the narrator; in the staged or filmed version of a play, the audience learns about these things through actions, speech, appearance and movement.

For the creative response question in the examination, you could be asked to write a creative piece using dramatic form and dialogue which reflects your source text. You would need to include stage directions that are in keeping with the original in your response.

Read the extracts below. Extract A is taken from early in Act 1 of *The History Boys* by Alan Bennett. A group of boys has returned to school, after achieving very good A-level results, to take entrance examinations for Oxford University. As you read, try to visualise the scenes and characters presented through both the stage directions and the dialogue. Extract B is taken from the opening of *A Streetcar Named Desire* by Tennessee Williams.

Extract A: *The History Boys*

(Though the general setting is a sixth-form classroom in a boys' school in the eighties in the North of England, when Hector first comes in, a figure in motorcycle leathers and helmet, the stage is empty.

His sixth-formers, eight boys of seventeen or eighteen, come briskly on and take Hector out of his motorcycle gear, each boy removing an item and as he does so presenting it to the audience with a flourish.)

Lockwood (*with gauntlets*): Les gants.

Akthar (*with a scarf*): L'echarpe.

Rudge: Le blouson d'aviateur.

(Finally the helmet is removed)

Timms: Le casque.

(The taking off of the helmet reveals Hector (which is both his surname and his nickname) as a schoolmaster of fifty or so. Dakin, a handsome boy, holds out a jacket)

Dakin: Permettez-moi monsieur.

(Hector puts on the jacket)

Hector: Bien fait, mes enfants. Bien fait.

(Hector is a man of studied eccentricity. He wears a bow tie.)

Commentary

Although Alan Bennett states that he has 'not included many stage directions or even noted changes of scene', this extract, which contains the first appearance of the boys and their teacher, Hector, does contain some guidance about both the scene and the actions of the boys.

In the opening sentence, the setting is given as a 'classroom' but details are left to be supplied by the set designer and director who will need to decide how to suggest the appearance of a northern school in the 1980s. The otherwise empty stage puts the focus on Hector. The removal of the motorcycle gear is reminiscent of a medieval squire removing armour from the knight he serves after a joust. This suggests that the boys both respect and admire Hector. Much of the opening dialogue is in French but the meaning is made clear by the stage directions, which tell the actors to hold the item being removed. We are told that Hector is 50 or so, a fact that is important in the development of the plot.

Dakin's handsome appearance also prepares the ground for later plot developments. Hector is described as 'a man of studied eccentricity'. This partly informs the actor how to play the role. The detail of the bow tie suggests one way in which this eccentricity should be represented.

Extract B: *A Streetcar Named Desire*

(The exterior of a two-storey corner building on a street in New Orleans which is named Elysian Fields and runs between the L and N tracks and the river. The section is poor but, unlike corresponding sections in other American cities, it has a raffish charm. The houses are mostly white frame, weathered grey, with rickety outside stairs and galleries and quaintly ornamented gables. The building contains two flats, upstairs and down. Faded white stairs ascend to the entrances of both. It is first dark of an evening early in May. The sky that shows around the dim white building is a peculiarly tender blue, almost turquoise, which invests the scene with a kind of lyricism and gracefully attenuates the atmosphere of decay. You can almost feel the warm breath of the brown river beyond the river warehouses with their faint redolences of bananas and coffee. A corresponding air is evoked by the music of Negro entertainers at a bar-room around the corner. In this part of New

> **Think about it**
>
> If you are studying *The History Boys*, consider whether it would be possible to cast a younger actor as Hector.

> **Link**
>
> To see another activity that includes a focus on stage directions, turn to p57.

> Orleans you are practically always just around the corner, or a few doors down the street, from a tinny piano being played with the infatuated fluency of brown fingers. This 'Blue Piano' expresses the spirit of life which goes on here.
>
> Two women, one white and one coloured, are taking the air on the steps of the building. The white woman is Eunice, who occupies the upstairs flat; the coloured woman is a neighbour, for New Orleans is a cosmopolitan city where there is a relatively warm and easy intermingling of races in the old part of town.
>
> Above the music of the 'Blue Piano' the voices of people on the street can be heard overlapping.)
>
> **Negro woman** (to Eunice): … she says St Barnabus would send out his dog to lick her and when he did she'd feel an icy cold wave all up an' down her. Well, that night when – – –
>
> **A man** (to a Sailor): You keep right on going and you'll find it. You'll hear them tapping on the shutters.
>
> **Sailor** (to Negro Woman and Eunice): Where's the Four Deuces?
>
> **Vendor**: Red hot! Red hots!
>
> **Negro woman**: Don't waste your money in that clip joint!
>
> **Sailor**: I've got a date there.
>
> **Vendor**: Re-e-ed h-o-o-t.
>
> **Negro woman**: Don't let them sell you a blue moon cocktail or you won't go out on your own feet!

Commentary

This play opens with an extremely detailed description of the setting. Although the buildings could be represented as described, Williams also writes of almost feeling 'the warm breath of the brown river' and the faint smell of 'bananas and coffee'. Here, the director must try to create a mood suggested by these stage directions. The sound of the music will help to suggest this. The fact that the two characters, one white, one black, are talking together and the comment that 'there is a warm and easy intermingling of races' in this city but, by implication, not in others reminds us that the play is set in a time when there was considerable segregation in the southern United States. However, at the time of writing the comment would have helped to describe how Williams saw the atmosphere of New Orleans' old town as 'warm and easy'. Similarly, a modern playwright would be unlikely to refer to one of their characters as 'Negro Woman'.

The dialogue suggests the liveliness of the street and the area with local colour provided by the selling of 'red hots' and a certain seediness by the reference to a clip joint.

■ Writing a creative response in narrative form

In the examination you are likely to be asked to write a narrative based on your knowledge of your set text. Even if you are studying only drama texts, you should make sure that you understand the narrative techniques described in Section A. In writing a narrative you have a chance to describe scenes, characters and relationships. Much of your information and interpretation will come from the dialogue. However, if your text has extensive stage directions you will also find these useful when you are describing scenes or characters. Questions might include such tasks as writing an additional extract or narrating the action from a different perspective.

Link

Remind yourself of the section on narrative techniques in Section A, p4.

Practical activity

1. Imagine you have come from another school to join the class featured in *The History Boys*. Write your impressions of the classroom, Hector and your fellow students as though you were telling your story in a novel using first person narrative.

2. Again using first person narrative, imagine you are walking through the street described in the extract from *A Streetcar Named Desire* and write your impressions, taking care to include smells, sounds, touch and tastes in your description.

For both pieces of writing, make sure you adapt as much information as possible from the texts.

Critical response activity

Read the following first scene of David Hare's play *Murmuring Judges* and comment on the stage directions and the dialogue, considering:

- the effect created by the stage directions
- the ways in which the dialogue makes you view Gerard and the judiciary
- where your sympathies lie at the end of this scene.

(*An empty stage. Then suddenly from nowhere they're all there – the judge, the jury, the battery of lawyers in wigs, the public, the police, the press, the ushers, the guards, and, at the centre of the forward-facing court, the defendants. The entire company of the law has appeared in the blinking of an eye.*

At the centre, the three defendants of whom **Gerard McKinnon** *is conspicuously the youngest, barely in his twenties, thin, wiry, tall, his dark hair down to his shoulders. Beside him, crop-haired, pale, in suits, two other defendants,* **Travis** *and* **Fielding**. *But the emphasis of the light is on* **McKinnon**, *and before you're ready he begins to speak. He has an Irish accent.*)

Gerard: I'm standing here, I'm thinking, oh God, it's coming, it's coming, it's finally happening, hold on, remember, this is happening to me. After it going so slowly, *slowly*, the standing, the waiting – God, is there anything in the world slower than a lawyer? – after all that, now suddenly, stop, hold on, suddenly it's going so fast …

Clerk: Has the jury reached a verdict upon which you are all agreed?

Juryman: We have.

Clerk: Do you find the defendant James Arthur Travis guilty or not guilty?

Juryman: Guilty.

Clerk: Do you find the defendant Michael Fielding guilty or not guilty?

Juryman: Guilty.

Clerk: Do you find the defendant Gerard Thomas McKinnon guilty or not guilty?

(*A slight pause*)

Juryman: Guilty.

(*The lights change again as Gerard struggles to interrupt*)

Gerard: And I want to say, yes, hold on, just a moment, take me back, I did meet these men, yes I did, but I thought at the time, part of me thought, this is stupid, I mean, I'm not *really* doing this, there's a part of me which isn't standing on this freezing pavement, thinking how did I get myself into this? So why is it now, only now, yes *now*, why is everything finally real?

(*The lights change back to favour the court*)

Judge: And now I will turn to the sentencing. Please, will the prisoners attend?

(*The lights focus on Gerard, his speech more insistent than ever*)

Gerard: Finally I get it, yes, it is happening, these men, every one of them silver-haired, judicious, informed, they will go home to their wives, to wine in fine glasses and the gossip of the Bar, they will walk the streets and complain about their lives, and I … (*He stops. More insistently*) And I …

(*The court is lit again*)

Judge: For Travis, eight years and six years to run concurrently. For Fielding, eight years and six concurrently also. For McKinnon … (*A pause*) Five years.

(*The lights change as if Gerard were at last alone. He is quiet.*)

Gerard: And I … the stuff of their professions … I will go to my gaol.

(*The lights fade to favour the whole court as the usher calls to make everyone stand*)

Practical activity

Re-write Gerard's experiences of the court and his sentencing as a first person narrative that would form the opening of a novel. Try to convey a sense of Gerard's voice by paying careful attention to:

- your lexical choices
- your style
- the content, especially Gerard's views of his situation and the judiciary.

Writing a creative response in dramatic form

One of the tasks which you might be set in the examination is to write an additional scene, based on your knowledge of the set text, in dramatic form. This scene might precede the action in the script, continue the play at the end or be one which could be inserted in between scenes in the existing text.

For this task you would not only have to match the language choices and dialogue used by the characters you are representing but also the kinds of stage directions given by the playwright.

Read the following extract from *A Streetcar Named Desire*, which is taken from the first scene of the play. Blanche is looking for her sister's house and she is clearly shocked by the area in which she finds herself when she arrives at her destination. Later on in the play we discover that Blanche has had to sell the family plantation and that she has come to her sister Stella for refuge.

(*Blanche comes around the corner, carrying a valise. She looks at a slip of paper, then at the building, then again at the slip and again at the building. Her expression is one of shocked disbelief. Her appearance is incongruous to this setting. She is daintily dressed in a white suit with a fluffy bodice, necklace and earrings of pearl, white gloves and hat, looking as if she were arriving at a summer tea or cocktail party in the garden district. She is about five years older than Stella. Her delicate beauty must avoid a strong light. There is something about her uncertain manner, as well as her white clothes, that suggests a moth.*)

Eunice (*finally*): What's the matter, honey? Are you lost?

Blanche (*with faintly hysterical humour*): They told me to take a streetcar named Desire, and then transfer to the one called Cemeteries and ride six blocks and get off at – Elysian Fields!

Eunice: That's where you are now.

Blanche: At Elysian Fields?

Eunice: This here is Elysian Fields.

Blanche: They mustn't have – understood – what number I wanted …

Eunice: What number you lookin' for?

  (*Blanche wearily refers to the slip of paper*)

Blanche: Six thirty-two.

Eunice: You don't have to look no further.

Practical activity

Imagine that you are introduced to Blanche as she seeks directions to find her sister's home. She arrives at the railway station and asks directions from a young man she meets in the street outside. Write a short piece of script dramatising this scene. You should pay particular attention to the:

- stage directions
- dialogue.

When you have tried the Practical activity, read the sample response and commentary that follows.

Sample response

(*Blanche appears on a street outside a railway station, carrying a valise. She looks at a slip of paper, then gazes around her as if hoping for inspiration. Her expression is bewildered. She is dressed all in white and looks delicate and feminine against the dirt and bustle of the street. She has a gossamer beauty which appears too fragile for the city. She approaches a man in his early thirties who seems to be waiting for someone. He is well dressed and waits comfortably, relaxed and smoking a cigarette. He notices her straight away but waits for her to make an approach. She smiles coquettishly at him but says nothing.*)

Man (*looking her up and down appreciatively*): Are you lost, little lady?

Blanche (*looking sideways at him*): Yes – yes I am. I sure would be grateful for your help. I'm looking for my sister's place – I've got the address right here. (*She consults the slip of paper again*) It's in Elysian Fields.

  (*The man looks at her with some surprise on his face*)

Man: Are you sure that's the right address, honey?

Blanche (*showing him the slip of paper*): I think so – that's what it says right here. I'm visiting my sister.

Man: Well, if you're sure, you go to the streetcar stop right over there (*He points across the street*) and you take the streetcar named Desire (*He looks at her significantly*). You ride on that for ten blocks, then get off and transfer to the one named Cemeteries. Ask the driver – he'll tell you where. Then you stay on for another six blocks and get off at Elysian Fields.

Blanche: Why, thank you kindly, sir. (*She starts to pick up her valise but he immediately moves to help her*)

Man (*picking up the valise*): That's too heavy for a lady like you. Let me help you. (*He walks over to the streetcar stop with her*) Maybe you'd like to give me a call. Here's my number. (*He gives her a slip of paper, which she tucks away in her bag*)

Commentary

In this sample response, the first stage direction comments directly on Blanche's expression, which is 'bewildered' here rather than 'shocked' as in the original when she actually sees her destination. The slip of paper is there in both texts. Blanche's appearance is shown but in less detail. Different words are chosen, for example, 'gossamer' for 'delicate'. It is important in this exercise to reflect the original but not to copy it.

In the extract from the set text, Blanche is clearly shocked by Elysian Fields. Here, she is still expecting the place to match its name. The sense that the place will not be as she expects is conveyed by the stage direction, which describes the expressions of surprise on the man's face. He is described as 'well dressed' so he would naturally be surprised at the equally well-turned-out Blanche's destination. The names of the streetcars are retained as they are obviously needed as part of the directions and they have a symbolic function in the play. Here, the man clearly finds Blanche attractive as the stage directions show and she responds flirtatiously to male attention. His significant look as he names the streetcar shows his interest in her as a woman. Blanche's uncertainty is shown in her words 'I think so'. This also shows the vulnerability she projects, which is again attractive to the man who goes on to help her with the valise and to offer her his number. There is a hint in this text that Blanche will not like her sister's neighbourhood.

The student uses an understanding of Blanche's effect on men and her reactions to them in other areas of the play as a basis for the presentation of her interaction with this man.

Practical activity

If one of your set texts is a drama text, choose a short section from the play. Think of a scene that could take place immediately before or after your chosen scene but which has not been included in the text. Write the scene taking care to reflect the:

- stage directions
- dialogue.

You should also make sure that the content is appropriate as an additional scene from your set text.

9 Form

This chapter covers:

- characteristics of a range of forms

- how to write a successful letters, article, diary entry or speech, using your set text as a stimulus.

When you look at a piece of writing, its form is often apparent from immediately visible features such as layout. For example, a letter is set out differently from a report or a newspaper article. The form chosen for a text depends on its purpose and audience.

A good proportion of creative response questions require you to write in a specific form and therefore you should build up your awareness of the characteristics of a range of forms.

Letters

If you are asked to write a letter you need to use the conventions that are appropriate for this form. These days you might communicate in writing with your friends by sending text messages, which use their own distinctive style and register (for example, 'RU OK. CU 2nite SalJ'). You might also communicate through informal emails and, less commonly, letters.

There are few conventions remaining for the informal letter beyond a greeting such as 'Dear Dave' and some form of rounding off the letter such as 'See you soon'. Nevertheless, the greetings and endings of informal letters will depend on their audience and purpose. If you are writing an informal letter in the examination, you need to make careful language choices to reflect the voice of the character you are representing in your answer as well as the period in which the source text is set. You would need to write more formally, for example, if you were asked to write a letter from Nelly Dean to a friend, commenting on how the relationship between Catherine and Hareton has developed since her return to Wuthering Heights as housekeeper. The novel was published in 1847 and its action takes place at a time when letters would generally have been both fuller and more formal.

Nelly Dean's voice is a well-educated one for a servant, so we can believe that she would commit her views to paper at some length. To help to make her narrative voice convincing, Emily Brontë shows her explaining to Lockwood in Chapter 7 that she is self-educated and loves to read, so you would need to convey those qualities in your letter.

Emily Brontë gives us an example of a letter when Isabella writes to Nelly Dean. It is detailed and written in a formal style and, although it gives us an insight into Isabella's mind through first person narrative, the style is very similar to that used by Nelly Dean throughout the novel. Your letter, written in Nelly Dean's voice, should convey the information you are asked to give and maintain the same level of formality shown in her narrative. For example, when Catherine is ill, Nelly relates: 'To obviate the fatigue of mounting and descending the stairs, we fitted up this, where you lie at present: on the same floor with the parlour; and she was soon strong enough to move from one to the other, leaning on Edgar's arm.' **Low frequency words** such as 'obviate', 'fatigue' , 'mounting' and 'descending', together with a complex sentence structure, create the level of formality that you would need to emulate in your letter. By contrast, **high frequency words** are words that are used very frequently and are therefore familiar to an audience. These terms describe how often words are used and therefore how familiar they are likely to be to

Link

See the sample questions on p81 for the full version of this question.

Key terms

Low frequency words: words that are not used commonly and are therefore not very familiar to an audience.

High frequency words: words that are used very frequently and are therefore familiar to an audience.

readers and listeners. Words such as 'bread', 'potatoes', 'bus', 'gossip' and 'walk' are used very frequently and are therefore described as high frequency, whereas words such as 'erudite', 'sanctimonious', 'risible' and 'parsimonious' are not used commonly and are described as low frequency. Of course, this definition is only a generalisation as many words fit somewhere in between. Nevertheless, the terms are useful tools in assessing the levels of formality of a text.

Even in emails the levels of formality vary greatly. You would not write an email requesting details of a job using a greeting such as 'Hi Emma'. You may find yourself needing to write formal letters to, for example, a bank, a potential employer, your local council or a newspaper. These letters tend to be important and there are conventional ways of writing them. If you ignore those conventions, the recipient of your letter may judge you harshly.

In the examination you might be asked to write a formal letter, for example from the headmaster in *The History Boys* to a parent; from Mr Smith, the Christian missionary, to a colleague of the District Commissioner in *Things Fall Apart*; or from Stella's doctor to her sister Blanche in *A Streetcar Named Desire*.

Formal letters

These are set out according to conventions although you will find variations when you look at letters from businesses, councils and other organisations that have their own corporate style. Letters from individuals are normally set out in the format shown below.

> **Think about it**
>
> What would be the consequences of failing to adopt an appropriate level of formality in any of the situations outlined above?

15 York Road
Easton
Leeds
LS6 5JT

5 October 2007

Mr James Breem
Manager
Reeds Bank plc
Bridge Street
Leeds
LS1 4AJ

Dear Mr Breem

I am writing to ask you if you would increase my overdraft limit to £3000 temporarily. I became unemployed on 16th September but I have just been appointed to a new post as a senior project development officer for Citicom plc. My salary will be £38,578 per annum but I will not be starting my new post until November 1st and my salary will be paid monthly in arrears. I would be grateful if you could help me to meet my expenses during the transition period by agreeing to my request.

Yours sincerely

S. J. Freely

Simon J Freely

If you know the name of the recipient as in the example above, you should use it in the opening salutation ('Dear Mr Breem'). The letter should then end 'Yours sincerely'. If you do not know the name of the person to whom you are writing, begin the letter 'Dear Sir/Madam' and end it 'Yours faithfully'. You will notice in the example above that the language is formal and there are no abbreviations or contractions.

If you are asked to write a formal letter in the examination, you could contextualise it by writing appropriate names and addresses if you wish, but do not spend a great deal of time on this. However, it should be clear that you are writing a letter so it must have an appropriate salutation and conclusion. The following example is from *Property* by Valerie Martin.

Dear Miss Favrot

Yours sincerely

Manon Gaudet

Practical activity

Try writing a formal letter in your own voice. Imagine you have been asked to write a reference for a friend who is applying to go to Africa as a trainee leader on a gap-year project. The organisation your friend wants to join is looking for qualities such as leadership skills, the ability to work in a team, physical fitness, sociability and a good sense of humour. Write the letter recommending your friend, making sure that you adopt an appropriate form and register.

After you have written a formal letter using your own voice, you need to attempt the more difficult task of writing in a particular form while conveying a sense of the voice of a character from your set text. For example, in *The Kite Runner* Amir returns from Kabul with the child who has suffered abuse in Afghanistan. He wants to adopt the boy, Sohrab, who is actually his half brother's son, and take him back to the USA. Your task might be to imagine that Amir writes to the American Embassy seeking permission to adopt Sohrab rather than visiting the embassy in person as he actually does in the novel (pages 284–9 of the recommended edition) and to write this letter using the information on these pages and from elsewhere in the novel as appropriate.

Practical activity

If you are studying *The Kite Runner* as one of your set texts, write the letter to the American Embassy as detailed above. Read the sample response and commentary below. If you are not studying this text, before you read the example and the commentary, think about how you would set out a letter like this and what style and register would be appropriate.

Sample response

48–50 Bahariya Road
Islamabad
Tel: 44987 6785432

5 October 2008
Mr R. Andrews
The Consulate of the USA
Islamabad

Dear Mr Andrews

I called at the embassy yesterday and was advised to write to you as you are not in your office this week. I am seeking to adopt my half brother's child and I would be so grateful for your help.

I was born in Afghanistan but have lived in the USA since 1981 and have since become a US citizen. My father and I fled from the Taliban but my half brother Hassan was not living with us at the time and he remained in Afghanistan.

I recently heard from an old friend of the family, Rahim Khan, who was very ill and living in Peshawar. He asked me to visit him. He did not tell me until I had arrived that he had news of my brother's terrible fate. I had not heard from Hassan since I left, communications being so difficult under the Taliban. Therefore, I did not know that Hassan had married and had a child, Sohrab, who is now 10 years old. My friend Rahim gave me the news that Hassan and his wife Farzana had moved back into our old family home. The Taliban coveted the house, and, on a pretext, they were both dragged out into the street and shot in the head. Rahim had heard that their child survived and was in an orphanage somewhere in the Karteh-Seh area of Kabul.

Rahim had told me of a refuge for Afghani children in Peshawar and he believed that if I could find Sohrab he would be safe there. He himself was dying but he was reassured about his responsibilities to his old friends when I told him that I would be going to Kabul to look for the child.

I found the conditions in Kabul even worse than I had expected. Life was cheap. I witnessed an execution by stoning. I found Sohrab at the orphanage in Karteh-Seh, an area that has been almost flattened by war. The orphanage itself was a makeshift place; the walls were damaged and the windows boarded up. Inside, conditions were squalid; the children were barefoot and dressed in badly frayed clothing not really sufficient to keep out the cold.

The director of the orphanage, Mr Zaman, had taken Sohrab in, knowing his identity. I was able to show him that I was the boy's half uncle and he agreed to let me take him in return for a donation to the orphanage. Sohrab was severely undernourished but he had heard all about me from his father and he was happy to come with me and seemed pleased with his change of circumstances. When we got to Pakistan, I found that my old friend had left Peshawar to spend time alone before his death. He had left no address and I could find no trace of the refuge he had told me about.

There was no other option but to bring Sohrab here with me to Islamabad. I have talked to my wife and we both sincerely want to give my brother's son a new home in the USA after all the trauma he has experienced. He has no one else in the world.

I am not familiar with the procedures for international adoption but as my brother's son is an orphan who has no other living relatives I hope you can help me to take him home with me to the USA.

I understand you will be back very soon and I would really appreciate it if you would contact me at my hotel, the details of which are given at the top of this letter.

Yours sincerely

Amir Karim

Amir Karim

Commentary

If you are studying *The Kite Runner* as one of your set texts, you will be aware that the story Amir tells here is not the same as the experiences narrated in the novel. In the book, Amir actually visits Raymond Andrews at the American Embassy and presents him with a version of the facts that he thinks will help his case.

> I gave him the version I had worked out in my head since I'd hung up with Soraya. I had gone into Afghanistan to bring back my half brother's son. I had found the boy in squalid conditions, wasting away in an orphanage. I had paid the orphanage director a sum of money and withdrawn the boy. Then I had brought him to Pakistan.

In the example above this information has been used as the basis of the story of the discovery of Sohrab given in the letter. The rest of the information in the letter is chosen and adapted selectively so that it does not conflict with this version of the story. The purpose of this letter is to persuade its audience, a consular official, that he should facilitate the adoption which Amir seeks. Although this is a formal letter, it needs to have some emotive content and language in order to affect Raymond Andrews's views. Details such as the shooting of Hassan, the execution by stoning and the condition of the orphanage are included to play on his sympathies. Lexical choices such as the verbs 'fled' and 'dragged' and the modifying 'terrible' fate are intended to bring out the horrors of Kabul from which Amir seeks to rescue this child. Nevertheless, the overall style is formal.

The letter is contextualised with some partial addresses. The invented details of the hotel are important because Amir gives the hotel as the place to contact him at the end of the letter. Amir knows the name of the recipient so he should use it in his salutation and conclude with 'Yours sincerely' rather than 'Yours faithfully'.

Amir is not given a surname in the novel as Afghans normally use only a first name. Sometimes, this is a double name, similar to the English Sally-Ann. An Afghan like Amir, who has moved to the USA, would usually adopt a surname as one would be expected in the US system. We are not given such a surname for Amir in the novel so one has been invented for the purposes of the letter.

Informal letters

It is just as important to give appropriate opening and closing words if you are writing an informal letter as a creative response in the examination. As in the letter from Isabella to Nelly Dean discussed on p61, you need to be aware of the period in which your text was written and the ways in which your characters interact in the text if both writer and recipient feature in it. In *The Kite Runner*, the central character Amir is married to Soraya. In the example below, a form of address taken from the novel is used to suggest Amir's voice and his relationship with his wife. It is important to contextualise your answer in this way if the source text lends itself to it.

Soraya jan

With all my love

Amir

■ Reports

If you are asked to write a report for the creative response question in the examination, it might be in the form of such things as a school report or a reference for a prospective employer which you may be familiar with from your own experience. For example, you might be asked to write a university reference for Rudge in *The History Boys*. In the play, set in the 1980s, a group of boys have returned to their northern grammar school after their A-levels to take entrance examinations for Oxford University. Rudge is considered by the teachers and the headmaster to be the odd one out of this talented group although he is gifted at sport. A university reference would normally contain comments on academic ability and the applicant's other skills and abilities.

On the other hand, you could be asked to write in a less familiar way, putting yourself in the position of one of the characters from your text who is writing a report to a third party. For example, in *Things Fall Apart*, the anger of the villagers has been so aroused that they burn the church although they do not harm the missionary, Mr Smith. Your creative response might be to write Mr Smith's report on the causes and outcome of these events for his Missionary Society and the District Commissioner. In the report you would need to convey events accurately and bring out the ways in which Mr Smith's view of events is radically different from that of the irate villagers.

🔍 Newspaper and magazine articles

Newspapers come in a variety of shapes and sizes and have differing styles, layouts and content. If you are asked to write a creative response in the form of a newspaper article, you need to pay careful attention to the type of newspaper specified in the question.

National newspapers

As the name implies, these are newspapers that are sold across the whole of the country. There are now three common formats for these: broadsheet, Berliner and tabloid. Although these categories refer to the size of the newspaper, they were originally also commonly associated with their style and content. Broadsheet newspapers (for example, *The Times*, the *Independent* and the *Daily Telegraph*) were formerly synonymous with a serious focus on reporting the news using a register appropriate for an educated adult audience. Tabloid papers (for example, the *Sun* and the *Mirror*) were generally categorised as being written for a less well-educated audience and as having a less serious content, focusing on gossip and scandal.

Conventions and fashions have gradually changed and the size of the paper is no longer a distinguishing feature, so it is more accurate to refer

Practical activity

If you are studying *The History Boys* as one of your set texts, imagine that the headmaster has compiled a reference for Rudge using comments from Irwin, Hector and Mrs Lintott. Write this reference bringing out the teachers' views of Rudge's qualities. If you are not studying this text, write a reference about yourself or someone you know well.

to the **quality press**, which targets a readership that expects serious news coverage and intelligent feature articles, and to the **popular press**, which offers a lighter and more entertaining read. The *Daily Mail* and the *Daily Express* are sometimes referred to as **middle-market newspapers**, occupying the ground between the quality and the popular press. Generalisations about these and the other newspapers can give only a very broad indication of the distinctions that exist between them. The best way to understand the range of British daily newspapers is, of course, to read them so that you gain first-hand understanding of their individual characteristics. Familiarising yourself with the different types of newspapers will help you to write convincingly in a style suitable for popular, middle-market or quality papers.

Regional newspapers

These papers usually contain some national news but serve a particular region. For example, the *Yorkshire Post* focuses on news and human interest stories from across all the counties within Yorkshire. It is a broadsheet newspaper having similar characteristics to the quality nationals but with an emphasis on regional stories and how national and international events particularly affect the region.

Local newspapers

You will be familiar with your own local newspapers. They normally serve a fairly limited area such as a town or a group of villages. Most are in tabloid format and they usually contain the name of the locality in their title, for example the *Ashford Messenger*, the *Leamington Spa Courier* or the *Witney Gazette*. They focus on local stories which can range from a very serious content such as a major fire in a local factory to light-hearted human interest stories such as 'Jam Tart Mystery at Vicarage'.

Writing a newspaper article as a creative response

The creative response examination question is likely to specify the type of newspaper for which you will be writing. Although some of the set texts are not by British writers, the same broad categories apply in other countries. Some topics would be appropriate for inclusion in a national newspaper, such as the story of Sohrab's adoption from *The Kite Runner* as part of an article on international adoption. Other topics, such as a profile of Dakin from *The History Boys* after he has successfully got into Oxford, would be appropriate for the local paper. Although the question may ask you to write in an appropriate form for a newspaper article, you should not spend time laying out your text in columns. However, you should give a name for the newspaper, an appropriate date, a **byline**, headlines and subheadings.

You need to make sure that your language choices and style are appropriate for the newspaper and its context and you also need to think about the structure and coherence of your article. Each paragraph should lead clearly on to the next.

Third person narration is normally used in newspaper articles but a journalist may seek to make the reporting more personal by using the first person. This is common where a reporter has first-hand experience of the subject, such as a story from a journalist who is living and working alongside a military unit in a war zone.

To achieve variety, immediacy and drama, reporters often use quotations and reports from eyewitnesses or neighbours and acquaintances. The

Key terms

Quality press: newspapers aimed at a readership expecting serious and detailed news coverage.

Popular press: newspapers aimed at a readership expecting light entertainment as well as news.

Middle-market newspapers: newspapers aimed at a readership expecting comprehensive news coverage but with a lighter touch than that of the quality papers.

Practical activity

Take one prominent news story on a particular day and compare the ways in which a range of newspapers cover it.

Key terms

Byline: the name of the writer shown at the top of a newspaper report or article.

Research point

Look at examples of the different kinds of newspapers described above and consider the varieties of language choices, style and content. You can find articles from most newspapers on their websites.

opening paragraphs of their reports often include the ages as well as the names of those who are quoted. Reporters have various methods of reporting what is said. The first is through direct speech in which the words of the person are (or should be) repeated verbatim and inverted commas (speech marks) are used to indicate the words spoken. For example, 'Neighbour, 34-year-old Sarah Jones, told me, "It was terrible. I tried to get to them but I couldn't get anywhere near." '

Reporters sometimes represent direct speech in ways that reflect the **idioms** used by speakers but with some compression and selectivity so that information can be given in a more concise manner. Look at the example below.

> 'I clearly saw the skeletal remains of a body. There was some clothing still there,' Forrester told the inquest into Ahmed's death. He saw a green T-shirt, khaki trousers and white shoes. Some jewellery was recovered later, he said.

Guardian Unlimited website, 8 January 2008

Here you can see that the journalist begins by using direct speech and moves into reported speech, suggesting a similar attention to detail to the direct speech without necessarily covering all the items. The words 'Some jewellery was recovered later, he said' appear to be direct speech and resemble the pattern of Forrester's speech but they are not placed in inverted commas to show that they are not a quote.

Another way of reporting what is said is by the use of **indirect speech** (reported speech). Here, the words spoken are expressed in the past tense. As they are reported and not quoted exactly, inverted commas are not used. For example, 'Neighbour, 34-year-old Sarah Jones, said that it had been terrible and that she had not been able to get anywhere near them.'

In your response, you need to remember the need for both variety and coherence in your writing to enable it to fulfil its dual purpose of entertaining readers while at the same time informing them.

■ Diary entries

Most adults record reminders of daily commitments in a diary, either paper-based or electronic. However, the kind of diary entry you might be asked to write as a creative response to your set texts is one in which you write down the character's thoughts and feelings in ways that reveal private motives, emotions or reactions to events.

Some diarists write with the intention of publishing their entries. This obviously affects the degree of personal revelation that the author is prepared to make. It also tends to make the style more polished and the content much more comprehensive. Others keep diaries without an intention to publish at the time of writing but are later persuaded to do so or perhaps have their writing published posthumously.

The diary form offers some good opportunities for a creative task. For example, in a response to a text that is written in first person narrative, you might be asked to write an extended diary entry about a significant incident that is mentioned in the text but referred to only in passing or about a later meeting between two characters after the end of the story. Another possibility might be to produce the diary entry from the point of view of one of the other characters, for example that of Manon's husband in the novel *Property*. Similarly, for a text written by third person narrators, such as *Wuthering Heights*, your task might be to write diary

■ Link

Look at the section on the representation of speech starting on p86 of Unit 2 for a further exploration of this topic.

💡 Key terms

Idioms: characteristic expressions used by speakers from particular groups. Formed from groups of words whose meaning is known through common usage rather than by their literal meaning, e.g. 'you're driving me up the wall'.

Indirect speech: the speaker's words are referred to but not quoted verbatim and are usually preceded or followed by verbs such as 'said' or 'reported'. The speaker's words are transformed into a past tense account.

■ Think about it

You may have kept this kind of diary yourself. If you have, think about your reasons for writing it.

entries in the voice of Isabella Linton, who is not one of the narrators, about her relationship with Heathcliff. For a dramatic text, you might write an extract from the diary of one of the characters, such as Posner in *The History Boys* or Blanche in *A Streetcar Named Desire*.

Prepared speech

You could be asked to write a prepared speech as a creative response in the examination. Some of the set texts lend themselves to this kind of response. For example, at the beginning of *The History Boys* Irwin is making a speech to a small group of fellow MPs. The context appears to be a strategy meeting but the speech is clearly a prepared one in which the speaker uses full sentences and carefully chosen lexis.

> **Irwin**: This is the tricky one.
>
> The effect of the bill will be to abolish trial by jury in at least half the cases that currently come before the courts and will to a significant extent abolish the presumption of innocence.
>
> Our strategy should therefore be to insist that the bill does not diminish the liberty of the subject but amplifies it; that the true liberty of the subject consists in the freedom to walk the streets unmolested etc., etc., secure in the knowledge that if a crime is committed it will be promptly and sufficiently punished and that far from circumscribing the liberty of the subject this will enlarge it.
>
> I would try not to be shrill or earnest. An amused tolerance always comes over best, particularly on television. Paradox works well and mists up the windows, which is handy. 'The loss of liberty is the price we pay for freedom' type thing.

Your task might be to write a speech for Irwin to make on television in which he gives his views on education; there is much more information available in the play about his views on this topic. You would need to pay particular attention to his **tone**, reflecting the tone of 'amused tolerance' and the use of **paradox** which he advocates here. The speech that he creates for his television appearance will have a significantly different purpose and audience from that of the extract. In the extract, Irwin is seeking to persuade his fellow MPs that his approach to presenting the bill is the best one for the task. His audience is sophisticated, but Irwin's rather cynical approach suggests that he might view his television audience as somewhat naive or he might adopt a condescending manner.

Practical activity

Using the information in the extract above, write the opening of a speech that Irwin makes on television about the bill to abolish trial by jury. If you are actually studying *The History Boys*, you should make education the topic of this speech instead as you will be able to include information from other areas of the play.

Practical activity

Imagine that one of the significant characters from your set text meets another character after the conclusion of the events in the text. Write a diary entry in the voice of this character. Try to convey as accurately as possible:

- the character's perspective on people and events
- the distinctive features of the character's language.

Link

When you have completed this activity, read the sample response and the examiner's comments on pp80–1.

Link

For a more detailed look at the features of prepared speech, see pp102–13.

Key terms

Tone: the mood or feeling of a text.

Paradox: an idea that seems to contradict itself, e.g. 'ignorance is bliss'.

Writing your creative response

Planning

In order to make a good creative response to your set text you need to have a framework in mind to enable you to approach the task efficiently. You can break the task down as follows.

Stage 1: analyse the question

Pick out the key words in the question and mark them clearly. These enable you to see what it requires. You can then use the key words to plan your response. They will specify some or all of the following requirements.

The source text

Does the question refer to:

- a specific part of your text, for example 'the opening section of Chapter 3'.
- the whole text?

The narrative voice

Are you required to write:

- as a first, second or third person narrator
- in the voice of a particular character
- in a specific role, for example as a journalist or a doctor?

The form

Does the question ask you to use a particular form, such as:

- a letter
- a report
- a newspaper article
- a diary entry
- a prepared speech?

The genre

Are you being asked to write, for example:

- a section from an autobiography
- the opening of a detective story
- a newspaper feature article
- a charity letter asking for funds to support famine relief work
- part of the screenplay for a film adaptation of a novel?

The content

What are you being asked to write about, for example:

- one character's feelings for another
- events described in the text
- a character's attitudes to a situation?

The audience and purpose

Once you have identified all the details above, consider:

■ the audience you are being asked to write for

■ the overall purpose of the piece.

Stage 2: use the source text

Remember that you will be writing about a text that you have studied, so you will have considered it carefully before the examination. You need to make sure, however, that you are writing appropriately for the specific task given in the question. Remind yourself of the following points.

Style

In all the questions you are asked to give careful consideration to your language choices and style. If you are writing in the voice of a specific character from your text, you need to reflect the language of that character. Consider:

■ lexis

■ imagery

■ grammar

■ dialect.

If you are writing as a character who does *not* feature in the source text such as a journalist or doctor, you need to decide what stylistic choices would be appropriate for that person.

Narrative voice

If you are asked to write, or choose to write, in the same narrative voice as that used in your set text, you need to look carefully at its features.

■ Is it written in the first, second or third person?

■ Do we trust the narrator?

■ Is the narrator an observer or a central character?

■ Is irony used?

■ Is the narrator omniscient or is the viewpoint restricted?

Stage 3: plan your own text

Use the key words you picked out from the question as the basis for your plan. Remember, the plan is there to make sure your answer fulfils all the requirements set out in the question or task. You can use pattern or linear notes but make sure you include all the elements of the task. Pattern notes are particularly useful for planning when you are working under tight time constraints. To construct the pattern as shown in Fig. 1 on p72, write the key words from the question in the centre. List the features that you need to cover under each heading in the boxes around the outside. You can then decide the order in which you want to present your points.

Linear notes are simply made as a list. If you use this method, you should put the key words as a main heading and the list below as subheadings. Worked examples of both types of notes are given for the sample question based on '55 Miles to the Gas Pump' from *Close Range* by Annie Proulx (see pp73–4).

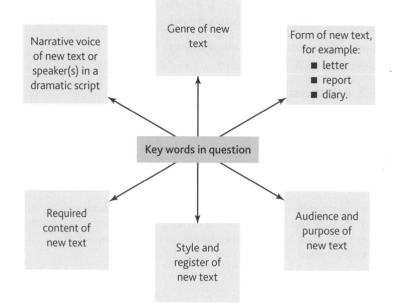

Fig. 1 *Writing a pattern note for creative interpretation tasks*

You can use the framework above to make this plan for your new text, making sure that you include brief notes on:

■ source text page references – to remind you where your information should come from

■ the voice in which you are writing – for example, Nelly Dean, Manon Gaudet, a Wyoming journalist

■ narrative voice

■ form – for example, letter, diary, report

■ genre – for example, novel, drama

■ content

■ audience

■ purpose

■ style – the language choices that you need to make to produce writing similar to the source text or different from it as specified by the question

■ register – the type of language choices that you need to make to fit the context and level of formality of your task.

The plan should be brief and to the point. Its purpose is to help you to think through what is needed and to provide you with a set of signposts to guide you as you write.

 Writing

You are now ready to begin writing your own response.

Read the short story '55 Miles to the Gas Pump' from Annie Proulx's collection *Close Range*, which is reproduced below in its entirety.

Rancher Croom in handmade boots and filthy hat, that walleyed cattleman, stray hairs like curling fiddle string ends, that warm-handed, quick-foot dancer on splintery boards or down the cellar stairs to a rack of bottles of his own strange beer, yeasty, cloudy, bursting out in garlands of foam, Rancher Croom at night galloping drunk over the dark plain, turning off at a place he knows to arrive at a canyon brink where he dismounts and looks down on tumbled rock, waits, then steps out, parting the air with his last roar, sleeves surging up windmill arms, jeans riding over boot tops, but before he hits he rises again to the top of the cliff like a cork in a bucket of milk.

Mrs Croom on the roof with a saw cutting a hole into the attic where she has not been for twelve years thanks to old Croom's padlocks and warnings, whets to her desire, and the sweat flies as she exchanges the saw for a chisel and hammer until a ragged slab of peak is free and she can see inside: just as she thought: the corpses of Mr Croom's paramours – she recognises them from their photographs in the paper: MISSING WOMAN – some desiccated as jerky and much the same colour, some mouldy from lying beneath roof leaks, and all of them used hard, covered with tarry handprints, the marks of boot heels, some bright blue with the remnants of paint used on the shutters years ago, one wrapped in newspaper nipple to knee.

When you live a long way out you make your own fun.

Read the following question.

> Imagine that you are a reporter for a regional newspaper and you are covering the inquest into one of the women found dead in the attic of the ranch house belonging to the Crooms. Write your report, using the information in the story as the basis for your answer.
>
> You should give careful consideration to your language choices and style. Write in an appropriate form for a newspaper article.

We will work through the framework above using this question as an example.

Stage 1: analyse the question

The key words in this question are highlighted for you below. You can do this directly on your question paper in the examination.

> Imagine that you are a reporter for a regional newspaper and you are covering the inquest into one of the women found dead in the attic of the ranch house belonging to the Crooms. Write your report, using the information in the story as the basis for your answer.
>
> You should give careful consideration to your language choices and style. Write in an appropriate form for a newspaper article.

When you have identified the key words, you can easily see the requirements of the task. You will need to use:

- source text page references – the whole text
- narrative voice – third person narrative, the most common voice for newspaper articles; perhaps some first person quotes
- form – an article for a regional newspaper
- genre – prose (non-fiction)
- content – the murders and some background to them and the characters involved
- audience – a wide social range of adults living in the region
- purpose – to inform and entertain (sell papers).

Stage 2: use the source text

This task does not require you to use the same style or narrative voice as the source text so you do not need to imitate the language choices made by Annie Proulx in the text. However, you still need to transform the details that she gives into your own text.

Stage 3: plan your own text

- ■ Source text page references – whole text.
- ■ The voice in which you are writing – a Wyoming journalist working as a court reporter.
- ■ Narrative voice – mixture of first and third person; include quotations in direct speech.
- ■ Form – newspaper article; context requires title for paper, date, headings, subheadings, byline.
- ■ Genre – newspaper reporting.
- ■ Content – inquest; aftermath of discovery of bodies; information about Rancher Croom's death.
- ■ Audience – wide social range of adults living in the region.
- ■ Purpose – to inform and entertain (sell papers).
- ■ Style – lexical choices could include some low frequency words but needs a mixture; some dialect could be used in representations of the evidence given by locals if this is quoted.
- ■ Register – suitable for a regional newspaper read by a wide social range; the primary concern is the accurate reporting of events.

Pattern notes can be a quick and efficient way of planning your examination answers. Read the example below.

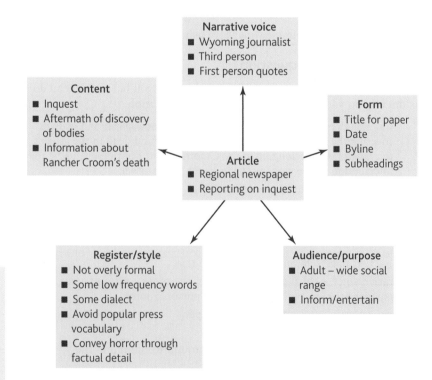

Practical activity

Using the plans above, write your answer to the examination question on '55 Miles to the Gas Pump'. Read the sample response below and the examiner's comments that follow.

Fig. 2 *A pattern note diagram for this question*

Sample response

THE WYOMING HERALD

Friday 9th June 1993

Inquest told of Discovery of Fifteen Corpses at Stony Mountain Ranch

By David Millar

The inquest into the death of Sarah Tyler, one of fifteen women whose remains were found at isolated Stony Mountain Ranch on 4th February this year, began today at the Wyoming State Court. The ranch is located in the hills beyond the small town of Carter Creek and was owned by Mr Sam Croom and his wife Esther.

> Follows word order common in news writing

The Crooms' nearest neighbour, seventy year old Agnes Salter, told the court that she had alerted the authorities after a distraught Esther Croom had arrived at her door.

> Age of the witness given

'I couldn't get no sense out of her at first,' Mrs Salter said. 'She was hollering fit to bust. But I took her inside and got her calmed down a bit and then she told me about the bodies. Esther's as tough as they come; she could handle an axe and chop wood as well as any man but I could see she was almost out of her wits with what she'd seen. I called the cops and kept her right there with me.'

> Mrs Salter's dialect represented. Direct speech is used to represent her actual words

Giving evidence, police spokesman Barry Waters said that when they'd reached the ranch after having picked up Esther Croom on the way, the place was deserted.

> Indirect speech used for variety

He said, 'Esther told us her husband hadn't let her into the attic for the last twelve years; he'd kept it padlocked and stuck warning signs everywhere. Naturally, she'd become suspicious. She told us that her curiosity had finally gotten the better of her and she'd sawed her way into the attic through the roof. Inside, she said, she saw bodies.' He continued, 'When we got to the ranch, we forced our way into the attic from inside the house. We found the remains of at least fifteen women, in varying states of decay. Some were dried out and some were mouldy. There were some marks on the bodies which looked like boot prints and handprints and some of the bodies were covered in blue paint.'

> Lengthy speech is condensed

> Direct speech is used to convey the gruesome details of the discovery

Esther Croom, 55, was then called to give evidence. 'I couldn't rest till I knew what was in the attic,' she said. 'When I saw the bodies I recognised some of them from the pictures in the papers even though they were in such a state. And the smell was terrible.' She went on to say, 'I had to get back down the roof and I don't know how I ever did it.' She then told the court about how she'd run to Mrs Salter's house for help.

Friends and family members described Sarah Tyler as a lively and popular eighteen year old who had enjoyed her job at Hank's Diner until her disappearance in September 1991.

> Indirect speech is used to sum up evidence given by a number of people. References to the victim's youth and popularity create empathy with the reader

The inquest will be resumed tomorrow.

The body of Mr Sam Croom was found in Stony Mountain Canyon, close to the Crooms' ranch on 4th February this year by police searching the area. At the March inquest into his death, a verdict of suicide was recorded.

> Factual information is provided for the reader. This helps to reinforce the context of the writing as a newspaper article

> Gives some further detail about the background to the case. No judgements are passed about possible connections to the deaths

Examiner's comments

The article is placed in its context of a regional newspaper by its title *The Wyoming Herald* (all of the Annie Proulx stories in the source text are set in Wyoming), the inclusion of a date, a headline, a subheading and a byline. The first sentence includes a syntactical pattern common in news writing 'whose remains were found at isolated Stony Mountain Ranch' omitting the definite article 'the'. The opening paragraph is clear and factual, fitting the style of the court reporter who must relate the proceedings accurately. These lexical choices are also appropriate for the wide social range of audience that you would expect for this kind of newspaper. The structure of the report is based on the order of events in the courtroom.

As is usual in court reporting, evidence presented by witnesses is quoted. The reason for Agnes Salter's appearance is summarised in third person narrative. Some of her actual words are then quoted as direct speech and so are meant to be represented as she delivered them. This provides an opportunity to represent some of the local dialect as suggested by the source text.

In reporting the police spokesman's words, indirect (reported) speech is used to sum up the first part of his evidence briefly, another common feature of writing used in newspapers. The most dramatic part – the discovery of the bodies – is quoted verbatim.

Esther Croom's evidence is related in a mixture of direct and indirect speech, thus avoiding covering the same material already reported in the representation of the policeman's words.

The comments about the victim from her friends and family are summarised and they are reported to encourage the reader to empathise with the victim and her family.

In the final paragraph, factual details about the death of Rancher Croom are included. The writer carefully avoids any suggestion that Mr Croom is responsible for the death of Sarah Tyler.

The article as a whole is given a coherent structure following the order of events in court. The writer has shown how the reporter would seek to maintain interest by using a variety of styles, particularly in the reporting of speech.

Additional details such as names are invented to provide a clear sense of the context of the writing. However, the content is firmly based on the source text. Overall, this is a very successful response.

For AO1, the writing is fluent and the structure coherent. Expression is precise and wholly appropriate showing a clear awareness of the range of lexis needed to represent different voices. The piece is stylish and errors are rare.

For AO4, the response is entirely appropriate for its intended audience (a wide social range of readers of a regional newspaper) and its purpose (to inform and entertain). The writer uses a variety of narrative techniques including third person narrative, direct and indirect speech which help to engage and maintain the reader's interest. The article is well contextualised, providing an appropriate name for the newspaper, a date, headline, byline and subheading. Careful attention is given to the accurate representation of facts. Anything that is speculative is reported by using direct, verbatim quotations. The content of the original story is very well adapted.

Technical accuracy

In this part of Unit 1 there are 15 marks for AO1 which refers to 'using accurate, coherent written expression'.

Although some consideration is given to the quality and accuracy of your expression in all of the areas covered in the examination, this aspect of your writing is given particular emphasis in your answer to the creative response question for Unit 1. You should therefore pay particular attention to the following:

- spelling
- punctuation
- grammar
- paragraphing
- **coherence**
- **cohesion.**

Think about it

Make an honest assessment of these five aspects of your own writing. Look carefully at feedback you have been given on your written work. If you identify areas of weakness, use the internet and library resources to help you to fill in gaps in your knowledge. Find a website or reference book that will give you good advice on aspects of correct usage and get into the habit of consulting it so that you can improve your quality of expression and your technical control. The addresses of some websites that may help are included in your e-resources.

Key terms

Coherence: the continuity of organisation and meaning that unifies a spoken or written text.

Cohesion: the grammatical and lexical devices, such as repetition and the use of pronouns and ellipsis, that link the parts of a written or spoken text.

Preparing for the examination

For the Unit 1 creative response question in the examination, candidates are required to write 'in a particular style, register or voice, based on a thorough knowledge of the text. They will be assessed on language use appropriate to the set task and on technical accuracy.'

This question is worth 45 out of the 75 marks available in the examination, split between Assessment Objectives 1 and 4.

■ For AO4, you will need to demonstrate expertise and creativity in using language appropriate for a variety of purposes and audiences. This Assessment Objective is worth 30 of the 45 marks for the creative answers (B).

■ For AO1 creative answers (B) 15 marks of the 45 available for this section are allocated for 'accurate, coherent written expression'.

You are advised to spend approximately 50 minutes on this question. To meet all these requirements, you need to demonstrate a thorough knowledge of your set text. This is just as important for the creative, text production question as for the analytical question as you need to understand the chosen text and the methods used by the writer. Your interpretation of material must be firmly rooted in the set text.

You also need to demonstrate:

■ clear awareness of the audience specified in the question

■ understanding of the purpose of your new text

■ knowledge of the style or styles used in the source text and an ability to respond to these according to the requirements of the question

■ awareness of the appropriate register for the set task

■ the ability to write in the form and genre specified in the question

■ good control of technical accuracy and expression

■ a well-structured and coherent response.

As always in an examination, there never seems to be enough time to cover everything that you have to do. You can help yourself by having a clear framework such as the one on pp70–1, which you can use to plan your answer. You need to be familiar with all the concepts listed above and you should gain as much practice as possible in writing in a whole range of different forms for a variety of purposes and audiences. This, together with a really good knowledge of the set text, will do a great deal for your confidence. It is also important to get used to the kinds of questions you will be asked and to practise answering them.

The kinds of questions you will face in this part of the examination follow a pattern. If you look at the specimen questions available on the AQA website you will see that they all have a similar structure. Here is a specimen question on *Things Fall Apart* by Chinua Achebe.

Things Fall Apart: **Chinua Achebe**

> In Chapter 5 we are told about the preparation for the Feast of the New Yam and how Okonkwo 'could never become as enthusiastic as most people'. Write about Okonkwo's feelings at this time, from his point of view.
>
> You should give careful consideration to your language choices and style, which should achieve a sense of Okonkwo's voice.

In the first part of this question the *situation* (the Feast of the New Yam), *point of view* (Okonkwo's) and the *content* (Okonkwo's feelings) are all specified.

In the second part of the question you are asked to give careful consideration to your *language choices and style*. You will always be asked to do this. There is then a further instruction to write in a way that conveys *a sense of Okonkwo's voice*. The requirement to write in a way that reflects a particular voice is a common one and you should be alert to this. You should also look out for an instruction to write in a particular genre although this is not specified in this question.

Sample questions and answers

Here are examples of the sort of creative response questions you will find in the examination. Other specimen questions for all the set texts are available on the AQA website.

Read Question 1 below and the sample response and examiner's comments that follow. For Questions 2 to 9, highlight the key words for each question and write a brief plan showing what you would need to include in your answer. Try writing complete answers to the questions on your set texts.

1 *Murmuring Judges*: **David Hare**

> In the opening scenes of the play, Irina is introduced as a new tenant in a law firm. Write about Irina's experiences from her point of view as though you were writing a diary.
>
> You should give careful consideration to your language choices and style, write in an appropriate diary form and convey a sense of Irina's voice.

Practical activity

Highlight the key words for this question as shown in the example on p73.

AQA Examiner's tip

Examiners are provided with a marking grid that details the requirements for each band of achievement. This grid is available on the AQA website. It is worth familiarising yourself with the kinds of things examiners are looking for.

Sample response

Monday 3rd September

Last day in court today for the armed robbery trial. No surprises in the verdicts or the sentences for Travis and Fielding ... but Gerard McKinnon? The jury had obviously thought twice about the verdict and, as for five years, that's absurd. I think we've really failed him there. On the way out we met Cuddeford – he seemed to be an old bosom buddy of my boss. They were scoring points off each other but Peter got round the fact he'd lost the case by trivialising it. Do any of them care about the people they're defending? They keep score – Cuddeford even called it a 'bowling average'. You would have thought I wasn't there but eventually he remembered to introduce me before he went on to more important things like his appearance on Desert Island Discs. Think his choice of Je Ne Regrette Rien just shows his smugness.

When they finally remembered I was there, Peter insisted on telling the story of the bright green dress I wore on the first day of the trial. Just shows how the judiciary is stuck in the past. Still, old Cuddeford was floored when I told him I'd raised a million pounds in four days! And Peter's a real self-interested cynic – I think he'd rather defend a politician from a sleaze charge than help someone like Gerard McKinnon to get any justice.

When I got back to chambers, Woody (Sir Peter's gopher) dropped a bombshell. He told me (didn't phrase it as a request) that I was going to take in a little Mozart with Sir Peter and then to go back to chambers and work late. And to think I'd just been with Sir Peter and he hadn't mentioned it. I told Woody what to do with the idea in no uncertain terms but he's a nice chap and he warned me turning the boss down wouldn't help my career. Talk about moral justice!

Thursday 15th November

I visited Gerard in prison today. Peter didn't want me to – in fact he was pretty hostile. He just sees all young criminals as the same. The prison was horrible. The warder who took me in had to warn me about shit packages on the ground – apparently, prisoners throw them out of the window because they can't stand the smell. There I was thinking it was some sort of protest. I liked Gerard. He's obviously suffering in that place and close to giving up. I tried to find out why he hadn't contacted us to ask for an appeal, the sentence was so obviously harsh. It turned out he was scared. Somehow we got to talking about me and love and he told me about himself and his girlfriend and children. I could see why he'd been desperate enough to get involved with the robbery and scared enough to lie when he was arrested because the others had threatened him and his family. He gave me a story too about one of the police planting Semtex. I don't know what to make of that.

Every instinct tells me Gerard is mostly a victim. We should fight his corner.

Saturday 17th November

Decided the only way to get Peter to fight the case would be to go to the opera with him as Woody told me to do. I felt such a hypocrite but even Helen Mirren would have been jealous of the way I played my part! He was putty in my hands and agreed to take it on. I felt a bit soiled, playing his games though, but I would never have been able to help Gerard otherwise. I suppose it's necessary to be pragmatic sometimes, but I can't say I like it.

Side annotations (left):

Irina's views about the trial are revealed

Lexis such as 'trivialising' is appropriate to Irina's voice as an educated woman

Details from the text are noted and adapted

Register is mainly informal but lexical choices such as 'Every instinct' reflect Irina's education

Side annotations (right):

Ellipsis creates informality appropriate for the diary

'Sir' is omitted from Sir Peter's name to show that privately she does not particularly respect him

Judgements are made on Sir Peter's character using apt material from the text

Informal punctuation – dashes are used

Apt use of content from the text. Irina is shown to reflect on her actions, one of the purposes of writing a diary

Examiner's comments

For AO1, the response is fluent and cohesive. Expression is precise and wholly appropriate. Errors are rare and the writing is stylish. There are some examples of informality in the punctuation of the piece but these are clearly intentional and designed to match the prescribed diary form.

For AO4, there is a clear sense of audience (the writer herself) and purpose (recording her experiences, perhaps for later use). A thorough knowledge of the set text is shown and Irina's experiences have been presented in a voice that is convincingly her own. There is some informality in her writing as is appropriate in a diary form but the lexical choices generally reflect Irina's high level of education. The writing is also contextualised by the provision of appropriate dates for the diary entries. The style is lively and engaging.

Sample questions from other texts

1 *Murmuring Judges*: **David Hare**

For the sample question and response on this text see p79.

2 *Wuthering Heights*: **Emily Brontë**

Imagine that Nelly writes to a friend who worked as housekeeper at Wuthering Heights until Nelly's return, telling her about events after her departure and focusing on the developments in relationship between Cathy and Hareton.

You should give careful consideration to your language choices and style. Write in an appropriate letter form which should convey a sense of Nelly's voice.

3 *Property*: **Valerie Martin**

Imagine that you are writing a novel using a third person narrator who is telling the story from Sarah's viewpoint. Tell this story beginning with Sarah's arrival at the Gaudets' plantation and adapting two or three scenes from the early part of the novel (up to page 23 of the recommended edition), bringing out her feelings towards Manon and Mr Gaudet.

You should give careful consideration to your language choices and style and convey Sarah's viewpoint.

4 *Things Fall Apart*: **Chinua Achebe**

In the last chapter of the novel we are told that the District Commissioner is planning to write a book. He feels that 'the story of this man who had killed a messenger and hanged himself would make interesting reading'. Write an extract from this book revealing his impressions of Okonkwo's behaviour.

You should give careful consideration to your language choices and style, which should achieve a sense of the District Commissioner's voice.

5 *The Kite Runner*: **Khaled Hosseini**

Before Amir visits the American Embassy in Islamabad to try to arrange to adopt Sohrab, he phones his wife and tells her everything that he has withheld before. Write this conversation, focusing particularly on Amir's feelings about his behaviour towards Hassan.

You should give careful consideration to your language choices and style, which should achieve a sense of Amir's and Soraya's voices.

6 *Close Range*: **Annie Proulx**

In *The Bunchgrass Edge of the World*, Ottaline's sister Shan sends a letter to her family in which she says she has 'Got into body building'. Imagine that Ottaline writes to Shan about her life on the ranch and her efforts to change it. Write this letter using an appropriate letter form.

You should give careful consideration to your language choices and style, which should achieve a sense of Ottaline's voice.

7 *The Importance of Being Earnest*: **Oscar Wilde**

In Act 2 of the play, Cecily Cardew reveals to Algernon Moncrieff, then disguised as 'Ernest Worthing', that she has kept a diary in which she has imagined she is engaged to him. She reads him part of an entry for 22 March, beginning 'Today I broke off my engagement with Ernest. I feel it better to do so.' Continue this entry and then write a second entry from Cecily's diary after her encounter with Ernest, showing how she feels about him after their meeting.

You should give careful consideration to your language choices and style. Write in an appropriate diary form and convey a sense of Cecily's voice.

8 *The Rivals*: **Richard Brinsley Sheridan**

In Act 1, Scene 2 of the play, Lydia Languish is talking to Julia Melville who has just arrived in Bath. Lydia refers to some letters she has previously written to Julia, informing her of her 'connection with Beverley'. Write one of these letters, showing how Lydia views romance and marriage.

You should give careful consideration to your language choices and style. Write in an appropriate letter form and convey a sense of Lydia's voice.

9 *A Streetcar Named Desire*: **Tennessee Williams**

Imagine that Stella writes to a close friend revealing her feelings about the decision to have her sister committed to an institution and her reasons for having done so. Write this letter using an appropriate letter form.

You should give careful consideration to your language choices and style, which should achieve a sense of Stella's voice.

10 *The History Boys*: **Alan Bennett**

Imagine that Irwin keeps a diary about his impressions of the school and its staff and pupils. Write an entry or entries from this diary in which Irwin gives his impressions of Hector and comments on his teaching style.

You should give careful consideration to your language choices and style, write in an appropriate diary form and convey a sense of Irwin's voice.

Learning outcomes for this section:

Knowledge, understanding and skills

Now that you have completed Section B of this unit, you should be able to:

- recognise the importance of a detailed knowledge of your set text to the production of a successful creative response

- understand the ways in which the author of your text presents its characters and plot

- understand and adapt the stylistic, and narrative or dramatic, techniques that the writer employs

- show that you can write in a range of forms and in different genres

- apply your knowledge and understanding appropriately in creating your own piece of writing, based on your knowledge of your set text, in the examination.

Transferable skills

Your study of this unit has provided you with a framework of terminology and concepts that you will be able to use in your study of Unit 2 and in your A2 studies. The skills you have acquired should include the ability to:

- use appropriate terminology in support of your analyses

- understand and adapt the techniques used by writers in the production of texts

- create a piece of your own work based on a set text

- write fluently and coherently.

Varieties of spoken English

This section introduces you to a range of features of spoken English and will equip you with a framework of terms and concepts to help you analyse these features. You will be considering how speech differs from writing and thinking about the influence of audience, purpose and context on speech. You will also look at many of the structures and patterns which are typical of spontaneous and planned speech. You will have the opportunity to consider a variety of speech texts, including spontaneous speech such as conversations, interviews and radio shows. You will also study a variety of prepared speech texts, such as political oratory from politicians both past and present as well as speeches from more familiar situations such as college talks and speeches at family events, focusing on aspects such as language, form and context, as well as audience and purpose.

In Section A of the examination, you will need to write an analytical comparison of spoken texts, which could also include other sorts of non-literary speech representation such as the text of an interview published in a magazine or an internet chatroom discussion. You will need to use a range of appropriate speech terminology to support your analysis, but should also continue to use the terms you acquired in Unit 1.

Your answers to Section A in the examination will be assessed for Assessment Objectives AO2 and AO3:

■ For AO2, you will need to show in detail that you understand and can analyse the ways in which structure, form and language shape your chosen speaker's meaning. (*15 marks*)

■ For AO3, you will need to show that you can compare texts effectively and that you can analyse the ways in which context affects both the production of speech and the way it is received. (*30 marks*)

Set texts: speech and style

You will be studying either a novel or a play for this section and part of the question will focus on the representation of speech. As you will see from your study of spontaneous speech, real conversations are often unplanned and can be unpredictable. Written transcripts of them reflect this immediacy and can present us with some difficulties of interpretation. Both novelists and playwrights aim to make the dialogue or the speech they give to characters sound natural and authentic, but in fact it is highly crafted. You will be exploring how writers achieve this.

Of course, writers do not simply seek to represent speech for its own sake; they aim to use it to develop characters and their relationships, explore themes, create mood, tension and suspense, and further the plot. For this part of the examination you are therefore asked to show how dialogue and other stylistic or dramatic techniques contribute to these other aspects of your text. You will look first at the use of dialogue in novels and then go on to look at how speech is represented in drama. Even if you are studying a play as your set text for this unit, you should still read the section on the novel and vice versa as many points are common to writing in both genres. In your response to the examination question for Section B you will also need to draw on the knowledge and understanding of literary and linguistic concepts and terminology which you have gained from the other areas of your studies in this subject.

There will be a short passage from each of the set texts printed on the examination paper and you will be asked to comment on this and one other episode of your own choice from your text. You are required to study only one text from the set list for this section but remember that you will not be allowed to take the text into the examination with you.

Your answers to Section B will be assessed for AO1 and AO2:

- For AO1, you will need to show your ability to choose relevant linguistic and literary concepts and terminology to help you analyse and write about your chosen text. The accuracy of your own written expression will also be assessed. (*15 marks*)
- For AO2, you will need to show in detail that you understand and can analyse the ways in which structure, form and language shape your chosen writer's meaning. (*15 marks*)

Features of speech

This chapter covers:

■ differences between written and spoken texts

■ the importance of context, audience and purpose in spoken communication.

🔖 Key terms

Mode: the medium of communication used, usually speech or writing.

Paralinguistic features: non-verbal aspects of communication such as intonation or pausing, which work alongside language to help a speaker convey the meaning effectively.

Pause: a short break in a spoken text, recorded in seconds.

Micropause: a very short pause in a spoken text.

So far in this book you have looked only at texts produced in the written **mode**, or written medium of communication. In this section you are going to consider speech texts, which have been produced in the spoken mode. There are some obvious differences between these two means of communication.

■ A piece of writing is a permanent record that can be read again and again, whereas an act of speech is ephemeral and exists only at the moment when it takes place (although, of course, records have often been made of famous speeches – you may well have seen and heard a recording of Martin Luther King's famous 'I Have a Dream' speech, for example).

■ A written text may be produced over time, with the writer drafting and polishing the work to achieve exactly the desired effect; spontaneous speech is usually much more immediate, even if there has been a degree of planning what to say. In the case of formal speeches, the planning is likely to be as thorough as it is for published written texts.

■ The audience for a written text is likely to be at a distance from the writer, both in terms of the time difference between when the text is read and the time when it was written (possibly up to hundreds of years apart for some works of literature) and in terms of the place where it was written and where it is read. However, the audience for many spoken events is likely to be present, or even participating, as speech is often a much more interactive form of communication than writing.

■ Speakers have the advantage of being able to use **paralinguistic features** such as placing stresses on particular words, pausing or modifying the tone and pitch of their voice as well as using body language, eye contact and gestures to convey their exact meaning. Writers, on the other hand, must resort to devices such as underlining or italicising key words for emphasis, or using punctuation such as exclamation marks, to create the same effect.

■ Critical response activity

Read the two extracts below, which are similar in that they both give an account of a boy in a dramatic situation. The first extract is a spoken account given by a nine-year-old boy called Tom. The **pauses** in his story are represented by (1.0) to represent the length of the pause in seconds. Very brief pauses, or **micropauses**, are represented by (.). The second extract is from the Young Bond novel *Silverfin* by Charlie Higson. Compare both texts, considering any similarities and differences between their language, structure and presentation. Check your answer against the commentary that follows.

Extract A: Tom's spoken account

I was playin with Mark an (.) we were skiddin on the grass cos it had been wet (.) but it had dried out and erm (2.0) er (1.0) er an it was still a bit slippy so we were skiddin and (.) I (.) I skidded a bit late (0.5) an we had some Jewson's bags (.) on the wa (1.0) not on the wall next t (.) behind the wall (0.5) an I skidded (.) an I came to this dry patch an I (.) just like nearly fell (.) kept meself up (.) put me f (.) M put one of me feet foot on the er (.) ma foot on the erm (1.0) Jewson's bags (0.5) an I wa I was trying to get me leg over the wall so I ended up sitting on it (1.0) what goes an happens I goes an flies straight over (.) scrapes all me face (.) I was like that (1.0) with ma hands over me face and erm (2.0) an I said to M (.) to my friend Mark that I was playin with (.) is it bleedin or anythink (.) and he said (.) I don't know you're covering your face up (.) an so I wen I just went dashin up the (.) steps screamin me head off (0.5) and erm (.) like erm ma mum started to (1.0) dab it with (.) cotton wool wet cotton wool and s (.) put some Germolene on an (.) then (0.5) just (.) that (.) night and (1.5) that evening and that night erm (.) an the next day (.) it wa we just had to kept putting (.) keep putting Germolene on and (1.0) like on the night (.) when I was sitting down watching TV (.) it just kept throbbin on an off (0.5) so it was like really horrible (.) an I think that's one of the worst accidents I've had.

Extract B: *Silverfin*

He froze. He'd lost touch with the wall and one leg was dangling in mid-air. Quickly he pulled it back up and found the rock. He hadn't been concentrating, just staring ahead, not looking up or down. Not that it would have made any difference. There wasn't enough light down here to see anything. He felt with his foot again: it was as he had thought, this was the end of the line. The walls of the shaft ran out … But what was below? How far was the water? How deep was it?

There were too many questions and no answers.

James suddenly had an image of the cell door opening, and Hellebore coming in with the ghastly MacSawney, seeing the grille on the floor, looking down into the shaft and finding him here, stuck like a rat up a drainpipe …

He let go.

There was a short painful moment as he scraped down the last two feet of the shaft and bumped his knees, and then he was in space, black space, like falling in a dream … It lasted only a short, terrifying moment, and then the freezing water hit him like a great fist and he was under it, not knowing which way was up or down.

Commentary

One of the first differences you probably noticed was the difference in structure. As you would expect of a literary text, Extract B is clearly structured into paragraphs, using a couple of short one-line paragraphs – 'There were too many questions and no answers' and 'He let go' – to create dramatic pauses. In comparison, Extract A has no paragraphs; instead it is presented as an exact **transcript** of Tom's words. It does,

Key terms

Transcript: an exact written representation of speech.

💡 Key terms

Utterance: a unit of spoken language, the end of which is indicated by a pause or a change of speaker. This term is often used to describe a 'spoken sentence' as an utterance may not follow the expectations and grammatical conventions of a written sentence.

Phonetic spelling: the spelling of words to represent exactly how they are pronounced.

AQA Examiner's tip

It is important not to think of spontaneous spoken language as in any way inferior to formal written language just because it does not follow the same expectations and grammatical conventions. It is better to think of spontaneous spoken language as a different but equally valid form of communication. You should therefore avoid saying things like 'Tom's speech is not written in proper English' or 'the grammar Tom uses is wrong'.

however, have a sense of structure: there is a clear beginning, middle and end to the narrative. Extract B uses a range of syntax, including questions such as 'But what was below?' to create a sense of James's uncertainty and tension. Extract A, on the other hand, reflects the grammar of spontaneous spoken language, with false starts, changes of direction and self-corrections. Rather than using the term 'sentence' in this context, **utterance** is used to describe a unit of speech. Tom's utterances in Extract A are clearly very spontaneous: in his excitement to tell the tale, he often has to correct himself ('we had some Jewson's bags (.) on the wa (1.0) not on the wall next t (.) behind the wall'). As he thinks of what he wants to say, he also includes plenty of 'erms' and 'ers'. In contrast, the Young Bond extract is obviously much more polished; it has been composed carefully using literary techniques such as the simile 'the freezing water hit him like a great fist' to add to the drama. Nevertheless, Tom's story still evokes a great sense of drama; for example, he uses lots of dynamic verbs such as 'skiddin', 'screamin', 'bleedin' and 'flies' to convey the excitement of the episode. His repeated use of the connective 'and' may seem childlike but it adds a sense of pace and continuity to the story. One final difference you may have noticed is that **phonetic spelling** has been used to represent Tom's pronunciation of certain words, such as 'anythink' and 'meself', which gives us a strong sense of his individuality. Extract B, of course, uses Standard English spelling, which is more typical of published writing.

■ Practical activity

Make a recording of someone you know describing a dramatic event and use this to create a transcript of what was said. Remember, when you are making a recording of spontaneous speech it is important to ask the speakers for permission to record them. You should also bear in mind that a speaker who is aware of being recorded may feel self-conscious, which could affect the spontaneity of their speech, so try to make your recording as unobtrusive as possible.

■ Context, audience and purpose

In Unit 1 we looked at the importance of awareness of the audience and purpose of a text in producing effective writing. These factors are just as important when considering spoken communication but, in addition, we need to consider the context in which the words are spoken.

Context

You will already be aware of the many different situations in which you use speech in your everyday life and how these affect the language choices and register of your speech. These situations vary according to who is present and the circumstances in which the speech takes place and they constitute its **context**. Both the audience and the purpose of the speech form part of its context.

💡 Key terms

Context: the social situation, including audience and purpose, in which language is used; this situation is an important influence on the language choices made by speakers and writers.

■ Practical activity

1. List as many different situations as you can think of in which you have used speech this week.

2. What aspects of your language use were specific to each of these situations?

Depending on your own circumstances, your list might include such things as:

- conversations with family
- talking with a group of friends
- talking on the phone
- giving a prepared talk in class
- addressing a meeting at work
- talking to small children
- attending a job interview.

Variations in language use do not fit readily into categories. However, we can make some broad generalisations about the features of different kinds of speech. In your conversations with friends the register is likely to be informal. The lexis used is likely to be held in common by the group and there will be little need for explanations. However, there can be great variations depending on, for example, the content of the conversation, the mood of the group or the time of day. Conversations between family members can vary greatly according to their purpose. For example, if a teenager is trying to get his parents to agree to help him to buy a motorbike there is likely to be a greater element of preparation and more carefully selected lexis than in a conversation about getting ready for school. A prepared talk will be planned and carefully structured and is likely to use a more formal register than a spontaneous conversation. It will have more of the features you would normally associate with a written text. It is helpful to think of the many different situations in which speech is used as being along a **continuum**, with casual conversation at one end and prepared speech at the other. Prepared speech has much in common with written texts.

Audience

The author of a text in the written mode is writing for an audience that is not physically present. Even a drama script that will eventually be performed to a live audience can only be written with an *intended* audience in mind. Spontaneous speech has an audience that is physically present and interactive. The responses made by the person or people hearing the utterance affect the dialogue that follows. In prepared speech, the speaker normally has a clear idea of the audience in advance of the presentation. There may be interaction between the audience and the speaker if the audience is physically present. However, a speech delivered on the radio or television will not have the instant feedback that is possible from a live audience.

The intended audience for speech, just as in writing, affects the lexical choices, register and content. Spontaneous speech is generally less structured than prepared speech but the divisions are not clear cut. A radio interview, for example, in which the interviewee has been invited to talk on a topic known in advance will be much more structured than a spontaneous conversation even though the words are not scripted. It might be closer on the continuum to prepared speech rather than spontaneous speech. Some prepared speeches, such as a prime minister's address to the nation in a crisis situation, would have a very wide audience whereas others might be delivered to a small interest group such as a support group for a local nature reserve receiving a talk on local birdlife. As for written texts, audiences can be broadly categorised by age, level of education, interests, etc. but these are loose and fluid categories that cannot account for the diversity of individual tastes and interests.

Key terms

Continuum: an imaginary line running from one extreme to another showing other possibilities in between. In discussing speech texts, a transcript of a casual conversation would be at one end and a formal, legal declaration such as the words of the wedding service or taking an oath in court at the other.

Link

Remind yourself of the section on 'Audience and purpose' on p41 of Unit 1.

Purpose

You have looked at the importance of a clear awareness of purpose to the authors of written texts. Looking at the speech continuum, conversations nearest the spoken end, such as chatty conversations between friends, may not have an overt purpose in mind other than social bonding – one of the main purposes of spoken language. There may, however, be a clear purpose; for example, persuading the group to go on holiday to a particular resort. As texts move closer to the prepared speech end of the continuum, the speaker's purpose often becomes more explicit. Speakers, like writers, aim to inform, persuade, entertain or argue. In your analysis of a particular text, these very broad purposes need to be related to an individual speaker's specific purposes. For example, in a political speech the speaker may try to entertain the audience in order to persuade it that the views of the opposition should not be taken seriously.

■ Critical response activity

Look at the short extracts below and consider the main purpose in each case.

Extract A

A. Excuse me. Could you tell me the way to the station?
B. Er (.) Let me think what's the best way to tell you (.) er (.) you go down there till you get to the market then go left down you know Bridge Street. It's right in front of you then.

Extract B

Good evening, ladies and gentlemen. Welcome to the first meeting of the Lemmingford Greenbelt Preservation Society. As you know, there is a proposal to build 500 new houses on Wilton Common, land that has been used by local people for generations.

Extract C

C. Hey (.) where were you last night? You missed it.
D. Missed what?
C. John and Karen that's what. You shoulda seen them (.)

The examples above are fairly straightforward and you should have been able to identify their purposes easily, although there might be some different ideas about the third example. As we consider in detail the different characteristics of speech, we will be looking at the ways in which the context affects both spontaneous speech and prepared speech.

13   Spontaneous speech

Key terms

Turn-taking: the pattern of spontaneous interactive speech in which participants cooperate or compete for the roles of listener/ speaker.

Adjacency pair: a pattern of speech in which one utterance is followed by an appropriate linked response.

In this section we will be looking at a variety of types of spontaneous speech, from interviews and broadcasts which are likely to have an element of careful planning involved in their production, to spontaneous informal conversations with no audience intended other than the immediate participants. Although spontaneous speech may at first seem random and unstructured, once you start to study it in detail you will see that there are, in fact, a number of patterns and structures that we all use as speakers in order to communicate effectively with others.

Turn-taking and adjacency pairs

One of the most prominent patterns that we follow as speakers in interactive speech such as conversations, discussions or interviews is that we take turns to speak. Unsurprisingly, this taking of turns has given rise to the linguistic term **turn-taking**. This may seem rather obvious, but in the examination you will need to do more than simply say 'the speakers take turns'. The concept of turn-taking becomes more interesting once you start to analyse the turn-taking and think about issues such as:

- who dominates the turns and why

- how speakers get a turn and gain control of the conversation

- who does not get a turn and why

- how speakers prevent others from getting a turn

- how speakers indicate that their turn is finished and that they are ready to pass the turn on to another speaker

- what happens when speakers deliberately flout the expectations we have about turn-taking.

When we take turns in interactive speech, the ways in which we speak and respond to each other tend to follow some typical patterns. For example, when one speaker asks a question, we usually expect the next speaker to respond with an answer, or if we say 'hello' to someone, we expect them to reply with a similar greeting. These typical pairings are known as **adjacency pairs** and these conventions help us to develop a conversation in a way that satisfies the participants. Of course, we often flout the rules of adjacency pairing for a variety of reasons; for example, if a student asks a teacher 'What does this poem mean?', the teacher may well respond not with an answer but with another question – 'Well, what do *you* think it means?' – thus passing the responsibility for the answer back to the student. Some of the typical adjacency pairs you are likely to come across are:

- a question followed by an answer

- a request followed by a reply, either positive or negative

- a greeting or farewell followed by an appropriate response

- a statement followed by a statement of agreement or disagreement

- a command followed by obedience or disobedience.

Critical response activity

Look at the following selection of adjacency pairs, gathered by a group of adult students at an A-level evening class. In each case, identify what sort of adjacency pair is being used and the context and purpose of each exchange.

STUDENT. Hello, can I rebook an appointment for my daughter?
DENTIST'S RECEPTIONIST. No, sorry, we can't as your daughter didn't turn up for her first appointment.

RECEPTIONIST. Good evening, Marks and Spencer Shoreham. How can I help?
STUDENT. Can you tell me if you have a top in stock?

STUDENT. Morning, Lina. How are you?
WORK COLLEAGUE. Fine, thanks. See you at break.

STUDENT. Geoff, the minutes of the last ODM asked us to look at presenting the report and how it can be improved.
GEOFF. Hang on a minute – I'll just finish this first, then we'll look at it.

BANK. Hello, Mrs Walker. My name is Andrew. How may I help you today?
STUDENT. I would like to know why I'm being charged a full account fee when I'm a member of staff, please.

FRIEND. Hi, Hugh. The meal is on for Friday after work. Are you still coming?
STUDENT. Yeah, that's fine. About sevenish, yeah? See you there.

Of course, none of these examples is a complete conversation and they would have continued with more adjacency pairs until the exchange was finished. Look at how the first exchange continues.

STUDENT. Hello, can I rebook an appointment for my daughter?
DENTIST'S RECEPTIONIST. No, sorry, we can't as your daughter didn't turn up for her first appointment.
STUDENT. I'm sorry, she's scared of dentists and must have been frightened. I'll have words with her and drag her in myself. So, can I please speak to the consultant?
DENTIST'S RECEPTIONIST. The consultant will ring you as soon as she finishes helping in theatre, as we have staff off sick.

Key terms

Chaining: the linking of a series of adjacency pairs to build up a conversation.

Phatic utterance: words spoken to establish social contact and express friendly intentions towards another person, rather than to convey significant information (e.g. nice day today).

Here the conversation begins with the adjacency pair of a request followed by a negative response. The student then responds to this with an apology and then starts a new adjacency pair with the next question, to which the receptionist gives a positive response. The way in which adjacency pairs link and develop in this way is referred to as **chaining**.

When you were thinking about the context and purpose of the adjacency pairs presented above, you probably noticed that many of them included expressions such as 'good evening', suggesting a relatively formal context, and 'morning' or 'hi', suggesting more informal situations. These expressions, which are not essential to the meaning or purpose of the conversation but help to open a dialogue and set an appropriate tone, are known as **phatic utterances**. Another example of this can be seen in the exchange where the student asks 'How are you?' and her colleague replies 'Fine, thanks.' You have almost certainly used this popular adjacency pair yourself and will realise that it has a purely social function. The speaker may not really be interested in her colleague's wellbeing; she just wants to greet and acknowledge her, perhaps as a preliminary to what she really wants to talk about. In fact, we are often put out or surprised if we ask someone 'How are you?' and get a detailed response about how terrible their life is rather than the standard reply: 'Fine, thanks'!

■ Interruptions and overlaps

Of course, when we talk with others our speech does not always fall neatly into the patterns described above. We do not always wait politely for someone to finish speaking before we take our turn and we do not always give the expected response. We may misjudge when someone has finished their turn and start to speak while they are still talking. We may feel angry or frustrated about what someone is saying or think they have been talking for too long and interrupt them. Alternatively, we may be so enthusiastic to join in with a discussion that we start to speak before the other speaker finishes. These **interruptions** and **overlaps** are natural features of spontaneous speech and you will need to be able to analyse why they occur.

> ### 💡 Key terms
>
> **Interruption:** when a speaker begins to talk before the previous speaker has finished, in an attempt to take over the conversation and gain control.
>
> **Overlap:** when a speaker begins to talk before the previous speaker has finished, perhaps because of their enthusiasm to join in the discussion or to show support for the speaker. An overlap is generally more cooperative and supportive, and less competitive, than an interruption.

💡 Critical response activity

Read the following transcript of a discussion from a local radio show called *Gobstopper*. The presenters, Bob Fischer (BF) and Mark Drury (MD) are talking about Middlesbrough Football Club, referred to in the transcript as 'Boro'. However, do not worry if you do not know about, or are not interested in, football; you just need to focus on the lively interaction between the two speakers rather than the content of the discussion.

- ▨ Where do the speakers interrupt or overlap with each other and why do they do so?
- ▨ What else do you notice about the language and speech of both speakers?

Key

(.)	Micropause
(1.0)	Pause in seconds
Underlining	Particular emphasis of a word
::	Elongation of sound
[	Overlap/interruption

MD. but now I have a <u>worry</u> (.) <u>another</u> worry

BF. you're always full of worries you

MD. yes I know but I have [another worry

BF.   [go on

MD. we've signed Zenden which (.) hurrah (.) good thing (.) good left-sided player (.) great

BF. yep

MD. <u>now</u> (1.0) um (.) I've been readin' the paper durin' the course o' the week an' suddenly there's all this talk of well (.) what do we do with Juninho (.) oh do we play him er as a as a striker or off a front man (.) I think [*in a groaning voice*] <u>no:::</u> (1.0) don't let's go <u>there</u> again

BF. it's exactly what yer gonna see

MD. don't let's go there again

BF. I think er I um uh (.) I would be <u>surprised</u> (0.5) n if not amazed if er Boro's formation against Bolton next weekend is not (.) erm Mendieta on the right (.) Zenden on the left (.) Greening and Boateng in the middle (.) Michael Ricketts up front with Juninho just ⌈ behind

MD. ⌊ and <u>there</u>

BF.　　　　　for one one

MD. and <u>there</u> (0.5) is the problem (0.5)

BF. go ⌈ on

MD. ⌊ when is Jonathan Greening gonna be dropped (.) ⌈ because

BF.　　　　　　　　　　　　　　　　　　　　　　　　　　⌊ I don't think he should be dropped (.) I thought he was <u>tremendous</u> against Leeds

MD. he was <u>awful</u> (.) he was ⌈ <u>awful</u>

BF.　　　　　　　　　　　　　　　⌊ rubbish (.) absolute rubbish

MD. awful awful awful

The first overlap you will have noticed occurs in lines 3 and 4. In this instance, Bob overlaps with Mark in a supportive manner – he has already shown light-hearted concern in the line 'you're always full of worries you' and the overlap 'go on' shows his encouragement and support for his friend. However, at line 11 Mark interrupts Bob with 'and <u>there</u>', perhaps in his enthusiasm for Bob's subject, and competes for control of the argument. Bob initially retains control by carrying on his point, but Mark repeats his interruption 'and <u>there</u>', enabling him to take over. The paralinguistic feature of emphasising the word 'there' helps him to assert control and dominate the conversation. Bob concedes to Mark at this point with another supportive 'go on', but as Mark knows he is now in control he interrupts Bob again during this utterance, cutting in with 'when is Jonathan Greening gonna be dropped?'. At this point, Bob, perhaps annoyed at Mark's competitive interruptions, himself interrupts, cutting across Mark with 'I don't think he should be dropped'. Finally, when Mark starts to repeat 'he was <u>awful</u>', Bob can see what is coming and interrupts him again with 'rubbish (.) absolute rubbish', thus directly challenging Mark's view and competing to win the argument. He repeats the word 'rubbish' after the interruption to ensure that his point dominates after the possible confusion of the overlap.

Link

Look back at the chapter on characters in Unit 1 for more information on, and a definition of, ellipsis.

Ellipsis

Because spontaneous speech is often fast-paced and informal, we do not always bother to include all of the words we might use if we were writing the same thing down in a grammatically complete way. This missing out of words is known as ellipsis. For example, in the above transcript from *Gobstopper* Mark Drury uses ellipsis when he says 'we've signed Zenden which (.) hurrah (.) good thing (.) good left-sided player (.) great', whereas if he were writing an article for the sports pages of a newspaper he might write something like 'Middlesbrough have signed Zenden, which is a good thing as he is a good left-sided player. This is a great decision.'

Mark's use of ellipsis in the discussion enables him to make several points very quickly and with an air of authority, adding pace to create a lively discussion for the audience to enjoy.

You may also have spotted an example of ellipsis in one of the adjacency pairs given on p92:

> FRIEND. Hi, Hugh. The meal is on for Friday after work. Are you still coming?
> STUDENT. Yeah, that's fine. About sevenish, yeah? See you there.

In this example, the student uses the ellipsis 'About sevenish, yeah? See you there' instead of saying 'the meal starts at about sevenish, yeah? I will see you there', as the informality of the context does not require such precision. The ellipsis creates a chatty informal tone appropriate to a conversation between friends. Although a feature of spoken language, you may also use ellipsis in writing for a variety of effects; for example, you may close a letter with a phrase like 'See you soon' or 'Hope you are well' to create an informal register and perhaps give the impression of talking rather than writing to a friend.

> **Think about it**
>
> In what spoken and written contexts is it appropriate and inappropriate to use ellipsis?

Fillers

Another feature of speech you may have commented on in your response to the *Gobstopper* transcript is Bob and Mark's occasional use of expressions such as 'um', 'er', 'uh' and 'erm', which are known as **fillers** as they literally 'fill' some of the pauses that are bound to occur in spontaneous speech. There are several reasons why you might use fillers when talking:

- You may feel nervous or uncertain of yourself.
- You may not be sure whether what you are saying is right.
- You may feel worried about offending the person you are talking to.
- You may want to create time to think about what you say next.
- You may want to indicate that it is still your turn to talk, even though you have not quite decided what to say – a silent pause could encourage another speaker to steal your turn.
- You may not be articulate enough to express what you want to say and therefore struggle to find the words you need.

> **Key terms**
>
> **Fillers:** sounds such as 'erm', 'um' and 'er', which speakers use to fill pauses in speech. Some speakers also use expressions such as 'y'know' and 'like' as verbal fillers.

In the *Gobstopper* transcript the most noticeable fillers are in Bob's utterance 'I think er I um uh (.) would be <u>surprised</u> (0.5) n if not amazed if er Boro's formation against Bolton next weekend is not (.) erm Mendieta on the right'. Here the fillers suggest that perhaps Bob, who has so far been the less dominant partner in the discussion, is suddenly a little nervous about taking centre-stage and may well be wondering if Mark will share his opinions. By using fillers, he also creates time for himself to order his thoughts and indicates to Mark that he is preparing to speak, thus sustaining his turn.

If you refer back to the section on features of speech on pp86–7, you will remember that fillers also featured in Tom's account of his accident ('and erm (2.0) er (1.0) er an it was still a bit slippy'). In contrast to Bob, Tom does not seem at all nervous here; he tells his story with a great sense of confidence and excitement. However, the frequent fillers and pauses in the transcript suggest that he is thinking about what to say next and what details he needs to include so that the story makes sense and has

> **AQA Examiner's tip**
>
> Remember, features such as fillers occur in speech for a variety of reasons and when evaluating them in the examination you must take into account the context in which they appear. Avoid over-generalised responses such as 'the fillers suggest the speaker is nervous'. Instead, look carefully at the example in front of you and give an answer that is specific to that example, bearing in mind its context. It is often sensible to be tentative and suggest, for example, that there are two or more possible interpretations of a speaker's use of fillers.

maximum impact on his audience. As Tom is only nine years old, the fillers and pauses may also suggest his age; he is not yet as articulate as an older speaker might be.

■ Practical activity

Comment on the use of pauses and fillers in the following exchange between a mother and daughter.

GIRL. er (.) Mum

MUM. yeah (.) what's the matter

GIRL. well erm (.) er you know it's Katie's birthday next week

MUM. ye:::s (.) what about it

GIRL.well erm (.) Katie's thinking of er having a er (.) a er (1.0) an all-night party (.) and erm (2.0) well I don't know what you (.) I mean what would you say if (.) um (.) would it be alright if (1.0)

MUM. if you went

GIRL.yeah

MUM. um (2.0) well um (1.0) let me think about it

■ Critical response activity

Write a full commentary on the *Gobstopper* transcript on pp93–4. Remember, it does not matter whether you are interested in football or not; your focus is the way in which the different speakers use language to communicate their thoughts rather than the subject matter. In your commentary you should consider:

■ features of speech, such as turn-taking, adjacency pairs, overlaps and interruptions, fillers, pauses and use of ellipsis

■ choice of vocabulary

■ the context, intended audience and purpose of the text.

(Note: you may find it useful to return to this task once you have finished studying this section on spontaneous speech and have developed a broader framework of terms and concepts to use in your commentary.)

■ Practical activity

Make your own transcript of a radio broadcast or family conversation and analyse how spoken language is used by the participants.

■ Side sequences and repairs

In the spoken texts you have looked at so far, the speakers remain relatively focused on their topics of discussion without digressing into other areas. However, you have probably noticed from your own experience that in spontaneous speech we often have to deal with interruptions, distractions and digressions from the main topic of conversation; for example, a parent talking to a friend may have to turn away from the conversation to deal with an interruption from their child, before returning to the main conversation or a point made by someone in a discussion may spark off a short debate about something different before the main topic of discussion is resumed. These brief digressions or interludes are referred to as **side sequences**. Look at the following opening exchange between an interviewer (I) and Mrs Cook (C), a female road sweeper, paying particular attention to the side sequence.

💡 Key terms

Side sequence: a sequence of utterances inserted into a conversation, which causes the main topic of the conversation to be temporarily suspended.

I. now Mrs Cook (.) you must be one of Britain's only roads (.) women road sweepers

C. well for a start call me Ame

I. Ame

> c. everybody else do
>
> I. ok (.) are you one of Britain's only road sweepers women road sweepers
>
> c. I'm the only one (.) in the whole of Gloucestershire

In this extract, Mrs Cook only responds to the interviewer's initial utterance *after* the three-line side sequence beginning 'well for a start call me Ame'. There are several reasons why she might side-step the question in this way and delay completing the expected adjacency pair: perhaps she does not like the abrupt formality of the interviewer's opening 'now Mrs Cook' with its lack of phatic utterance and decides to use the side sequence to create a more informal atmosphere for the interview; perhaps she uses it as a means of gaining control over the interviewer and situation; perhaps she objects to being seen only as a road sweeper and wants to divert the focus of the interview on to her as an individual for a moment.

Whatever Mrs Cook's reasons, the side sequence certainly has an impact on the interviewer. He changes his initial statement 'you must be … ' to a question 'are you … ?', which seems much more confrontational and designed to force Mrs Cook to respond how *he* wants this time. When you read the complete transcript on p99, you may also notice this slightly aggressive confrontational attitude when the interviewer uses a **tag question** in the utterance 'well you're not a road sweeper then are you?'. He also seems a little flustered by the side sequence, repeating the same mistake he began to make in the first line – 'road sweepers women road sweepers' and is forced to correct himself. This sort of self-correction is known as a **repair** and you have already seen an example of this in Tom's account of his accident in the section on features of speech (see p87). Repairs are common in spontaneous speech; unlike in writing where you have the opportunity to reflect on and change what you have written before your intended audience sees it, in spontaneous speech you have to think and speak simultaneously, which often leads to mistakes. In Tom's case, when he says 'an we had some Jewson's bags (.) on the wa (1.0) not on the wall next t (.) behind the wall' we can see he uses the repair simply to put right a mistake and clarify the description for his audience. However, there are other reasons why you may use a repair in your speech:

- You may pick up signals from your audience that what you are saying is too difficult for them to understand or too boring, and so change or shorten what you are saying.

- You may realise that what you are about to say may cause offence, and so adapt and amend your language.

- You may suddenly think of a better or more interesting way to express yourself and so go back and 'cross out' what you have started to say.

💡 Key terms

Tag question: a phrase tagged on to the end of a statement to turn it into a question, e.g. 'We're going to the zoo today, aren't we?' Words such as 'right', 'yeah' or 'OK' can also be used with the same function, e.g. 'See you at sevenish, yeah?'

Repair: a self-correction in spontaneous speech.

Practical activity

In the following extract, two people are attempting to make an omelette together. There are several examples of repairs in this extract; when you have identified them, comment on why they might have occurred. Then compare your ideas to the commentary which follows.

Speaker 1. right (.) put the (.) perhaps you could put the (.) eggs in the bowl

Speaker 2. how many

Speaker 1. three (.) I think (.) three

Speaker 2. now what

Speaker 1. beat them light just <u>lightly</u> while I (.) melt this (.) butter (1.0) OK (1.0) now pour (.) can you pour the eggs in

Speaker 2. OK (.) is that OK

Speaker 1. yep (.) now (.) I need a sp (.) can you pass me that spoon (.) I mean <u>spatula</u>

Speaker 2. there y'go (2.0) shall I put this cheese on now

Speaker 1. oh (.) yeah (.) OK (*turns away for a few moments*)

Speaker 2. right (.) I'm gonna get it out now (.) it's done

Speaker 1. wha' (.) do you know what you're

Speaker 2. yeah yeah (1.0) you just sorta <u>flip</u> like (2.0)

Speaker 1. <u>Oh</u> (.) you've made a complete (.) that's a (.) well (.) it's a bit of a mess isn't it

Speaker 2. I'll have (.) I can have it

Commentary

The first repair occurs in the opening utterance, when Speaker 1 begins to tell Speaker 2 what to do with the imperative 'put', but then changes this with the **hedge** 'perhaps you could put', which softens the impact of the instruction, making it sound less bossy. Further on in the transcript another repair occurs when Speaker 1 says 'beat them light just <u>lightly</u>' – the repair here enables Speaker 1 to put more emphasis on 'lightly', suggesting that Speaker 2 is already overdoing it. In the same utterance, Speaker 1 also amends 'now pour' to 'can you pour' – the switch from an imperative to an interrogative here once again softens the request. Speaker 1 certainly takes a more dominant role in the activity, but seeks to minimize this impression in this way. Speaker 1 also makes a repair in the change from 'I need a sp' to 'can you pass me that spoon', perhaps realising that just making the statement 'I need..' may not make their intention clear enough to Speaker 2. At the same time, Speaker 1 amends 'spoon' to 'spatula', using the repair to simply correct a mistake. Finally, at the end of the extract we assume that Speaker 1 intends to say 'you've made a complete *mess*' or something similar. Probably realising that this sounds accusatory and could offend, thus spoiling an otherwise cooperative activity, Speaker 1 opts to repair this. After a false start with 'that's a', suggesting a struggle to find an appropriate alternative, Speaker 1 settles on the more neutral-sounding 'it's a bit of a mess', which doesn't target Speaker 2 quite so personally. The tag question 'isn't it' encourages Speaker 2 to agree, thus maintaining the collaborative atmosphere.

Accent and dialect

Read the whole interview with Mrs Cook, the road sweeper. As you read, pay attention to the way her **accent**, or the way she pronounces words, is conveyed, and also the way her regional identity comes across through her use of **dialect** terms and grammatical constructions in comparison to the language of the interviewer.

Key terms

Hedge: a word or phrase such as 'maybe', 'perhaps' or 'sort of', used to soften the impact of what is said or to make speech sound more polite.

Accent: the characteristic pronunciation, features and speech rhythms of a speaker, usually related to regional or social influences.

Dialect: a variety of a particular language characterised by distinctive features of accent, grammar and vocabulary and used by people from a particular geographical area or social group.

I. now Mrs Cook (.) you must be one of Britain's only roads (.) women road sweepers

C. well for a start call me ⌈ Ame

I. ⌊ Ame

C. everybody else do

I. ok (.) are you one of Britain's only road sweepers women road sweepers

C. I'm the only one (.) in the whole of Gloucestershire (.) after twenty six year (.) nineteen thirty nine when war broke out (.) I seed the advertisement in the newspaper (.) and our dad said to I well he said if thee carsn't do that as good as some of the men he said that's a poor job (.) well I thought myself well I wouldn't let the old man down so I had a go (.) that's nineteen thirty nine and I'm still going strong

I. why did you start really

C. well it was on account of the money (.) they was paying (.) they was paying more for an hour than what I was getting where I was before

I. what do you actually have to do in your work

C. all sorts sk (.) it's got grass-cutting to do (.) in the winter put down the grit (.) it's got siding (.) channelling (.) I've even put up signposts (pronounced zineposties)

I. what

C. even put up signposts

I. indeed (.) ⌈ yes

C. ⌊ yes

I. and all those come under your work (.) well you're not a road sweeper then are you

C. no (.) I er I'm classed as a road worker (.) I do all the jobs all (.) all but the manual labour which is carried out by the men

I. now (.) which is your area

C. all round Hutton (.) Coombe (.) Sinnel (.) Blackwaters and er all round World's End Lane and up Sinnel Lane again and that's my worst piece on my area is Sinnel Lane (.) all the fish and chip paper is chucked up the bank and the kids is on the top of the lane scorting the bloody stones down (.) and it ain't a bit of good to sweep it up because it's just as bad ten minutes after

I. they're a mucky lot up there

C. they do (.) and it ain't no good to have litter baskets

I. isn't it

C. not a bit of ⌈ good (.)

I. ⌊ why's that

C. and it ain't no good to tell em (.) cos they'll say all right to thee face and behind thee back there's (.) b and we's just as bad as ever

I. mm (.) yes (.) well (.) do you think they're a clean lot or a dirty lot round here

C. well (.) take em on average and they been't too bad (.) but still there's (.) there's ways and way (.) means for improvement

Elision: the running together of words or the omission of parts of words, e.g. 'gonna' for 'going to' or 'y'know' for 'you know'.

In this exchange, a sense of Mrs Cook's Gloucestershire roots is partly conveyed through the representation of her accent in words such as 'zineposties' and abbreviated forms such as 'cos' for 'because' and ''em' for 'them'. You probably noticed something similar in Tom's account of his accident on when he described 'skiddin' and 'playin' – the dropped letters here give us a sense of his voice and accent. Equally, the **elision** or running-together of words can give us more of an impression of how someone speaks; for example, in the *Gobstopper* transcript on pp93–4 the elided form 'gonna' was used for 'going to', which gives us a sense of how the speakers spoke. In contrast, the interviewer in the Mrs Cook transcript gives no sign of an accent in his utterances.

However, the main way we gain such a strong impression of Mrs Cook's regional identity is through her use of dialect – in other words, her use of non-standard language which is typical of a group of speakers from a particular area of the country. For example, she uses the words 'scorting' and 'thee', neither of which we would expect in contemporary Standard English but which are characteristic of a regional dialect. Apart from her choice of individual words, Mrs Cook also uses non-standard grammar, such as 'ain't' in marked contrast to the interviewer's standard 'isn't', and 'they been't too bad' for 'they aren't too bad', also typical of her dialect. It is a mistake to believe that dialect speakers must be 'stupid' or 'uneducated' and don't use 'proper' English. In fact, dialects are interesting and valid varieties of English. After all, Mrs Cook comes across here as a hard-working, confident woman who holds her own with the rather posh Standard English-speaking interviewer and is proud of her regional identity.

■ A framework for analysing spontaneous speech

This section will have helped you to build up a framework of appropriate specialist terms, which you will be able to use in Section A of the examination for this unit. The concepts, terms and ideas covered in this section can be organised into different areas as follows, to create a logical structure for the analysis of any spontaneous speech text.

■ Audience, purpose and context: what influence do these factors have on the nature and style of the spoken text?

■ Structural features of spoken language: what can we learn about the attitudes of the speakers involved from analysing the use of turn-taking, adjacency pairs, side sequences, repairs, interruptions and overlaps?

■ Vocabulary features: what can we learn about speakers' attitudes and intentions from their use of particular vocabulary choices, as well as phatic utterances, hedges and dialect terms?

■ Style: how do features such as ellipsis, elision and the representation of a speaker's accent help us to create an impression of the speaker?

■ Non-verbal features: what do non-verbal aspects of speech such as fillers, pauses, intonation and emphasis reveal about speakers' feelings and attitudes?

Critical response activity

Using the above framework where relevant, compare the transcript of the interview with Mrs Cook with the following transcript of part of a conversation between a boy called Tom and his parents, in which they discuss Tom's recent work experience. Our suggestions for questions to consider are:

- How do the interviewer in the Mrs Cook transcript and the parents in the transcript below elicit responses from Mrs Cook and Tom respectively?
- How do Tom and Mrs Cook express their feelings about work?
- How do the various speakers in both transcripts reveal their attitudes towards each other?
- How do the personalities of the different speakers in both transcripts emerge?

Key

(.)	Micropause
(1.0)	Pause in seconds
<u>Underlining</u>	Particular emphasis of a word
::	Elongation of sound
italics	Elongation of sound

TOM. anyway (.) I've had a <u>fantastic</u> week (.) s'been <u>really</u> (.) <u>really</u> (.) good (3.0) an' an' (.) an' I'm not really sure (1.0) er (0.5) that I want to go to college <u>now</u>

DAD. what's been so good about it then Tom

TOM. we::::ll (1.0) I've been given some (1.0) re <u>responsibility</u> (.) an' (.) an' I've been doin' stuff which I kinda (.) <u>really</u> enjoy (.) an' that's <u>dead</u> important (.) to *me* anyway (1.0)   an' I wanna(.)

MUM.   so you thin' (.) sorry (.) go on

TOM. right (.) all I wanna do is mountain bikin' (1.0) either in a shop (.) or try to do something with it (.) y'know (.) erm (1.0) <u>professionally</u> (0.5) or or (.) do a qualification in engineering or whatever

MUM. but you'd need to continue at school for that

TOM. no no (.) no you don't (.) the lads at the Bike Scene[1] (.) they're doin' erm (.) NVQs[2] in Bike Maintenance (.) they're the first in the <u>country</u> to do it (.) I could train on the job (.) the told me that durin' me work experience

DAD. so can we get this straight then (.) y'you (.) you've decided that yer wanna leave school next year (.) an' get a job (.) <u>preferably</u> something to do with mountain bikin'

TOM. well (0.5) yeah:::: (.) that's what I've been sayin'

DAD. I suppose that's what work experience is all about (.) findin' out what you want to do

MUM. what about sixth form though

TOM. well (1.0) at the moment (.) this is what <u>I::</u> want to do

[1] *The name of a shop*
[2] *A national qualification*

i Research point

In this section there has been space to cover only some of the main aspects of spontaneous spoken language. You might find it useful to use the internet or a library to research other theories about spoken language including Face Theory, the Politeness Principle and the Cooperative Principle, as well as exploring accent and dialect in more depth.

14   Prepared speech

Prepared speech has many characteristics in common with writing and speakers often have their whole text written in advance either by themselves or sometimes by speechwriters. However, a good speech text has to offer an additional dimension to a written one. It will be designed to offer opportunities for the speaker to enhance its content by using non-verbal features such as tone of voice, pauses, gestures, facial expressions and other paralinguistic features. Like a drama script, a prepared speech gains its impact from both text and performance.

Practical activity

List as many contexts as you can think of in which a prepared speech would be given. Think of your own ideas before looking at the suggestions below.

It is not only politicians and campaigners who prepare speeches before delivering them. Many other people give presentations and lectures to live audiences, for example about their special interests, their travels or topics on which they are experts. There are also family occasions, such as weddings and funerals, where speeches are made.

Your list might look something like this:

▦ a political leader at the annual party conference

▦ a speaker giving a presentation on climate change

▦ a chef giving a presentation on food preparation

▦ a teacher giving a talk on applying to university

▦ a sales presentation

▦ the best man at a wedding

▦ a student giving a talk to a class about a scene from a Shakespeare play

▦ a local resident addressing a protest campaign group

▦ a television presenter giving the commentary on a wildlife programme

▦ a news reporter giving a report for radio from a war zone

▦ a business entrepreneur trying to convince potential investors of the worth of their product.

Practical activity

Look at the list of examples of prepared speech and identify the purpose and audience for each point given.

As you will see, there is scope for considerable variation in levels of formality across these contexts even though all are examples of prepared speech. The television wildlife commentary has many features in common with a drama script whereas the best man at a wedding is likely to include more comments that are improvised, perhaps in response to his audience's reactions. Prepared speech, just as speech in general, can be fitted in along the continuum between speech and writing.

Persuasive speaking

Link

Remind yourself of the section on imagery starting on p13, where we
looked at ways in which writers use imagery to create an imaginative response in the audience. Speakers also use imagery to make their points vividly and you need to be alert for the effects created by it.

Many planned speeches are delivered with the intention of persuading the audience to accept a particular point of view or of rallying people to a cause. Since ancient times, individuals have always needed to develop techniques to help them to persuade an audience effectively. The Greek philosopher Aristotle, born in 384 BC, set out principles for persuasive argument that still influence writers and speakers today. These principles are known as **rhetoric** and they are concerned with how a speech is structured, the devices that can be used to affect the audience through comparisons or contrasts, methods of emphasising points and ways of addressing the audience. Most of these principles apply to both spoken and written texts.

Look carefully at the extracts below, which are taken from David Cameron's speech to the Conservative Party conference in October 2005 before his election to the leadership of the party in December 2005. The paragraphs have been numbered to help in our analysis. This speech was generally considered to have had a decisive effect on the outcome of the contest.

Extract A

1. We meet in the shadow of a third consecutive election defeat, defeated by a government that has complicated the tax system, dumbed down the education system, demoralised the health system and bankrupted the pension system.

2. It has made promises that no one believes, passed powers to a European Union that nobody trusts and set up regional assemblies that nobody wants and nobody ever voted for. And still we were defeated. We were defeated by a government that won fewer votes than any in history.

3. But let's not blame the electoral system. Let's not take comfort in solid but slow progress. Let's have the courage to say: they've failed – but so have we.

4. And let's resolve here, at this conference, when we put defeat behind us, failure behind us, to look ourselves in the eye and say: never, ever again.

5. I joined this party because I love my country. I love our character. I love our people, our history, our role in the world. This is the only party that understands, and is proud of, what we have been and who we are.

6. I joined this party because I believe in freedom. We are the only party believing that if you give people freedom and responsibility, they will grow stronger and society will grow stronger.

7. I joined this party because I believe in aspiration. This party, the Conservative Party, is the only party that wants everybody to be a somebody – a doer, not a done-for.

8. That's the spirit we have to recapture. I want people to feel good about being a Conservative again.

9. Aspiration is enabled by education; how cruelly it is disabled by Labour today, when one-fifth of children leave primary school unable to write properly, when one million schoolchildren play truant each year and when the very essence of aspiration – social mobility – is going backward in this country.

Key terms

Rhetoric: the technique of using language persuasively in order to influence the opinions and behaviour of an audience.

Research point

Search on Google for 'David Cameron October 2005 Conservative Party Conference', which should give you a link to the text of the whole of this speech on the Guardian Unlimited website.

Commentary

Extract A is taken from the beginning of the speech. The first four paragraphs set the scene. David Cameron immediately addresses the 2005 election defeat for the Conservative Party, a difficult issue to cover. The opening of a speech is vital in gaining the interest and empathy of the audience. To do this, he addresses the audience directly using the first person pronoun 'we', creating a sense of inclusiveness. There are few metaphors used in this speech but he opens with a reference to the 'shadow' of defeat implying to the audience that they need to move into the sunlight of victory. He acknowledges the degree of the electoral failure but actually attacks the government's record powerfully in doing so. He uses a pattern of words beginning with 'd' which emphasises a series of emotive verbs – 'defeated', 'dumbed down', 'demoralised' – and ends with a further emotive verb: 'bankrupted'.

Repetitions and patterns are important in spoken texts. In the second paragraph of this speech you can see that Cameron has used a list of related words and phrases: 'that no one believes', 'that nobody trusts', 'that nobody wants and nobody ever voted for'. Lists of three related words or phrases are particularly memorable and such **triplets** are used frequently in persuasive speaking. Here, the triplet is used to suggest that the government has not carried out the wishes of the people.

You can see a similar pattern in paragraph 3: 'let's not blame', 'let's 'not take comfort', 'let's have the courage'. In this case there is a movement from the negative 'let's not' to the positive 'let's'. This contrasting of ideas is called **antithesis**. Here, it leads on to the upbeat message of paragraph 4: 'And let's resolve here, at this conference, when we put defeat behind us, failure behind us, to look ourselves in the eye and say: never, ever again.'

These first four paragraphs, by addressing the problem of the electoral defeat, allow the speaker to look to the future. He identifies strongly with his audience using the personal pronoun 'ourselves', rallying them not to accept defeat again. The structure of the opening paragraphs enables him to set out his case with clarity and to move coherently to the next phase of the speech. Cameron is then able to move on to a section in which he identifies his personal values and shows that they are embodied by the ideals of the Conservative Party. Mirroring the structure of the opening, he uses four linked paragraphs to make his point. You will notice that paragraphs 5–7 each begin with the same words: 'I joined this party because' followed by three different reasons: 'I love my country', 'I believe in freedom', 'I believe in aspiration'. This pattern of **repetition and replacement** is frequently used to reinforce and develop points in persuasive speeches. Here, these paragraphs are closely linked by the repetition so that the values of both Cameron and the party are clearly set out.

Cameron's use of the first person pronoun 'I' shows that he joined the Conservative Party because it already shared his values. The positive abstract nouns he uses, such as 'freedom', 'responsibility', 'aspiration', all serve to show the audience that these are the right values to hold. The triplet in paragraph 3 – 'I love my country. I love our character. I love our people' emphasises his own passion for the values he lists. This second group of four paragraphs concludes with another positive message, this time using the first person pronoun assertively: 'I want people to feel good about being a Conservative again', helping him to establish his credentials as a leader.

After these opening paragraphs, Cameron moves on to a detailed criticism of the performance of the government, which is introduced in paragraph 9. Most political speeches disparage the record of opposing parties and the central part of Cameron's speech is no exception: 'Aspiration is enabled by education; how cruelly it is disabled by Labour today'. Here, you can see that the antithesis of the verbs 'enabled' and 'disabled' is used to present a picture of what is seen as the failure of Labour's education policy. Aspiration is personified to create a vivid image of injury.

💡 Key terms

Triplet: a pattern of three repeated words or phrases.

Antithesis: the juxtaposition of contrasting words or phrases to create a sense of balance or opposition between conflicting ideas.

Repetition and replacement: a pattern in which some words or phrases are repeated and others replaced, e.g. 'We must plan for a strong economy, we must plan for full employment, we must plan for a healthy nation.'

Extract B

10. Everyone knows that education, like our other public services, desperately needs radical reform. And who is the man standing in the way? Gordon Brown, the great roadblock. Everyone knows that our economy needs lower and simpler taxes. Who's standing in the way? The great tax riser and complicator, Gordon Brown.

11. Everyone knows that business needs deregulation to compete with China and India. Who is standing in the way? The great regulator and controller, Gordon Brown. How are we going to stop him? Tony Blair can't. God knows, he's tried hard enough. There's only one group of people who can stop him – and that is us in this room. There's one thing Gordon Brown fears more than anything else: a Conservative Party that has the courage to change. So let's give him the fright of his life.

Commentary

In this extract, taken from the middle of the speech, the content changes from issues to personalities. In 2005, Gordon Brown was, of course, not yet prime minister and much was made in the media of the relationship between him and Tony Blair. Cameron uses the opportunity to make some humorous references to Gordon Brown, seen as the likely successor to Tony Blair. A metaphor referring to Gordon Brown as 'the great roadblock' suggests that he is already in control and stubbornly resisting deregulation. The jibe is continued in the words: 'How are we going to stop him? Tony Blair can't', which suggests that the leadership has already passed to Gordon Brown. A triplet pattern is used again in these two paragraphs to highlight Cameron's view of Brown's obstructiveness. He is referred to as 'the great roadblock', 'the great tax riser and complicator' and as 'the great regulator and controller', jokes which are designed to appeal to his audience and made memorable by the use of this pattern. Although he is speaking to an audience of Conservatives, Cameron would also have been aware that this speech, and his references to Gordon Brown, would be widely reported and help to establish him with the wider electorate as well as with his own party.

Extract C

12. By changing our culture we can change politics, too. When I meet young people, they tell me how sick they are of the whole political system – the shouting, finger-pointing, backbiting and point-scoring in the House of Commons. That's all got to go.

13. I want young people to see politics not as a waste of time but as a way to change the world. I want every young person in this country with ideas and talent and energy to say, 'Yes, I want to make a difference. I've got something to offer. I will get involved.'

14. So let's build together a new generation of Conservatives. Let's switch a new generation on to Conservative ideas. Let's dream a new generation of Conservative dreams.

15. There is a new generation of social entrepreneurs tackling this country's most profound social problems.

16. There is a new generation of businessmen and women who are taking on the world, creating the wealth and opportunity for our future.

17. We can lead that new generation. We can be that new generation, changing our party to change our country. It will be an incredible journey. I want you to come with me. We'll be tested – and challenged. But we'll never give up. We'll never turn back. So let the message go out from this conference: a modern, compassionate conservatism is right for our times, right for our party and right for our country.

18. If we go for it, if we seize it, if we fight for it with every ounce of passion, vigour and energy from now until the next election, nothing, and no one, can stop us.

Commentary

This is the closing stage of the speech. Structurally, this is just as important as the opening because the words used here give the message that the speaker wants his audience to put into action. These paragraphs focus on a strong theme: change, youth and a new approach. Paragraphs 12 and 13 mention 'young people' three times and comparisons are made using the negative participles 'shouting, finger-pointing, backbiting and point-scoring' to show the old way and the antithesis of the positive triplet ' "Yes, I want to make a difference. I've got something to offer. I will get involved" ' to show the new.

The next four paragraphs focus on this theme. The phrase 'new generation' is repeated seven times in these paragraphs, giving a powerful emphasis on change, and it is applied to many aspects of life: social, business and political.

Paragraph 17 gives the message the speaker wants his audience to carry away: 'a modern, compassionate conservatism is right for our times, right for our party and right for our country'. Once again, you can see the use of triplets to reinforce the message. This pattern is also used in the rousing close to the speech where the audience is promised success: 'If we go for it, if we seize it, if we fight for it' and exhorted to devoting 'every ounce of passion, vigour and energy' to achieving it. Most speeches aim to reach a climax at the end and this one does so very successfully.

This speech gives you an example of a carefully constructed piece of rhetoric. It appeals to emotions and values rather than giving the tactics of how the changes might be achieved. It fulfils its aim of raising support and commitment effectively. Of course, as with a drama script, you need to see and hear the text delivered to appreciate it fully.

The prepared speech above contains many of the features common to persuasive speeches and you need to have a framework to help you to analyse a prepared speech systematically so that you can make an effective comparison of its text with a different text in the examination. If you work through the framework below, you will be able to comment on the features of a prepared speech text.

Practical activity

1. If you were one of David Cameron's political opponents, what would you criticise about this speech?

2. Write the opening paragraphs of a speech that is designed to undermine Cameron's case.

■ Informative speaking

Many prepared speeches are given with the primary intention of giving information to the audience. As with all speeches, there may also be other elements involved. Information might be absorbed more readily, for example, if there is an element of entertainment. Information can also be presented in ways which have an element of persuasion. Consider, for example, the following statements:

■ When you leave university, you need to plan how you will manage the debt you have accumulated.

■ When you leave university, you need to plan how you will manage repayments on your investment.

Here, the word 'debt' has negative connotations whereas 'investment' is positive.

■ Practical activity

List as many examples as you can think of in which you have heard speeches that have giving information as their main purpose.

Your list will depend on your own experience but might include such things as:

■ a lecture on a topic such as applying to university

■ a presentation to a management team on sales figures

■ a talk by a gap-year student on their experience

■ a lecture on emergency first aid

■ a presentation on healthy eating

■ a demonstration by a chef.

As with all speeches, the audience is an important factor. A presentation on healthy eating might be delivered to a range of different age groups and the language chosen will vary accordingly.

Many speakers do not use a full script for their speech, instead using notes, prompt cards or presentation software and improvising aspects of the speech according to the audience. The final text is what is actually spoken and it will vary each time it is delivered, although the gist remains the same.

■ Critical response activity

Look at the two extracts below, which are taken from a lengthy lecture on applying to university given first to an audience of students and then to an audience of parents. The PowerPoint slide, which the speaker used for both presentations, is shown on the right.

■ What information is conveyed in both presentations?

■ Choose some examples of rhetorical devices that the speaker has used.

■ How has the material been adapted for the audience of parents?

Where should I study?

Area
Town or campus
Cost

Extract A: *presentation given to students*

When you're thinking about where you want to study you need to remember you're going to spend three or four years there, maybe more and you need to go to a place that suits you. Do you love cities or hate them? If you go on a visit to London, do you love the crowds and the atmosphere or do you worry about getting squashed by the doors on the tube trains?

There are different kinds of university and you should try to visit at least one of each type if you can before making up your mind. Travel is expensive, so at this stage you can save yourself some money by looking at local universities. A lot of universities give virtual tours on their websites so you can have a look around without actually going there.

Some universities are very much a part of the town or city they belong to whereas others are set apart on a campus which may be a few miles away from the nearest town. Both have advantages. If you like the atmosphere of a city, you'll probably prefer one of the universities that are in the heart of a city, such as Leeds. If you'd like to be mainly with other students, a campus might suit you better.

Cost is also something you really need to think about. These days, many more students have to live at home while they are at university simply because of the cost. Still, there are loans and grants to help you so you don't have to give up on the idea of moving away from home if that's what you really want to do. We'll be looking at these in detail later on.

You also need to think about how well you'd cope with living away from home. I hope you won't be bringing your washing home to your parents! How many of you know what a loaf of bread costs, for example? Or, if you are thinking of self-catering, how much does heating and lighting cost? And what about things like toilet rolls? Try working out how much you spend each week including everything.

There are different options for living away from home, for example halls of residence run by the university, self-catering university accommodation and independently rented accommodation.

Extract B: *presentation given to parents*

You can help your son or daughter to make a good decision about where to study. They're going to spend three or four years there, maybe more, and they need to go to a place that suits them. You know them well. Do they enjoy cities or hate them? If you go on a family visit to London, do they love the crowds and the atmosphere or do they worry about getting squashed by the doors on the tube trains?

There are different kinds of university and you should encourage them to visit at least one of each type before they make up their minds. I appreciate that travel is expensive and this can be a real worry. However, it really is important for students to get a clear picture so they can make a good decision and not want to drop out later. They can save themselves – or you – some money by looking at local universities. A lot of universities also offer virtual tours on their websites so encourage them to look at these as well.

Some universities are very much a part of the town or city they belong to whereas others are set apart on a campus which may be some miles away from the nearest town. Both have advantages. For those who like the atmosphere of a city, one of the universities which are in the heart of a city, such as Leeds, would be a good choice. For those who would prefer to be mainly with other students, a campus university might be better.

Cost is something students really need to think about. I know this will be a real worry for many of you. We will be looking at the help that is available in detail later on. These days, many more students have to live at home while they are at university simply because of the cost. You may be looking forward to your son or daughter being out of your hair or you may feel worried about how they'll cope.

You can give them a bit of help with this now. How many of your sons and daughters do their own washing now? Do they know what a loaf of bread costs, how much money goes on heating and lighting or even the price of toilet rolls? How many of you would be prepared to let your son or daughter run your house for a week for practice? I see a few intrepid hands raised! But for the rest of you, encourage them to work out how much they spend each week including their share of household costs.

There are different options for living away from home, for example halls of residence run by the university, self-catering university accommodation and independently rented accommodation.

Commentary

Information conveyed in both presentations

Students should:

- think about their personality and reaction to different places
- visit different kinds of university locally and use virtual tours
- consider town and campus universities
- look at how cost can influence choice
- learn budgeting and other practical skills
- find out about different types of accommodation.

Rhetorical devices

Although these speeches are designed to give information there is also an element of persuasion, not towards a particular point of view but to encourage students to do some research. Some rhetorical devices are employed, for example antithesis is used in the first paragraph to contrast the characteristics of cities with their opposites and also in paragraph 4 of the parents' speech: 'You may be looking forward to your son or daughter being out of your hair or you may feel worried about how they'll cope.' The audience is addressed directly using the second person pronoun for most of the speech in both cases and occasionally the first person 'we' is used to create a sense of inclusion. The third person 'they' is used in the parents' version to refer to their children. The speaker gives personal opinions too: 'I hope you won't be bringing your washing home to your parents!' and 'I see a few intrepid hands raised!' Both of these comments provide an element of entertainment. The speaker has also used a triplet – 'bread', 'heating and lighting' and 'toilet rolls' – to emphasise the importance of students gaining practical experience of costs.

How the presentation has been adapted for parents

Contractions are used less frequently, making the speech a little more formal as the parents are visitors whereas the students are in their own environment. The sentence 'You know them well' is included to show parents that they have a special capacity to help and to make them feel valued in this process. Paragraph 2 includes more detail about the importance of visiting universities and stresses the issue of money twice: 'I appreciate that travel is expensive' and 'They can save themselves – or you – some money'. The words 'I appreciate' suggest to the audience that the speaker understands their concerns about how much the process will cost them.

Paragraph 4 shows an appreciation of the kinds of worries parents are likely to have about how students will cope away from home in comparison to the implication in the student version that students are prevented from moving out mainly because of cost.

Paragraph 5 looks at issues of coping in both cases. The suggestion that students be allowed to run their family home for a week is not included in the student version. The speaker has clearly included this in the parents' version to both amuse and shock the audience. The intention is to make them think about the level of practical knowledge their offspring have so that they will help to get their sons and daughters to acquire a bit more understanding of money.

The speaker then moves on to look at options for accommodation. As the information here is purely factual, there are no differences between the two versions of the presentation.

Your task in the examination will be to compare two extracts. They may be very different, for example a spontaneous text and a prepared speech, or they may be of similar types. The themes might be the same but the audiences different. As in the speech above, you need to compare the extracts carefully and illustrate your points with close reference to the text.

Link

We will be exploring comparing extracts and making close references to the text in Chapter 15, Preparing for the examination.

Speaking to entertain

Speeches designed to entertain take place in a whole range of contexts from the stand-up comedian in a working men's club to a dramatic monologue on television, from the after-dinner speaker at the Women's Institute to a rap artist on the radio. One of the most challenging contexts for many people who are not used to speaking in public is the best man's speech at a wedding.

Practical activity

Look at the extract below which is taken from an example of a best man's speech.

- What features make the speech entertaining?
- How does the speaker make the speech appropriate for his audience?

To start off, I'd like to thank Nigel for his kind words to our beautiful bridesmaids, Rachel and Ellie. Don't they look amazing? They've done a wonderful job. And in spite of the hideous weather, they managed to get Katy to the church, pretty much on time, and looking gorgeous even though she had to be carried over the lake at the entrance. Where's Walter Raleigh when you need him?!

I'd like to join Nigel in thanking everyone for coming, through the wind and rain, to share their special day. In case there is anyone out there who hasn't bought me a drink yet, I'm Dave, Nigel's oldest friend (at least I feel very old today!). When Nigel asked me to be his best man I thought 'Why's he asking me?' and 'How did I manage to deserve this honour?' Then it came to me:- he knows I'm the only one of his long suffering friends who hasn't yet got a good enough reason to turn him down. Mind you, I didn't have to think about it for long; the free booze opportunities at a wedding are outstanding, and I knew that if I turned him down I wouldn't get invited.

I'm especially thrilled to have the opportunity to give this speech. I mean, what man wouldn't jump at the chance of showing himself up in front of such a distinguished set of people?! Of course, I'm already plotting how to pay him back for the privilege, although I think we took care of some of that at last night's stag party! I have to congratulate Nigel on managing to untie himself, find some clothes and get back from Edinburgh in time for the service.

This is my first time as best man and I'm told I'm supposed to give you the low down about Nigel. I'd better be a bit careful what I say, though –he'll be returning the favour in November. Nigel and I were in primary school together – my first real memory of him is when he was making faces at me through the school railings and got his head stuck. The fire brigade were very impressed. And he just went on from there – knocking himself out sliding on a tea tray in a quarry, falling out of trees, spilling beer ….. As you all know, he didn't stop there – he first met Katy when she was a nurse on his ward after he'd fallen off next door's roof trying to rescue their cat. Good job she's going to be around to look out for him from now on.

But seriously, the most important thing today is the happy couple. Congratulations Katy and Nigel! Nigel – you've done really well for yourself. And Katy, - well, I'm sure you'll work on him.

Commentary

Best man's speeches are meant to follow some conventions. For example, they begin by thanking the groom for his compliments to the bridesmaids. Here, the speaker does this and then makes an impromptu topical reference to the weather using hyperbole in describing a large puddle as a 'lake' and making a reference to Sir Walter Raleigh and his cloak.

Paragraph two fits the conventional pattern of thanking the guests. The speaker uses self-deprecating humour '(at least I feel very old today)'and moves on to make an ironic reference to the '*honour*' of being a best man. This part of the speech ends with the comical assertion that his motive for accepting the invitation to be best man is the risk of losing '*the free booze opportunities.*'

The ironic references to his own role as best man continue in paragraph three '*I'm especially thrilled to have the opportunity to give this speech*' and '*I'm already plotting how to pay him back for the privilege*' humorously emphasise the discomfort of the best man's lot. He involves the audience referring to them with a further hint of irony as '*such a distinguished set of people*' At the end of this paragraph he lets the audience in on the (possibly fictitious) events of the stag night using a triplet: '*untie himself, find some clothes and get back from Edinburgh*' to reinforce the comical image of the bridegroom's predicament.

The asyndetic list of incidents in Nigel's accident prone life leads into the **bathos** of 'spilling beer', followed by the rather absurd attempted rescue of a cat which resulted eventually in the wedding.

The congratulations to the happy couple are conventional and include an inference that the bride has got the better part of the bargain. '*And Katy – well I'm sure you'll work on him*'

The audience for a best man's speech is usually mixed. There will be friends and family of both bride and groom and these will usually include some children and others who might be offended by some kinds of language and content. The jokes and anecdotes in this extract are appropriate for a mixed audience and are entertaining whilst avoiding the sexual innuendo which sometimes features in speeches made at weddings.

Key terms

Bathos: a sudden descent from elevated language or subject matter to the ordinary or the commonplace. Often used for comic effect.

■ Practical activity

There are many sites on the internet which give examples of speeches and advice on how to give them. Use a search engine or have a look at the links in your e-resources to find more examples of speeches, for example, wedding speeches, persuasive speeches, political speeches and a whole range of other types of speeches on the BBC website. You need to make yourself as familiar as possible with different kinds of prepared speech.

💡 A framework for analysing prepared speech

When you are analysing a prepared speech text in the examination, remember that you have only the words of the speech in front of you and that you cannot hear the speaker's tone of voice, see facial expressions and gestures or hear the emphasis that is put on particular points. Nevertheless, it is possible to see from the written text some of the features that the speaker clearly intends to emphasise. You need to bear in mind that repetition, which might seem over-used in a written text, is often memorable in a spoken one. The framework below will help you to consider the features of a prepared speech in a logical order. Remember, in the examination you will be comparing two texts; you need to understand the features of each of these to make an effective response.

Context, audience and purpose

■ What is the speech intended to achieve?
■ Who will hear the speech?
■ What is the medium for delivery of the speech (e.g. television, radio, live audience)?

Methods of addressing the audience

■ Choice of personal pronouns.
■ **Rhetorical questions**.
■ Tone.
■ Use of humour.
■ Use of shock tactics.
■ Use of exclamations.

Structural features

■ The arrangement of the content and the ways in which this contributes to the overall effect.
■ The coherence of the speech and how this is achieved.
■ The ways in which the speech creates interim and final climaxes.

The language used

■ Emotive words and phrases.
■ Comparisons that use figurative language such as metaphors, similes and personification.
■ Contrasts that are made using devices such as **antonyms**, antithesis, **oxymoron** and paradox.

Features of repetition

■ Use of triplets.
■ Alliteration.

💡 Key terms

Rhetorical question: a question that implies its own answer and is used not to ellicit information but to achieve a persuasive effect (for example, 'Are we to stand idly by while our rights are trampled by a dictator?').

Antonym: a word or phrase that is opposite in meaning to another, e.g. 'hot and cold', 'fat and thin'.

Oxymoron: when apparently contradictory terms are placed together, e.g. 'bitter sweet'.

■ Repetition of words, phrases and structures.

■ Repetition of ideas using synonyms.

Features of emphasis

■ Use of irony.

■ Hyperbole.

■ **Understatement**.

■ Bathos.

Not all of these features will be present in every text but you should always consider them.

■ **Critical response activity**

Using the framework on p112, analyse the following extract from the beginning of President Kennedy's inaugural speech, which was delivered in Washington on 20 January 1961. In your answer, focus particularly on:

■ Kennedy's use of persuasive language

■ the ways in which he seeks to unify the different factions that will hear his message.

Vice-president Johnson, Mr Speaker, Mr Chief Justice, President Eisenhower, Vice-president Nixon, President Truman, reverend clergy, fellow citizens: we observe today not a victory of party, but a celebration of freedom – symbolising an end, as well as a beginning – signifying renewal, as well as change. For I have sworn before you and almighty God the same solemn oath our forebears prescribed nearly a century and three-quarters ago.

The world is very different now. For man holds in his mortal hands the power to abolish all forms of human poverty and all forms of human life. And yet the same revolutionary beliefs for which our forebears fought are still at issue around the globe – the belief that the rights of man come not from the generosity of the state, but from the hand of God.

We dare not forget today that we are the heirs of that first revolution. Let the word go forth from this time and place, to friend and foe alike, that the torch has been passed to a new generation of Americans – born in this century, tempered by war, disciplined by a hard and bitter peace, proud of our ancient heritage, and unwilling to witness or permit the slow undoing of those human rights to which this nation has always been committed, and to which we are committed today at home and around the world. Let every nation know, whether it wishes us well or ill, that we shall pay any price, bear any burden, meet any hardship, support any friend, oppose any foe, to assure the survival and the success of liberty.

This much we pledge – and more. To those old allies whose cultural and spiritual origins we share, we pledge the loyalty of faithful friends. United, there is little we cannot do in a host of cooperative ventures. Divided, there is little we can do – for we dare not meet a powerful challenge at odds and split asunder.

■ **Key terms**

Understatement: the deliberate adoption of restrained language, often to achieve an ironic or humorous effect.

AQA **Examiner's tip**

You will not earn marks merely for feature spotting, such as 'James Smith uses a metaphor here.' To gain credit, you need to comment on *how* the metaphor works and the effect it produces.

15   Preparing for the examination

For the Section A question in the examination, the question 'will have two pieces of speech which could be transcribed spontaneous speech, prepared oratory or any other type of speech representation from a non-literary context. Candidates will be required to compare how the speech texts differ by focusing on features of spoken English and how form and context can help to shape meaning.'

This question is worth 45 marks out of the 75 marks available in the examination, split between Assessment Objectives 2 and 3.

■ For AO2, you will need to show in detail that you understand and can analyse the ways in which structure, form and language shape your chosen speaker's meaning. *(15 marks)*

■ For AO3, you will need to show that you can compare texts effectively and that you can analyse the ways in which context affects both the production of speech and the way it is received. *(30 marks)*

You are advised to spend approximately 50 minutes on this question, as opposed to 40 minutes on your choice of question in Section B, as this question is worth more marks. However, even though you will spend more time on this response, you still do not have long, so think about the following tips to help you make the most of your time:

■ Make sure you know, understand and can use a range of terms which will enable you to analyse both prepared and spontaneous speech texts. Many appropriate terms and concepts have been covered in this section to help you with this.

■ Do not forget that you will need to use many of the framework terms discussed in Unit 1 of this book where they are relevant or appropriate.

■ Remember to focus closely on the texts and include specific examples from both texts to illustrate your points.

■ When you only have a short time to produce your work, it can be tempting to start writing straight away. However, it is always a good idea to spend a few minutes thinking about the extracts and planning a well-structured response.

■ As two-thirds of the marks for this question are given for AO3, which requires you to explore relationships between texts, it is essential that you *compare* the extracts closely. More guidance on this is given below.

The kinds of question you will come across in this examination will be similar in pattern. You can expect to be presented with two extracts of spoken language, which are likely to be linked in some way. You will be asked to compare them in terms of the speakers' choices of vocabulary and the grammatical, stylistic and speech features, as well as being asked to comment on the influence of context on the ways in which the speakers convey their attitudes and ideas. You will be asked to compare two different kinds of spoken text so may have to compare an extract of prepared speech with a transcript of spontaneous speech. Alternatively, one of the texts might be a representation of speech from a different sort of context, such as the transcript of an interview presented in a magazine or an extract of dialogue from an internet chatroom. Whatever the contexts, the extracts you are given will include features of spoken language and the same range of terms and concepts you have learned to analyse prepared and spontaneous speech will still apply.

Drawing comparisons

Remember, the focus of AO3 is on effective comparison of the spoken texts and the significance of the context in which they are produced and their form, so you must make explicit links between the texts, their respective forms and where the speeches take place. If a student writes something like 'the context of Extract A is quite formal' and 'the context of Extract B is quite informal', the comparison here is left implicit – no explicit link between the two statements is made. However, if the student rewords this to 'the context of Extract A is quite formal, *whereas* the context of Extract B is *relatively* informal', a much clearer comparison and contrast is being made between the given extracts. Do not forget that comparisons can focus on similarities *and* differences, and some of the **discourse markers** suggested below will help you to create explicit, confident comparisons between the two texts.

Discourse markers to draw similarities:

- Similarly …
- Likewise …
- Like …
- Equally …
- In comparison …
- As in …

Discourse markers to draw differences:

- In contrast …
- Whereas …
- While …
- Unlike …
- However …
- In comparison …
- On the other hand …

As you need to compare both spoken texts, it is not a good idea to write about one first and then the other. You really need to write about the texts at the same time and alongside each other, integrating your comments on both extracts. It is also not a good idea to try to compare the texts chronologically, section by section. It is much better to focus on comparing similar aspects and features of both texts, regardless of whether they appear at the beginning, middle or end of the extracts. For example, both texts might include examples of triplets which you want to comment on but, in the first extract, the triplet appears in the opening utterance and in the second extract at the end. By comparing the extracts in chronological order, you would therefore miss the opportunity to compare the use of the triplet, just because they did not appear at similar places in the texts. A framework to help you structure your comparison in an appropriate way is suggested below.

Key terms

Discourse markers: words or phrases that give structure to speech or writing, enabling a writer or speaker to develop ideas, relate points to each other or move from one idea to the next.

Approaches to structuring your answer

There are many approaches to answering the question in Section A which would produce equally valid responses. It is up to you to decide on the best way for you to tackle this task. However, the framework suggested below is one way of approaching a comparison between spontaneous and prepared speech, which may help you structure your response.

- *Compare* the audience, purpose and context of the extracts.
  Comment on how these factors influence the speakers.
  Keep your comments fairly brief and general initially, but remember to keep returning to these key aspects throughout your answer.

- *Compare* how the different speakers address their respective audiences.
  Comment on any links you can see between the tone of the two texts. Include features such as the speakers' choice of pronouns or rhetorical questions used to address the audiences.

- *Compare* the language choices made by the different speakers.
  Consider issues such as emotive language, figurative language, contrasts and hyperbole, which could appear in both sorts of text, as well as features such as phatic utterances, hedges and use of dialect terms.

- *Compare* the style of delivery of the different speakers.
  You could think about the occurrence of features such as ellipsis, elision and the use of contractions, as well as the representation of accent and any other stylistic features such as repetition.

- *Compare* the structural features of both texts.
  Consider the arrangement and organisation of the prepared speech in comparison to turn-taking, adjacency pairs, side sequences, repairs, interruptions and overlaps which you may well find in the spontaneous speech transcript.

- *Compare* any non-verbal aspects of the texts.
  Although you are unlikely to find the fillers and pauses typical of spontaneous speech in a prepared speech, pauses may be indicated in different ways such as through punctuation and paragraphing, and intonation may be indicated by underlining or exclamation marks.

- *Provide* a conclusion.
  Sum up your key findings about the influence of context on the production of the two texts.

Sample questions and answers

Try answering the examination question below. Then read the sample response and examiner's comments that follow.

1   Read Text A and Text B. Text A is a transcript of a conversation between a father and his 11-year-old son. Text B is an extract from a speech made in 1983, shortly before the general election, by the Labour politician Neil Kinnock.

    a   Compare how the speakers use language to influence their listeners. In your answer you should comment on:

        i   the choice of vocabulary and of grammatical, stylistic and speech features

        ii   the influence of context on the ways in which speakers convey attitudes and ideas.

Key

(.)	Micropause
(1.0)	Pause in seconds
::	Elongation of sound
[	Overlap/interruption

Text A

SON. da::d (.) d'you wanna cup of coffee

DAD. erm (.) okay (.) that'd be nice

(There follows a five-minute gap where a cup of coffee is made in the kitchen)

SON. there you go

DAD. thanks very much

SON. what about a biccy

DAD. erm (.) go on then

(Son goes out to get a biscuit from the kitchen)

DAD. I'll have a kitkat

SON *(from kitchen)*: right

SON. there y'are (.) what you watching

DAD. oh its erm (.) just some programme about er (.) the printin industry

SON. oh (2.5) da::d (1.0) y'know you said that I could have a new deck for me birthday

DAD. mmm (.) deck

SON. yeah skateboard deck (.) cos it's like (.) erm all scuffed an' (.) like wrecked and stuff

DAD. what (.) you only got it for Christmas for God's sake

SON. yeah (.) but I use it all the time an it's completely wrecked so (.) I need it now

DAD. yer not havin a new one (.) it (.) you'll have to wait till yer birthday

SON. aawww plea::se

DAD. no way (.) no chance

SON. [but dad

DAD. [no (.) no (0.5) you'll have to save up

SON. huh (.) well I would (.) if I got enough pocket money

DAD. I'm not falling for that'n neither

SON. yeah but (.) like it's it's not fair (3.0) an' it's only thirty four ninety nine on the net (.) which is a rea::lly good price

DAD. fff (.) thirty four ninety nine (1.0) on yer bike

SON. well thanks a lot *(Slams door)*

Text B

If Margaret Thatcher is re-elected as Prime Minister, *I warn you.*

I warn you that you will have pain –
When healing and relief depend upon payment.

I warn you that you will have ignorance –
When talents are untended and wits are wasted, when learning is a privilege and not a right.

I warn you that you will have poverty –
When pensions slip and benefits are whittled away by a government that won't pay in an economy that can't pay.

I warn you not to go into the streets alone after dark or into the streets in large crowds of protest in the light.

I warn you that you will have defence of a sort –
With a risk and at a price that passes all understanding.

I warn you that you will be home-bound –
When fares and transport bills kill leisure and lock you up.

I warn you that you will borrow less –
When credit, loans, mortgages and easy payments are refused to people on your melting income.

If Margaret Thatcher wins, she will be more a Leader than a Prime Minister. That power produces arrogance and when it is toughened by Tebbitry [a reference to Conservative Cabinet Minister, Norman Tebbit] and flattered and fawned upon by spineless sycophants, the boot-licking tabloid Knights of Fleet Street and placemen in the Quangos, the arrogance corrupts absolutely.

If Margaret Thatcher wins –
I warn you not to be ordinary.
I warn you not to be young.
I warn you not to fall ill.
I warn you not to get old.

B. MacArthur (ed.), The Penguin Book of Twentieth-Century Speeches *(1999)*

Sample response

These two texts both have very different audiences and contexts. Text B would probably have had a large audience present, presumably at an event like a political rally, and the speaker might well expect his speech to make the television or radio news as well, thus giving him the sense of addressing an even broader audience than those present. The speaker has therefore used very powerful language and many rhetorical features to suit this very important public context. In contrast, Text A has a purely domestic context, with no audience other than the two speakers themselves. The language is therefore much more informal in comparison to Text B. However, both Neil Kinnock and the son in Text A have a similar purpose in that they both want to persuade their audience to share their point of view and inspire their listeners to a particular course of action – vote Labour in Text B and buy the son a new skateboard in Text A – and this does lead to some similarities in language.

Both texts are linked by the fact that all the speakers use the pronouns 'I' and 'you'. There would not really be an alternative to this in Text

A, as the father and son are talking to each other, but it does create a homely domestic intimate feel to the chat. The son also uses the noun 'dad' to address his father more frequently than might be usual, drawing attention to their relationship perhaps to sound particularly affectionate and therefore appeal to his better nature. The elongated sound of 'da::d' used in a couple of places suggests a wheedling tone, again to sound affectionate. Similarly, Neil Kinnock uses the pronouns 'I' and 'you' as he also wants to create a sense of intimacy between himself and the listener. He makes the speech seem more personal in this way and the audience feel as if they are being addressed directly, and are thus more directly affected by the message.

As well as this use of pronouns, there are some other similarities which can be drawn between the language choices in both texts. For example, both use emotive language to try and influence their listeners. This is more obvious in the Kinnock speech: as its context is that of a public political speech, he uses features or oratory, such as antithesis – 'pain' compared to 'healing and relief' and 'ignorance' compared to 'talents' and 'wits'. This is done to emphasise how terrible things could be if people do not vote for him. The son in Text A tries to make an impact on his dad's emotions through his language. For example, he chooses quite dramatic verbs such as 'scuffed' and 'wrecked' to describe the skateboard, which compares to Kinnock's dramatic, hyperbolic use of language. He also tries to bribe his dad with a 'biccy' – this abbreviated form of the word sounds childish and friendly and appeals to the dad's emotions.

All three speakers in both texts use different techniques to make their points emphatically to their listeners. The son uses intensifiers such as 'completely' to exaggerate his claim and 'only thirty four ninety nine' to try to persuade his dad it is a bargain. He also uses the elongation of sound in 'rea::lly' to emphasise the value. On the other hand, the dad uses dismissive colloquial phrases such as 'for God's sake' and 'on yer bike' to emphasise his view, and also interrupts his son with 'no' to gain control of the conversation. Kinnock's speech is equally emphatic, partly created through the use of striking alliteration such as 'wits … wasted' and 'leisure … lock', but mainly created through the repetition of 'I warn you'. The sustained repetition of this phrase leaves the listener with a key idea to remember and gives the speech a great sense of melodrama.

This repetition provides the main structure of Text B: Kinnock uses the phrase, then follows it with a variety of emotive images as discussed above. The paragraph beginning 'If Margaret Thatcher wins' breaks this pattern briefly although its insistent alliteration maintains the rhythm. The pace intensifies, however, in the final lines, as the phrases become shorter and the expression 'I warn you' comes closer together. As a spontaneous conversation from a domestic context, the structure of Text A is, of course, quite different, although, like Kinnock, the boy is aiming to make an impact on his listener through the way he structures his speech. For example, the boy deliberately entices his father into conversation by asking questions: 'd'you wanna cup of coffee', 'what you watching'. His father answers the questions, thus completing the expected adjacency pair and in this way he is drawn into the boy's plans for the discussion.

In terms of style, the Kinnock speech is much more formal and polished, suiting its formal context. Text A is much more informal and the informality is created through features such as the elision of 'y'are' and 'y'know' and contractions such as 'I'm'. There are some fillers in Text A: the dad's 'erms' suggest he is perhaps suspicious of the son's questions and offers, and the son's 'cos it's like (.) erm all scuffed an (.) like wrecked and stuff' suggest he is perhaps embarrassed to admit what's happened and he is struggling to get the right words for the right impact. This is in contrast to the obvious fluency of the prepared speech.

There are also a few pauses in Text A. The longest pauses come when the son waits after the dad has told him about the television programme before launching into his request. He does not want to seem too keen to get on to the subject of the skateboard, so pauses, perhaps to suggest he is genuinely interested in what the dad said. Towards the end of the exchange there is also a long three-second pause; the boy seems to have run out of ideas for his argument but then comes up with a new approach by mentioning the bargain price. On the other hand, in Text B the short lines and paragraph layout imply that Kinnock also pauses often during his speech. This would probably have the effect of making the speech sound very ominous, the pauses allowing Kinnock's audience to really reflect on the importance of his words.

In conclusion, the different contexts of both speech extracts have led to many differences in the formality of the language used and the style of delivery. However, both the boy and Kinnock try to persuade and influence their listeners: Kinnock through his use of rhetorical features and emotive language and imagery, and the boy through his affectionate childish appeal.

Examiner's comments

For AO2, this candidate has given a secure and coherent reading of both texts, with close focus on a good range of examples. Close comparison is maintained throughout with detailed consideration of similarities and differences between the texts. The response is well constructed and coherent and shows evident understanding of the features of the texts. There is a range of thoughtful points made about speech and how it works. The candidate has produced a strong response, but does not quite achieve full marks, as there is no really profound or illuminating analysis here; for example, the student could have explored some of the emotive language in Text B in much more depth.

For AO3, the candidate gives a clear sense of the different contexts for the two texts and finds some worthwhile points of comparison. There is close focus on the texts, with equal coverage given to both, and the comparison covers the structure, form, language and mode of the two texts with assurance. This is a confident comparison, but again this response does not quite achieve the originality of ideas required for full marks despite being a skilful and secure comparison. In one or two places the texts are not entirely integrated; for example, the comparison of the use of pronouns is a little clumsy.

Practical activity

Look up the mark scheme for this unit on the AQA web site and use the grid provided to assess your own response.

Learning outcomes for this section:

Knowledge, understanding and skills

Now that you have completed Section A of this unit, you should be able to:

- explain a range of varieties of spoken English

- use an appropriate framework of terms and concepts to enable you to analyse the features of spoken English

- show understanding of the importance of language form and context in your analysis of speech

- make an effective analytical comparison of two spoken texts

- integrate the knowledge you gained in Unit 1 with the new material covered in this section

- apply your knowledge and understanding appropriately in comparing the two speech texts in the examination.

Transferable skills

Your study of this section will form a basis from which you will be able to look at the representation of speech in novels and plays in Section B. In Section B, you will also need to apply the concepts and terminology you have learned in Unit 1.

16 Use of dialogue and other stylistic techniques in novels

Link

Refer back to the chapter on character on p15 of Unit 1 for more information and ideas about the use of dialogue in prose fiction.

Key terms

Reporting clause: a phrase such as 'he said' or 'she replied', which accompanies spoken language and indicates who is speaking.

Dialogue can play a significant part in the revelation of character and relationships in novels, as well as in the development of themes. In order to make the dialogue sound convincing and to bring their characters to life, novelists represent speech using a range of techniques. Writers may incorporate some of the features of real spontaneous speech in their dialogue. However, despite this appearance of realism, speech and dialogue is represented in novels in a stylised manner.

Direct and indirect speech

Most writers include at least some direct speech as a means of presenting dialogue in their work, in order to give the reader an immediate direct impression of their characters and to convey a sense of character through voice. Direct speech, such as ' "It's raining," he said', is usually categorised by the inclusion of speech marks around the actual words spoken and a **reporting clause** such as 'he said' or 'she replied'. Occasionally, some writers may choose to omit the speech marks to create a particular effect; for example, if *Close Range* by Annie Proulx was one of your set texts for Unit 1, you may already have noticed this in the story 'The Half-skinned Steer'.

> Winking at Rollo the girlfriend said, yes, she had said, yes sir, Tin Head eats half his dinner and then he has to take a little nap. After a while he wakes up again and goes outside stretching his arms and yawning, says, guess I'll finish skinning out that steer. But the steer ain't there. It's gone. Only the tongue, laying on the ground all covered with dirt and straw, and the tub of blood and the dog licking at it.

Here, Proulx has blurred the distinction between the girlfriend's voice and the narrative viewpoint. However, this is still in the form of direct speech, as the girlfriend's exact words are given, creating a vivid impression of her personality, along with the reporting clause 'she said'. Alternatively, a writer might choose to convey a character's words indirectly in the form of indirect or reported speech; for example, ' "It's raining," he said' becomes 'he said that it was raining' in indirect speech. If Annie Proulx had chosen to write the above example in indirect speech, the extract would begin:

> Winking at Rollo the girlfriend said that Tin Head had eaten half his dinner and then had to take a little nap. After a while he had woken up again and had gone outside stretching his arms and yawning, saying that he guessed he would finish skinning out that steer.

In this case the girlfriend's words are no longer presented exactly as she said them and as a result some of her colourful character is downplayed. Also, the necessary switch to the past tense makes the story she is telling seem much less dramatic, entertaining or immediate.

Critical response activity

Read the following extract from *Great Expectations* by Charles Dickens, in which Pip encounters the convict Magwitch on the marshes for the first time. Magwitch is holding Pip upside down and has asked him to bring him some 'wittles' (food) and a blacksmith's file so that he can remove the chains from his legs.

- Comment on Dickens's use of direct and indirect speech in the extract.
- What effect do these different choices have in this context?
- What else do you notice about the speech presented in this extract?
- Compare your ideas to the commentary that follows.

He gave me a most tremendous dip and roll, so that the church jumped over its own weather-cock. Then, he held me by the arms in an upright position on the top of the stone, and went on in these fearful terms:

'You bring me, to-morrow morning early, that file and them wittles. You bring the lot to me, at that old Battery over yonder. You do it, and you never dare to say a word or dare to make a sign concerning your having seen such a person as me, or any person sumever, and you shall be let to live. You fail, or you go from my words in any partickler, no matter how small it is, and your heart and your liver shall be tore out, roasted and ate. Now, I ain't alone, as you may think I am. There's a young man hid with me, in comparison with which young man I am a Angel. That young man hears the words I speak. That young man has a secret way pecooliar to himself, of getting at a boy, and at his heart, and at his liver. It is in wain for a boy to attempt to hide himself from that young man. A boy may lock his door, may be warm in bed, may tuck himself up, may draw the clothes over his head, may think himself comfortable and safe, but that young man will softly creep and creep his way to him and tear him open. I am a keeping that young man from harming of you at the present moment, with great difficulty. I find it wery hard to hold that young man off of your inside. Now, what do you say?'

I said that I would get him the file, and I would get him what broken bits of food I could, and I would come to him at the Battery, early in the morning.

'Say, Lord strike you dead if you don't!' said the man.

I said so, and he took me down.

'Now,' he pursued, 'you remember what you've undertook, and you remember that young man, and you get home!'

'Goo-good night, sir,' I faltered.

'Much of that!' said he, glancing about him over the cold wet flat. 'I wish I was a frog. Or a eel!'

Link

Refer back to the chapter on writing articles on p66 of Unit 1 for more information about direct and indirect speech.

Commentary

You almost certainly noticed that Magwitch's words are all presented in the form of direct speech, which in this context makes his presence seem much more real, intense and threatening. By giving us Magwitch's exact words, precisely as he says them, Dickens is able to create a unique impression of the character; for example, Magwitch's idiosyncratic pronunciation of 'partickler' and 'pecooliar', as well as the habit of replacing a 'v' sound with a 'w' as in 'wain' and 'wery', means that we are able to 'hear' Magwitch's voice, thus making him appear more strange and yet more real to us. These peculiarities would almost certainly have been lost in indirect speech. In contrast to Magwitch, some of Pip's words are presented as indirect speech, perhaps reinforcing the impression that Pip has been overwhelmed by the monstrous convict's presence. Dickens shifts the focus entirely on to Magwitch rather than Pip at this point and achieves this through contrasting direct with indirect speech. However, Dickens reverts to direct speech for Pip when he says 'Goo-good night, sir', as this enables him to convey Pip's fear and nervousness through the stuttering repetition of 'Goo-good'.

Free direct speech

In the extract above, the reporting clauses such as 'said the man', 'he pursued', 'I faltered' and 'said he' clarify for the reader who is speaking and often give us an idea of the character's tone or manner of speaking. However, writers often choose to miss out these reporting clauses when presenting dialogue, perhaps to add pace or intensity to the scene, and direct speech presented in this way is known as **free direct speech**. This is a technique used to great effect by Anita Shreve in the novel *Eden Close*, as we can see in the following extract, where the central character Andy is talking to Eden, who is blind, about her mother's reaction to the fact that Andy washed Eden's hair the previous day.

> I thought you wouldn't come.'
>
> 'I nearly didn't.'
>
> 'She's warned you off.'
>
> 'She's very concerned about you.'
>
> 'You think so.'
>
> 'Yes, I do.'
>
> 'Then why are you here?'
>
> 'Well, I think she's concerned, but I'm not convinced she's right.'
>
> 'I told her I washed it myself, but she didn't believe me. It's the part. I never get it right.'
>
> Her hair is freshly brushed, the part he made yesterday still straight.
>
> 'I want to ask you something,' he says.
>
> 'What is it?' she says after a time.
>
> 'Was it very bad?' he says. 'In the beginning, I mean. I never knew until today what happened, where you were.'
>
> She hesitates. 'There are things about the beginning I don't remember,' she says. 'And what is bad? Worse than before? Worse than now?'
>
> 'You must have loved Jim very much,' he says.
>
> 'He was my father.'
>
> 'I know.'
>
> 'No you don't.'

Key terms

Free direct speech: direct speech presented without, or with minimal, reporting clauses such as 'he said'. Some writers also omit the speech punctuation in free direct speech.

Commentary

Here, the extract begins with a number of lines of free direct speech. This, combined with the shortness and simplicity of the lines, recreates a sense of the tension between Andy and Eden and the intensity of their feelings at this point. Our attention is focused entirely on the two characters, without any distraction from the narrator. Later on, the extract switches to direct speech, with reporting clauses such as 'he says' and 'she hesitates'. The conversation has moved on at this point from discussing Eden's hair to her traumatic experience as a teenager, and the direct speech here creates a much more hesitant, tentative mood. For example, in the line ' "Was it very bad?" he says. "In the beginning, I mean. I never knew until today what happened, where you were," ' the insertion of 'he says' creates a pause in Andy's speech, suggesting a hesitation as he wonders how to approach such a difficult subject. The earlier intensity returns at the end of the extract with the return to free direct speech at the mention of Eden's father.

▮ Critical response activity

Read the following example of direct and free direct speech from *The Lovely Bones* by Alice Sebold. Comment on the effects achieved by using these techniques in this extract of dialogue between Lindsey and her father.

'What was the phone call?' my sister asked.

'What phone call?'

'I heard you say that thing you always say about Susie's smile. About stars exploding.'

'Did I say that?'

'You got kind of goofy. It was a cop, wasn't it?'

'No lies?'

'No lies,' Lindsey agreed.

'They found a body part. It might be Susie's.'

It was a hard sock in the stomach. 'What?'

'Nothing is ever certain,' my father tried.

Lindsey sat down at the kitchen table. 'I'm going to be sick,' she said.

'Honey?'

'Dad, I want you to tell me what it was. Which body part, and then I'm going to need to throw up.'

My father got down a large metal mixing bowl. He brought it to the table and placed it near Lindsey before sitting down.

'Okay,' she said. 'Tell me.'

'It was an elbow. The Gilberts' dog found it.'

He held her hand and then she threw up, as she had promised, into the shiny silver bowl.

Free indirect speech

Just as free direct speech omits the expressions such as 'he said' and 'she said' from the dialogue, **free indirect speech** omits the phrases such as 'he said that' from indirect speech while still seeming to report the words of a character. Jane Austen often uses this technique, as we can see in the following extract from *Persuasion* in which the heroine Anne hears about life in Bath from her snobbish sister Elizabeth and father Sir Walter.

> They had the pleasure of assuring her that Bath more than answered their expectations in every respect. Their house was undoubtedly the best in Camden Place, their drawing-rooms had many decided advantages over all the others which they had either seen or heard of, and the superiority was not less in the style of the fitting-up or the taste of the furniture. Their acquaintance was exceedingly sought after. Everybody was wanting to visit them. They had drawn back from many introductions, and still were perpetually having cards left by people of whom they knew nothing.

This extract could have been written in indirect speech ('they said that their house was undoubtedly the best in Camden Place') as Austen is clearly reporting the words and language of Elizabeth and Sir Walter. However, by using free indirect speech Austen subtly withdraws herself from the narrative, allowing the characters to reveal their own snobbishness in their own words. Austen's own viewpoint as narrator here seems to have blended with Elizabeth and Sir Walter's viewpoint. There is great irony in the discrepancy between what is said and what is meant, because, although Austen does not explicitly challenge the characters' opinions of themselves, her readers understand, of course, that Austen is really mocking them by the way she presents them.

As we can see, Austen uses the technique of free indirect speech for ironic effect. However, different writers may use this approach to create different effects. If you come across this technique in one of your own set texts, remember to analyse its impact in the context of that book rather than assuming it will always be used with the same purpose or intentions.

Spontaneous speech in a literary context

When presenting speech and dialogue, many writers include or adapt some of the typical features of spontaneous speech we studied in Section A of this unit in order to create vivid naturalistic portrayals of their characters. For example, in the following extract from *Emma*, in which the heroine is talking with her garrulous neighbour Miss Bates about the latter's niece Jane Fairfax, look out for how Jane Austen uses several of the features of spontaneous speech to create a realistic impression of Miss Bates.

> 'Oh! yes – Mr Elton, I understood – certainly as to dancing – Mrs Cole was telling me that dancing at the rooms at Bath was – Mrs Cole was so kind as to sit some time with us, talking of Jane; for as soon as she came in, she began inquiring after her, Jane is so very great a favourite there. Whenever she is with us, Mrs Cole does not know how to shew her kindness enough; and I must say that Jane deserves it as much as anybody can. And so she began inquiring after her directly, saying, "I know you cannot have heard from Jane lately, because it is not her time for writing;" and when I immediately said, "But indeed we have, we had a letter this very morning," I do not know that I ever saw anybody more surprised. "Have you, upon your honour!" said she; "well, that is quite unexpected. Do let me hear what she says." '

Emma's politeness was at hand directly, to say, with smiling interest –

'Have you heard from Miss Fairfax so lately? I am extremely happy. I hope she is well?'

'Thank you. You are so kind!' replied the happily deceived aunt, while eagerly hunting for the letter. – 'Oh! here it is. I was sure it could not be far off; but I had put my huswife upon it, you see, without being aware, and so it was quite hid, but I had it in my hand so very lately that I was almost sure it must be on the table. I was reading it to Mrs Cole, and since she went away, I was reading it again to my mother, for it is such a pleasure to her – a letter from Jane – that she can never hear it often enough; so I knew it could not be far off, and here it is, only just under my huswife – and since you are so kind as to wish to hear what she says; – but, first of all, I really must, in justice to Jane, apologise for her writing so short a letter – only two pages you see – hardly two – and in general she fills the whole paper and crosses half.'

Commentary

In this extract we can see that Miss Bates dominates the turn-taking expected in a social context such as this, partly by the speed with which she talks and partly because Emma is obliged by the social conventions of politeness, particularly valued in that era, not to interrupt. Emma asks the question 'I hope she is well?' which is clearly intended as a phatic utterance. However, Miss Bates misinterprets this, and completes the adjacency pair with a rambling monologue rather than the more socially acceptable 'Yes, thank you.' In these ways we are given the impression of a lonely woman, desperate for an opportunity to talk but who lacks the social skills we expect in conversation. In addition, Austen represents the pauses typical of spontaneous speech with dashes and suggests something of the nature of real speech by including repairs in Miss Bates's dialogue, notably in the first few lines of the extract, suggesting her rather flustered excitable character. Austen includes frequent digressions here, another typical feature of spontaneous speech. Through using these techniques she creates a realistic representation of Miss Bates's disorganised outpourings of speech.

You can see here how the framework of terms you learned in Section A in order to analyse spontaneous speech can equally be applied to the analysis of dialogue in a literary context. Remember, though, that your analysis of the representation of speech in your set text should be supplemented by the analysis of other stylistic features, using the framework of terms you learned in Unit 1.

Link

Remind yourself about monologues by referring back to Chapter 4 on dramatic techniques in Unit 1.

Critical response activity

Read the following extract from *Eden Close* by Anita Shreve. At this point in the novel, the father of the central character, Andy, has just emerged from the neighbouring house where a dramatic incident has just occurred. He tells his wife and son what has happened.

- What features of spontaneous speech has Shreve incorporated into the dialogue here?
- How do these features help to reflect the context of this scene?
- What impressions do we get of Andy's parents through the use of these features?

'Go inside now. Take the boy. They're bringing Jim out.'

'Jim?' his mother said quickly.

'It's bad. You go on in. Quick, now.'

But his mother would not move. 'What happened?' she demanded. 'Tell me.'

His father raised his arms, as if he meant to shepherd his family back to shelter. But when he saw she would not move, he lowered them. He stabbed the barrel of the rifle into the gravel, like a stick. He looked at the ground. He sighed – a deep, exhausted sound.

'Jim is dead,' said his father. 'Eden's been shot, but she's still alive.'

His mother brought her hands to her mouth. Andrew heard a high, strangled murmur.

'But how?' she asked. 'Who?'

'I don't know. It looks like, *looks like*,' his father said, faltering, repeating himself, 'and I think Edith was trying to say this, a man broke in while she and Jim were out, Jim was out, and Jim found him in Eden's room. He was' – his father hesitated, looked at Andy, searched for the proper wording – '*assaulting* Eden, and the man had a gun – we heard the shots … Eden somehow got in the way … a struggle, I think…. Edith saw the man on the stairs … He had a mask … She found them both.' His father stared. 'I saw her in the bedroom … covered, covering … '

🔍 Idiolect

If you compare the speech of some of the characters in the extracts you have looked at so far, such as Magwitch or Miss Bates, you will notice that each character has a distinctive individual style of talking. All speakers, whether real or fictional, use language in a way that is unique to them, using particular words and phrases, pronouncing words in a particular way or using particular grammatical constructions. This individual variety of language is known as an **idiolect**.

In the extract from *Great Expectations* on p123, we saw that Magwitch's distinctive idiolect was represented in his unusual pronunciations such as 'pecooliar' and 'wery', as well as through his use of some non-standard grammar such as 'ain't' and 'I am a Angel'. If *Great Expectations* is your set text for this unit or you have read any other works by Dickens, you will know that Dickens creates highly individual idiolects for many of his characters, often distorting and exaggerating the idiosyncratic patterns of their speech to the point where some might say the characters become almost **caricatures** rather than realistic portraits. The blacksmith Jo Gargery in *Great Expectations* is a good example of this. Dickens gives his speech several unique features, such as his repeated use of the elided phrase 'I meantersay' and his constant choice of 'old chap' or 'old fellow' to address Pip, as well as his unique pronunciation of 'Ram-page', and, like Magwitch, his use of a 'w' for a 'v' in words like 'welwet' and 'weal-cutlets'.

In a long novel such as *Great Expectations* or *Wuthering Heights*, you are likely to encounter a much wider variety of speech styles than you will find in a text with a more limited number of characters such as

💡 Key terms

Idiolect: a combination of habitual language choices that is unique to an individual speaker, seen in such features as pronunciation, choices of vocabulary, phrasing and grammatical patterns.

Caricature: a portrayal of a character in which certain features are exaggerated, usually for comic effect.

Samuel Beckett's *Waiting for Godot*, which we will be looking at on p138. However, although few writers use such extreme forms of idiolect as Dickens, most novelists, in much more subtle ways, create distinctive identities for their characters through the ways they speak. Look at this extract from *Enduring Love* by Ian McEwan, where the narrator Joe meets his stalker Jed Parry for the first time.

> Of course, I didn't think of any of this at the time. All I heard was a whine of powerlessness, and I relaxed. What he said was, 'Clarissa's really worried about you? I said I'd come down and see if you're alright?'
>
> My silence was hostile. I was old enough to dislike his presumption of first names, or, for that matter, of claiming to know Clarissa's state of mind. I didn't even know Parry's name at this point. Even with a dead man sitting between us, the rules of social engagement prevailed. As I heard it later from Clarissa, Parry had come over to her to introduce himself, then turned away to follow me down the hill. She had said nothing to him about me.
>
> 'Are you alright?'
>
> I said, 'There's nothing we can do but wait,' and I gestured in the direction of the road, one field away.
>
> Parry took a couple of steps closer and looked down at Logan, then back to me. The grey-blue eyes gleamed. He was excited, but no one could ever have guessed to what extent.
>
> 'Actually, I think there is something we can do.'
>
> I looked at my watch. It was fifteen minutes since I had phoned the emergency services. 'You go ahead,' I said. 'Do what you like.'
>
> 'It's something we can do together?' he said as he looked about for a suitable place on the ground. The wild thought came to me that he was proposing some form of gross indecency with a corpse. He was lowering himself, and with a look was inviting me to join him. Then I got it. He was on his knees.
>
> 'What we could do,' he said with a seriousness which warned against mockery, 'is to pray together?' Before I could object, which for the moment was impossible because I was speechless, Parry added, 'I know it's difficult. But you'll find it helps. At times like this, you know, it really does help.'

Here Parry's speech is made distinctive by what McEwan refers to as his 'interrogative style', or his habit of turning statements such as 'Clarissa's really worried about you' into questions – 'Clarissa's really worried about you?' His repeated use of this feature betrays Parry's personal insecurities and his neediness, as he constantly seems to seek a response from Joe. Joe himself says that this habit suggests someone 'too hesitant and apologetic to say how things were in the world'. Also in the extract we see a marked contrast between Joe's restrained rational comments and Parry's gushing emotional style.

Practical activity

Choose a character from your set text and carefully identify the features that give your character a distinctive style of speech or idiolect.

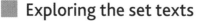

Exploring the set texts

So far in this chapter you have focused on the representation of dialogue and how the framework of terms used to analyse real speech covered in Section A, along with the new concepts and terms introduced in this section, can also be helpful in the analysis of a literary text. However, in the examination you will need to integrate this approach with an analysis of any other stylistic features and techniques used in the extract given in the examination paper. Read this extract from *Great Expectations* and the commentary that follows for some ideas on how you can achieve this.

The time so melted away, that our early dinner-hour drew close at hand, and Estella left us to prepare herself. We had stopped near the centre of the long table, and Miss Havisham, with one of her withered arms stretched out of the chair, rested that clenched hand upon the yellow cloth. As Estella looked back over her shoulder before going out at the door, Miss Havisham kissed that hand to her, with a ravenous intensity that was of its kind quite dreadful.

Then Estella being gone and we two left alone, she turned to me and said in a whisper:

'Is she beautiful, graceful, well-grown? Do you admire her?'

'Everybody must who sees her, Miss Havisham.'

She drew an arm round my neck, and drew my head close down to hers as she sat in the chair. 'Love her, love her, love her! How does she use you?'

Before I could answer (if I could have answered so difficult a question at all), she repeated, 'Love her, love her, love her! If she favours you, love her. If she wounds you, love her. If she tears your heart to pieces – and as it gets older and stronger it will tear deeper – love her, love her!'

Never had I seen such passionate eagerness as was joined to her utterance of these words. I could feel the muscles of the thin arm round my neck, swell with the vehemence that possessed her.

'Hear me, Pip! I adopted her to be loved. I bred her and educated her, to be loved. I developed her into what she is, that she might be loved. Love her!'

She said the word often enough, and there could be no doubt that she meant to say it; but if the often repeated word had been hate instead of love – despair – revenge – dire death – it could not have sounded from her lips more like a curse.

'I'll tell you,' said she, in the same hurried passionate whisper, 'what real love is. It is blind devotion, unquestioning self-humiliation, utter submission, trust and belief against yourself and against the whole world, giving up your whole heart and soul to the smiter – as I did!'

When she came to that, and to a wild cry that followed that, I caught her round the waist. For she rose up in the chair, in her shroud of a dress, and struck at the air as if she would as soon have struck herself against the wall and fallen dead.

Commentary

If you were to analyse this extract focusing on aspects of spontaneous speech, you might comment on the use of adjacency pairs and the way in which the dialogue opens with a question and answer exchange. However, Miss Havisham's enquiry is very much a **closed question** (rather than the more **open question** 'What do you think of Estella?'), thus directing and controlling Pip's response. Miss Havisham begins another adjacency pair with the question 'How does she use you?' but does not wait for Pip's response this time – the way she dominates and controls the turn-taking here reflects the strength of her passion at this point. You could also use your knowledge of the features of prepared speech to analyse this extract, as Miss Havisham uses several triplets such as 'Love her, love her, love her!' in order to emphasise her point. She also uses other rhetorical features such as **parallelism** in the repetition and replacement seen in 'If she favours you, love her. If she wounds you, love her. If she tears your heart to pieces … love her, love her!' These features perhaps suggest that this is a speech Miss Havisham has been thinking about and planning for a long time, waiting for an opportunity to speak – hence the passion with which she delivers it.

If you consider your knowledge about features of language gained in Unit 1, you will see that there are many other aspects of style to explore here. For example, you could look at some of the lexical choices in the extract, such as Miss Havisham's choice of the verbs 'bred' and 'developed' to describe Estella's upbringing, which make her sound more like an animal than a human being, or the verb 'possessed' in the phrase 'the vehemence possessed her', which has demonic connotations. You could also consider the syntactical choices in the extract; for example, Miss Havisham uses many imperatives such as 'Love her!' to show the forcefulness of this shadowy character while the many exclamations convey her frenzied excitement. In addition, you could look at the figurative imagery in the extract: the opening metaphor 'The time so melted away' sets a strange other-worldly tone for the extract while the metaphor of 'her shroud of a dress' has sinister connotations of death. Equally, the literal imagery of Miss Havisham when 'She drew an arm round my neck, and drew my head close down to hers' suggests the intimacy of lovers, which, combined with language such as 'ravenous intensity', 'passionate eagerness' and 'hurried passionate whisper', is in stark contrast to the imagery and language associated with death, such as 'withered arms', 'yellow cloth' and 'shroud'. The effect of the contrast here is, as Pip says, 'quite dreadful'.

Key terms

Closed question: a question phrased in such a way that offers the respondent only a limited choice of possible answers, usually Yes or No, or a one-word answer, e.g. 'Do you like cheese?'

Open question: a question phrased in an open-ended way so that the respondent can answer in a wide range of ways, e.g. 'What sort of food do you like?'

Parallelism: the repetition of the structure of a phrase or sentence, often for rhetorical effect, e.g. 'That's one small step for man, one giant leap for mankind.'

Critical response activity

Read the following extract from *The Lovely Bones*. Use the questions to help you to analyse the use of dialogue and other stylistic features in a similar way to the commentary on the extract from *Great Expectations* above.

- What use is made of direct and free direct speech in the extract?
- What features of spontaneous or prepared speech can you identify in the extract and how do these help you to interpret the text?
- What other features of language are significant here?

'What I'm saying, Lindsey, is that we all miss Susie,' Mr Caden said.

She did not respond.

'She was very bright,' he tried.

She stared blankly back at him.

'It's on your shoulders now.' He had no idea what he was saying, but he thought the silence might mean he was getting somewhere. 'You're the only Salmon girl now.'

Nothing.

'You know who came in to see me this morning?' Mr Caden had held back his big finish, the one he was sure would work. 'Mr Dewitt. He's considering coaching a girls' team,' Mr Caden said. 'The idea is all centered around you. He's watched how good you are, as competitive as his boys, and he thinks other girls would come out if you led the charge. What do you say?'

Inside, my sister's heart closed like a fist. 'I'd say it would be pretty hard to play soccer on the soccer field when it's approximately twenty feet from where my sister was supposedly murdered.'

Score!

Mr Caden's mouth opened and he stared at her.

'Anything else?' Lindsey asked.

'No, I … ' Mr Caden reached out his hand again. There was a thread still – a desire to understand. 'I want you to know how sorry we are,' he said.

'I'm late for first period,' she said.

■ Critical response activity

Remember, in the examination you will need to comment in detail on the extract given in the examination paper, as well as one other episode of your choice, so it is important to think about *linking* extracts from your set text. Below are two extracts from *Eden Close* by Anita Shreve, which are connected as they both focus on the relationship between Eden and Andy. Use the following questions to help you analyse both extracts.

■ How are features of spontaneous speech used in both extracts to express the relationship between the characters? Think in particular about phatic utterance, turn-taking and adjacency pairs.

■ What use does Anita Shreve make of direct and indirect speech, or free direct and indirect speech?

■ How is a sense of each character conveyed through their individual language choices?

■ What other features of language and style do you notice in both extracts? Think particularly about the use of imagery and metaphor.

■ How has Andy and Eden's relationship changed between the two extracts?

Extract A

'Hello,' she says.

She is holding herself still, her gaze seemingly directed toward a window beside him.

'I wanted to see you,' he says. He shakes his head. 'To speak with you, I mean.' He stands in the center of the linoleum floor, uncertain as to whether he should sit at the table, make himself at home, or not. She has not invited him to. Perhaps, he thinks, she has no sense now, as he does, of the awkwardness of a conversation conducted standing stiffly face to face. Though she cannot see him, he feels uneasy in front of her. His arms and hands are appendages that seem no longer to belong to him. He folds them across his chest in unconscious parody of her stance.

'I thought. Yes,' she says elliptically.

A quick intake of air she cannot fail to hear betrays his nervousness. 'So how are you?' he asks. It is an inane question, and instantly he regrets it.

She gives the faintest of shrugs. 'I am always all right,' she says evenly.

He searches for the next sentence as if hunting for a trail that will lead him out of an unfamiliar wood. All his choices seem lame.

'It's been a long time,' he says.

She doesn't answer him. Instead she turns her head so that she is looking at him so acutely he wonders fleetingly if perhaps he has got it wrong – and she can see after all. Her stare is uncompromising. He tries to imagine what it is that she 'sees': his presence must be to her a voice in a vast inky sea.

'Your mother is dead,' she says.

Her words startle him. The sentence is bald, unadorned. Almost unfeeling. But he realizes that he likes the frank statement. Likes not hearing an expression of sympathy, likes not hearing the words I'm sorry for the hundredth time. The fact is a simple one: His mother is dead, and she has said only that.

Extract B

On her own, she can go no farther than the cornfields, so he takes her hand and leads her to a damp grassy patch beneath the tallest tree, the tree most encumbered by vines and hence the one providing the coolest shade. She sits, leaning against the tree for support, her legs stretched out in front of her. She reaches for the hem of her dress and brings it to her face, wiping her forehead, her upper lip, the top of her chest. Her thighs, uncovered, are white, with a fine down of golden hairs. She smooths her dress along her legs, covering herself.

'You can tell me,' she says.

'Tell you what?' he asks.

'How it looks. Is it how it was?'

He surveys the landscape nearest them. 'It is,' he says, 'but more so. The trees are covered with vines. The water is much the same. Do you remember the color?'

She shakes her head.

'It's gold,' he says, 'from the minerals.'

'Gold,' she repeats.

'And here … ' He stands up and walks to the mass of lilies. He snaps one off its stem and brings it back. He puts it in her hand.

'Do you remember these?' he asks. 'They're lilies. Red. They've grown wilder, thicker along the banks. It's hard to say if anyone's been here recently. There's no obvious debris left behind, no trampling.'

The hymn he has heard before is quieter here. She fingers the long crimson petals in her lap.

'You're going swimming,' she says.

'Oh, I don't know,' he says, picking up a stone in his hand. He looks at the water. He would like a swim. The surface of the pond is glassy, undisturbed but for the arcs of water bugs.

'You could come too,' he says. 'You could swim in your dress. It would dry in the sun on the walk back, and you could change before she got home.'

She shakes her head. 'I don't need to swim. I am just all right here.'

17 Use of dialogue and other dramatic techniques in plays

Link

Look back at the section on dialogue on p33 to remind yourself of the ways in which dialogue is used to develop plot, character and conflict. Then look at the section on stage directions on p54 as a reminder of how stage directions can influence the presentation of dialogue in a play.

In drama, the dialogue represented in the script is actually spoken by the characters on stage. Together with the stage action and the set, it is the means by which the dramatist reveals character and develops the themes and plot of the play. However, just as in the novel, the dialogue is stylised. No audience would want to hear all the fillers, repairs, overlaps and interruptions that characterise spontaneous speech.

There is a great variety of ways of representing speech in drama. As in speech texts, there is a continuum, ranging from dialogue which is as close as possible to spontaneous speech at one end to poetic speeches at the other. Most modern dramatists write in prose and seek to give the illusion of spontaneous speech, although there was some revival of poetic drama in the interwar years, most notably in the work of T. S. Eliot. Shakespeare and his contemporaries used verse extensively. Poetic drama continued into the Restoration period, notably in the works of Dryden, but its importance diminished as comedies written in prose became popular. We will be looking at Shakespeare's use of poetry on p142 but we will begin by looking at the ways in which dramatists writing in prose represent speech.

Read the passage below, which is taken from the beginning of Harold Pinter's play *The Caretaker*. The script of this play opens with lengthy and detailed stage directions that give explicit details of the set and go on to describe the movements, appearance and clothing of the three characters in the play before dialogue begins. The extract begins after Mick, who does not speak at all at this point, has left the stage leaving the audience wondering what his role will be.

Critical response activity

1 In what ways does the dialogue do the following?
  ▪ Resemble spontaneous speech
  ▪ Differ from spontaneous speech
  ▪ Reveal the character of the speakers and the relationship between them.

2 What effect would the physical appearance of Aston and Davies, as described in the stage directions, have on your view of their characters?

(*Aston and Davies enter, Aston first, Davies following, shambling and breathing heavily. Aston, in his early thirties, wears an old tweed overcoat and under it a thin, shabby dark blue pinstripe suit, single breasted, with a pullover and faded shirt and tie. Davies, an old man, wears a worn brown overcoat, shapeless trousers, a waistcoat, vest, no shirt, and sandals. Aston switches on the light, puts his keys in his pocket and closes the door. Davies looks about the room.*)

Aston: Sit down.

Davies (*moving down R*): Thanks. (*He looks about*): Uuh …

Aston: Just a minute. (*He looks around for a chair, sees one lying on the bed up C, moves and picks it up*)

Aston: Sit down? Huh – I haven't had a good sit down – I haven't had a proper sit down – well, I couldn't tell you …

Aston (*placing the chair down R of C*): Here you are. (*He crosses to the bed L*)

Davies (*following Aston*): Ten minutes off for tea break in the middle of the night in that place and I couldn't find a seat, not one. All them Greeks had it, Poles. Greeks, Blacks, the lot of them, all them aliens had it. And they had me working there – they had me working … (*He moves C*)

(*Aston sits on the bed L, takes a tin of tobacco and papers from his pocket and rolls a cigarette*)

Davies (*he watches Aston*): All them Blacks had it, Blacks, Greeks, Poles, the lot of them, that's what, doing me out of a seat, treating me like dirt. When he come at me tonight I told him.

(*Pause*)

Aston: Take a seat.

Davies: Yes, but what I got to do first, you see, what I got to do, I got to loosen myself up, you see what I mean? (*He loosens himself up*) I could have got done in down there. (*He exclaims loudly, punches downwards with closed fist, turns his back to Aston and stares at the wall up C*)

(*A pause. Aston lights his cigarette.*)

Aston: You want to roll yourself one of these?

Davies (*turning*): What? No, no, I never smoke a cigarette. (*He pauses then moves to R of Aston*) I'll tell you what, though. I'll have a bit of that tobacco for my pipe, if you like.

Aston (*handing Davies the tin*): Yes. Go on. Take some out of that.

Davies: That's kind of you mister. Just enough to fill my pipe, that's all. (*He takes a pipe from his pocket and fills it*) I had a tin, only – only a while ago. But it was knocked off. It was knocked off on the Great West Road. (*He holds out the tin*) Where shall I put it?

Aston: I'll take it.

Davies (*handing the tin to Aston*): When he come at me tonight I told him. Didn't I? You heard me tell him, didn't you?

Aston: I saw him have a go at you.

Davies: Go at me? You wouldn't grumble. The filthy skate, an old man like me – I've had dinner with the best.

(*A pause*)

Aston: Yes, I saw him have a go at you.

Commentary

Just as in spontaneous speech, the speakers take turns, with Davies having more utterances and seeming to dominate the conversation. However, Aston is clearly the host here and the imperatives he uses such as 'Take a seat 'and 'Take some out of that' show that he tries to control the situation. Davies does not actually sit down, however, and he is allowed to speak at length. There is therefore some ambiguity about who is in control of the situation. You will have noticed some typical adjacency pairs which give an impression of a spontaneous conversation. For example:

> **Aston**. You want to roll yourself one of these?
>
> **Davies** (*turning*): What? No, no, I never smoke a cigarette.

There are also fillers such as 'Uuh', 'Huh' and 'well' at the beginning of the extract but far fewer of these than there would be in spontaneous speech. They serve to give an impression of the hesitancy that characterises natural conversation without making the dialogue tedious and difficult to follow. The fillers here help to suggest that Davies is unsure of himself in his new situation. There are also examples of repairs, such as 'I haven't had a good sit down – I haven't had a proper sit down' and 'they had me working there – they had me working'. Again, there are fewer examples of these than would be normal in spontaneous speech but they are used here to suggest both natural conversation and Davies's hesitancy. Unlike spontaneous speech, there are no interruptions or overlaps but there are hesitations and pauses which create a sense of awkwardness.

> **Davies**: Yes, but what I got to do first, you see, what I got to do, I got to loosen myself up, you see what I mean? (*He loosens himself up*) I could have got done in down there. (*He exclaims loudly, punches downwards with closed fist, turns his back to Aston and stares at the wall up C*)

His exclamation and the action of punching the air suggest his tension and need to fight as well as his inability to cope, as his bravado in the words 'When he come at me tonight I told him. Didn't I? You heard me tell him, didn't you?' demonstrate.

Unlike spontaneous speech, much of the dialogue is written in full sentences, making it easier for the audience to follow but still maintaining the illusion of naturalistic dialogue. There is some repetition which is more characteristic of prepared speech; for example 'All them Greeks had it, Poles. Greeks, Blacks, the lot of them' and 'All them Blacks had it, Blacks, Greeks, Poles, the lot of them'.

The description of Aston, whose clothes are neat but shabby, contrasts sharply with that of Davies, whose shambling movements and lack of a shirt suggest he is a vagrant. This appearance affects our perception of the dialogue, helping to suggest that Aston is in the dominant position as host but also that Davies may be trying to exploit him. His words 'I'll have a bit of that tobacco for my pipe, if you like' develop this idea further. Davies does not accept what he is given, instead stating what he wants ('I'll have') – innocuous here but developed later on in the play. Aston's pocketing of the keys also helps to introduce the fact, confirmed by the opening words 'Sit down', that he lives in the room they are in.

Read the extract below, which is taken from the opening stages of the play *Waiting for Godot* by Samuel Beckett. Beckett's work influenced Pinter and other later writers.

■ Critical response activity

Discuss the representation of speech in the extract below and show how the dialogue reveals aspects of the characters and their relationships.

Vladimir: One daren't even laugh any more.

Estragon: Dreadful privation.

Vladimir: Merely smile. (*He smiles suddenly from ear to ear, keeps smiling, ceases as suddenly*) It's not the same thing. Nothing to be done. (*He pauses*) Gogo.

Estragon (*irritably*): What is it?

Vladimir: Did you ever read the Bible?

Estragon: The Bible … (*He reflects*) I must have taken a look at it.

Vladimir: Do you remember the Gospels?

Estragon: I remember the maps of the Holy Land. Coloured they were. Very pretty. The Dead Sea was pale blue. The very look of it made me thirsty. That's where we'll go, I used to say, that's where we'll go for our honeymoon. We'll swim. We'll be happy.

Vladimir: You should have been a poet.

Estragon: I was. (*With a gesture towards his rags*) Isn't that obvious.

   (*Silence*)

Vladimir: Where was I … how's your foot?

Estragon: Swelling visibly.

Vladimir: Ah yes, the two thieves. Do you remember the story?

Estragon: No.

Vladimir: Shall I tell it to you?

Estragon: No.

Vladimir: It'll pass the time.

   (*Pause*)

   Two thieves, crucified at the same time as our Saviour. One – – – –

Estragon: Our what?

Vladimir: Our Saviour. Two thieves. One is supposed to have been saved and the other … (*He searches for the contrary of saved*) … damned.

Estragon: Saved from what?

Vladimir: Hell.

Estragon: I'm going. (*He does not move*)

Vladimir: And yet … (*He pauses*) … how is it – – – – this is not boring you I hope – – – – how is it that of the four Evangelists only one speaks of a thief being saved. (*He pauses*) Come on Gogo, return the ball, can't you, once in a way?

Commentary

You will have noticed some features which are similar to the text from *The Caretaker*. Vladimir actually refers to one of the features of spontaneous speech, the adjacency pair, in the metaphor 'Come on Gogo, return the ball, can't you, once in a way?' However, for most of the extract, the characters do respond to one another in chained adjacency pairs that resemble natural speech.

The interruption in the lines:

> Two thieves, crucified at the same time as our Saviour. One – – – –
>
> **Estragon**: Our what?

resembles spontaneous speech but, as in the Pinter extract above, there are few of these.

There is a side sequence, as is common in spontaneous speech, when Vladimir asks 'how's your foot?' The relationship between the two is also brought out by the number of questions Vladimir asks, suggestive of a parent–child relationship.

The stage directions make an important contribution to the effect of the dialogue because of their influence on the production of the play and the delivery of the dialogue. They are a key part of the text for the reader. In the example below, Vladimir's smile appears artificial and tragic-comically exaggerated and brings out the characters' feelings of hopelessness.

> **Vladimir**: Merely smile. (*He smiles suddenly from ear to ear, keeps smiling, ceases as suddenly*) It's not the same thing. Nothing to be done. (*He pauses*) Gogo.

Pauses and silences reflect the situation of the characters who have nowhere particular to go and nothing to do.

The dialogue suggests the relationship between the two characters is close and longstanding but not straightforward. Each appears from the dialogue to meet different needs in the other. Vladimir refers to Estragon as 'Gogo' and Estragon does not object to the name, suggesting it is affectionate rather than derisive. Vladimir dominates the dialogue by introducing topics to a somewhat reluctant Estragon and showing that his need to talk is stronger than his companion's.

Like the Pinter extract, this extract appears to be a spontaneous dialogue but it is in fact carefully constructed to represent a natural conversation, not to mimic it exactly.

The following extract from Peter Shaffer's play *Equus* is part of a session in which a deranged boy, Alan Strang, talks about his first encounter with a horse to his psychiatrist, Martin Dysart. The boy is 17 in the play but here he is relating an experience he had as a child.

■ Critical response activity

Discuss the representation of speech in the extract below and show how the dialogue brings out:

■ its context as part of a therapy session

■ the shift in time from the present to the past

■ the relationship between Alan and Dysart.

Alan [*sullenly*]: On a beach …

(*He steps out of the square, upstage, and begins to walk round the circle. Warm light glows on it*)

Dysart: What?

Alan: Where I saw a horse. Swizzy.

(*Lazily he kicks the sand and throws stones at the sea*)

Dysart: How old were you?

Alan: How should I know? … Six?

Dysart: Well, go on. What were you doing there?

Alan: Digging.

(*He throws himself on the ground, downstage centre of the circle and starts scuffing with his hands*)

Dysart: A sandcastle?

Alan: Well, *what* else?

Dysart [*warningly*]: And?

Alan: Suddenly I heard this noise. Coming up behind me.

(*A young Horseman issues in slow motion out of the tunnel. He carries a riding crop with which he is urging on his invisible horse, down the right side of the circle. The hum increases*)

Dysart: What noise?

Alan: Hooves. Splashing.

Dysart: Splashing?

Alan: The tide was out and he was galloping.

Dysart: Who was?

Alan: This fellow. Like a college chap. He was on a big horse – urging him on. I thought he hadn't seen me. I called out: Hey!

(*The Horseman goes into natural time, charging fast round the downstage corner of the square straight at Alan*)

And they just swerved in time.

Horseman [*reining back*]: Whoa! … Whoa there! *Whoa!* … Sorry! I didn't see you! … Did I scare you?

Alan: No!

Horseman [*looking down on him*]: That's a terrific castle!

Alan: What's his name?

Horseman: Trojan. You can stroke him if you like. He won't mind.

Commentary

As this is a conversation between Dysart, the psychiatrist, and his patient, Alan, it is natural for Dysart to take a lead, which he does by asking questions to prompt Alan's memories. The stage direction 'Lazily he kicks the sand and throws stones at the sea' begins a section of dialogue in which Alan appears to regress to his 6-year-old self. The vocabulary is mixed, with some expressions such as 'urging him on' being appropriate to the 17-year-old Alan and others, such as the simple question 'What's his name?', fitting the recreation of his speech as a 6-year-old. Dysart appears to be in control of the relationship, dealing with Alan's petulant 'Well, what else?' with a warningly spoken 'And?' There is a resistance to this control shown by the way Alan calls Dysart 'Swizzy' as he wants to suggest that Dysart has broken their earlier bargain to answer each other's questions in turn. The dialogue between Alan and Dysart consists of chained adjacency pairs that remain on the topic of Alan's memory of his first meeting with a horse. The conversation between Alan as a 6-year-old and the horseman appears more spontaneous with the non sequitur of 'That's a terrific castle!' followed by 'What's his name?'

The extracts above are taken from plays written in the 20th century. These modern playwrights all use stylised representations of spontaneous speech. We will now look at Shakespeare's representation of speech in an extract taken from Shakespeare's *Othello*, Act 2, Scene 3. Cassio has been involved in a drunken fight that Iago has set up to destroy his reputation. Read it carefully and think about the ways in which speech is represented. This extract is written in prose although much of the dialogue in this play is in verse.

In the extract you will recognise some features of spontaneous speech as well as some of the rhetorical features we discussed when we were looking at prepared speech. In contrast to the extracts from *The Caretaker* and *Waiting for Godot*, there are no stage directions other than 'Exeunt all but Iago and Cassio.'

Critical response activity

1 Carefully identify:
- the ways in which this extract differs from spontaneous speech
- the similarities to spontaneous speech
- the rhetorical features that you can identify and the effects they create.

2 What impression do you gain of the relationship between the two characters?

(*Exeunt all but Iago and Cassio*)

Iago: What, are you hurt, lieutenant?

Cassio: Ay, past all surgery.

Iago: Marry, God forbid.

Cassio: Reputation, reputation, reputation! O, I have lost my reputation, I have lost the immortal part of myself – and what remains is bestial. My reputation, Iago, my reputation!

Iago: As I am an honest man I thought you had received some bodily wound; there is more of sense in that than reputation.

> Reputation is an idle and most false imposition, oft got without merit and lost without deserving. You have lost no reputation at all, unless you repute yourself such a loser. What man, there are ways to recover the general again. You are but now cast in his mood, a punishment more in policy than in malice, even so as one would beat his offenceless dog to affright an imperious lion. Sue to have him again and he's yours.

Commentary

You will have noticed that even though Iago dominates the conversation, the speakers take turns without interrupting each other. Although dramatists do sometimes use overlaps, these can make it difficult for the audience to follow what is going on. There are no fillers and few pauses. Iago's long speech is much more carefully structured and coherent than any utterances would be in a natural conversation. Generally, complete sentences are used. Nevertheless, some features of spontaneous speech are kept. Both speakers address the same topic and the adjacency pairs appear natural. One speaker controls the conversation but he does respond to the words of the other. Direct addresses such as 'What man' contribute to the impression that this is a real conversation.

The most obvious rhetorical device used here is the repetition of 'reputation', which is the theme of the dialogue. Cassio introduces the word with a triplet 'Reputation, reputation, reputation' followed by the repetition of 'I have lost' and further repetition in the last utterance creating a second triplet of 'reputation'. All of this emphasises the extremity of Cassio's despair about his situation. The metaphor of physical wounding 'past all surgery' reinforces this. Iago's reply begins with dramatic irony 'As I am an honest man'. The audience is perfectly aware that he is not.

Iago seeks to manipulate Cassio by making an unsubstantiated assertion, common in persuasive speeches: 'Reputation is an idle and most false imposition.' As the audience is already aware of Iago's duplicity, this creates an immediate understanding that reputation is indeed as valuable as Cassio perceives it to be. It is followed by a series of assertions in which Iago claims that Cassio is not in as much trouble as he thinks he is (and actually is). The speech builds to the imperative urging 'Sue to have him again and he's yours.' Iago is clearly in control of the conversation and the whole situation. His words here set up the element of the plot in which Cassio asks Desdemona to be his intermediary with Othello and Iago uses this to provoke Othello into jealousy. In the play, Iago speaks in both prose and verse, showing a chameleon-like ability to adapt his manner of speaking to match the situation. Here, his prose is bluff, manly and encouraging ('What man, there are ways to recover the general again') but his purpose is actually to deceive.

Poetic techniques

Of the playwrights set for the examination for this unit, only Shakespeare writes in verse so we will be looking at some of the poetic techniques he employs in his plays. In Shakespeare's plays, higher-ranking characters generally speak in verse whereas those of the lower orders and comic characters speak in prose. However, this is a very broad generalisation and you need to be aware of more subtle shifts, even within the speech of a single character. In more domestic, informal or secretive exchanges

Practical activity

Look again at the extracts in the chapters on drama beginning on pp24 and 54. Analyse the features of the dialogue and what is conveyed by it in the same way as you have done for the extracts above.

or when the character's state of mind is disturbed, a shift to prose for a high-ranking character is not uncommon. You need to be alert to the dramatic reasons for such changes. In the speech below, Othello has been convinced of his wife's infidelity. His loss of control is indicated by the fact that he speaks in prose and his words switch abruptly from a violent expression of his desire for vengeance to a description of Desdemona's sweetness showing the immense stress he is under.

> Ay let her rot and perish, and be damned tonight, for she shall not live. No, my heart is turned to stone; I strike it and it hurts my hand. O the world hath not a sweeter creature; she might lie by an emperor's side and command him tasks.

Blank verse

Shakespeare's plays, in common with those of many of his contemporaries and some later dramatists, were written largely in blank verse, intermingled with some prose. Blank verse was originally used in classical Greek and Latin poetry. It was introduced into England in the 1540s and it became the standard verse form of Elizabethan and Jacobean drama. It does not rhyme and is written in **iambic pentameters**, which are discussed below. Most of the verse in Shakespeare's plays is written in this form although there are exceptions such as songs, which usually rhyme, chants such as those used by the witches in their spell-making in *Macbeth* and the **rhyming couplets** that sometimes round off a speech. Iago's soliloquy at the end of Act 1 is completed in this way and it is a good example of how the rhyming couplet can make a powerful impact, in this case conveying Iago's unscrupulous and evil nature:

> I have't. It is engendered. Hell and night
> Must bring this monstrous birth to the world's light.

Iambic pentameters

In English, words with more than one syllable (**polysyllabic words**) have a stress on one of these; for example in the word 'painting' the first syllable 'paint' is stressed. If a word is **monosyllabic**, it will be stressed or not according to its importance and its position within an utterance or verse line.

An iambic pentameter is a line of verse with five stressed syllables and five unstressed ones. To look at the pattern of stresses in a line that creates this rhythm, it is usual to show where the stresses fall as follows:

- Stressed syllables are marked with a forward slash (/).
- Unstressed syllables are marked with a cross (x).

Looking at the following line from *Othello*, you can see this pattern of stressed and unstressed syllables:

> x / x / x / x / x/
> They do discharge their shot of courtesy

If you tap out this rhythm it goes 'de *dum*, de *dum*, de *dum*, de *dum*, de *dum*'. Marking a line of verse in this way is called scansion or scanning.

Key terms

Pentameter: a line of verse containing five feet.

Iambic pentameter: a line of verse with five iambic feet.

Rhyming couplet: two lines of verse in which the words at the ends of each line rhyme.

Polysyllabic words: words with more than one syllable.

Monosyllabic words: words with only one syllable.

💡 Key terms

Feet: units of rhythm consisting of particular patterns of stressed and unstressed syllables.

Iamb: a foot with the rhythm: unstressed/stressed (x /).

End-stopped line: a line of verse with a punctuation mark at the end to indicate a pause.

Enjambement: continuity of the sense and rhythm from one line of verse to the next without end-stopping.

Caesura: a pause in the middle of a line of verse indicated by a punctuation mark.

■ Practical activity

Try writing about 10 lines of a poem or speech in iambic pentameters. When you have finished, read the lines aloud, or ask someone else to do so, to see how well you have succeeded.

Metre

The rhythm of a line of poetry can be measured in this way and the term used to describe it is metre. The metre is built up from the pattern of stresses and it is described in terms of small rhythmic units called **feet**. The original Latin or Greek names for these are still used. The line from Othello above has five feet, each containing an unstressed syllable followed by a stressed one (x /). This is known as an **iamb**.

Enjambement and caesuras

In Shakespeare's earlier plays, the rhythms tended to be much more regular than in later plays such as *Othello*. Many of the lines in the earlier plays were **end-stopped lines**, that is they had a punctuation mark at the end of the line creating a pause at that point. Later on, the ends of lines less frequently corresponded with pauses and the sense continued easily into the next line. This is called **enjambement** and it makes it much easier for an actor to deliver verse which is stylised in a way that can resemble natural speech. Lines of blank verse often have a natural break within them, which is marked by punctuation and very helpful to the actor in speaking the line. This break is called a **caesura**.

In the lines below, Othello is giving orders to stop a brawl:

> He that stirs next to carve for his own rage
> Holds his soul light; he dies upon his motion.
> Silence that dreadful bell; it frights the isle

You can see here that the enjambement of the first line enables the actor to convey both his authority and a threat. The semicolons in the middle of the second and third lines mark the caesuras. They give an opportunity for the actor to pause and look at each of the combatants and then to issue general orders to his attendants. The speech sounds measured and controlled, in sharp contrast to the chaotic fight which he stops. However, in the speech below the frequent end-stopping, pauses and side-sequences show his mental disintegration:

> Proceed you in your tears, –
> Concerning this sir – – O, well-painted passion – –
> I am commanded home. – Get you away;
> I'll send for you anon.

Shared lines

Often, lines of verse are shared between two, or occasionally more, characters helping to create an illusion of a more natural conversation. For example, in the speech below where Iago seeks to encourage Othello's suspicions, the shared lines bring out both Othello's reaction, and the way in which Iago immediately capitalises on it, in a manner which resembles spontaneous speech. The words 'did' and 'why' overlap, showing Iago's urgency.

> *Iago*: She did deceive her father marrying you;
> And when she seemed to shake, and fear your looks,
> She loved them most.
>
> *Othello*: And so she did
>
> *Iago*: Why, go to then:
> She that so young could give out such a seeming,

Sentences

Although blank verse (and indeed any verse) is written in lines, it is also written in sentences. In order to understand what the speaker is saying, you need to follow the sentence structure carefully even though the structure of the lines of verse may cut across it. Many of the sentences in Shakespeare's verse are very complex with a number of **subordinate clauses** and **phrases** and it is easy to lose track of the meaning if you do not follow them carefully.

The language of Shakespeare's poetry

Imagery

The imagery Shakespeare uses in his poetry is often highly charged and it makes a great contribution to the dramatic impact of his verse. For example, Iago's metaphors of the ewe and the ram near the opening of the play are used to incense Brabantio by giving an animalistic and racist view of Othello. The intensifier 'old' is also intended to increase Brabantio's disgust:

> Even now, now, very now, an old black ram
> Is tupping your white ewe.

Equally effective is the kind of literal imagery used by Othello when he stops a potential brawl in Act 1, Scene 2:

> Keep up your bright swords for the dew will rust them.

Shakespeare makes use of a wealth of metaphors and similes and often uses personification to great effect. Remember, however, that when you are writing about these rhetorical features you must do more than just identify them; you need to focus on what they contribute to the drama.

Antithesis

In both the quotations above, antithesis is used to present a contrast. As in prepared speech this device is very useful in the presentation of contrasts and conflicts and Shakespeare uses it frequently. Emilia's words after Othello has killed Desdemona express her outrage at what he has done and her desire to make him understand the truth:

> O the more angel she,
> And you the blacker devil.

Patterns of language

Poetry gains much of its characteristic nature from the patterns within it. The rhetorical techniques that we looked at when considering prepared speech are also used in dramatic texts and in poetry. Consider Mark Antony's famous speech in Julius Caesar:

> Friends, Romans, countrymen, lend me your ears;
> I come to bury Caesar, not to praise him
> The evil that men do lives after them;
> The good is oft interred within their bones

💡 Key terms

Subordinate clause: this depends on the main clause, e.g. in the sentence 'I went to a salesroom where I saw a great sports car', the clause 'where I saw a great sports car' cannot stand alone.

Main clause: a part of a sentence that is grammatically independent and may exist alone or alongside a subordinate clause.

Phrase: in the hierarchy of grammatical units, the phrase comes between word and clause. There are five types of phrase:
Noun phrase (e.g. *the red dress*)
Verb phrase (e.g. *will be running*)
Adjective phrase (e.g. *nice hot lovely*)
Adverb phrase (e.g. *quite inexcusably*)
Prepositional phrase (e.g. *wherever*)

 Examiner's tip

A surprising number of candidates describe verse extracts as prose and vice versa. Remember that Shakespeare often uses some prose sections within his plays as well as blank verse. When you are writing about an extract, it is important to identify accurately whether it is written in prose or verse.

■ Link

Remind yourself of the information on imagery on p13 and of the discussion of rhetoric in the chapter on prepared speech on p102.

Of course, the context of this speech is actually political; Mark Antony seeks to persuade his audience towards his point of view about the murder of Caesar. You will have noticed the opening triplet 'Friends, Romans, countrymen' and the antitheses that follow. You will also have recognised the parallel phrasing of 'the evil' and 'the good'.

Lists

Shakespeare often builds up a vivid picture by writing detailed lists. For example, Othello speaks of how he told Desdemona's father about his past adventures giving a strong impression of the exciting and dangerous life he has led:

> Of moving accidents by flood and field
> Of hair-breadth scapes i' the imminent deadly breach,
> Of being taken by the insolent foe,
> And sold to slavery; of my redemption hence

Desdemona, hearing this, becomes strongly attracted to Othello. You will also have recognised the way the repetition of words and structures helps to link all these literal images together here.

Patterns of sound

Patterns can also be created by repetition of sounds. **Alliteration** links words by repeating the initial consonants. **Assonance** is the repetition of vowel sounds and **consonance** the repetition of consonant sounds other than at the beginnings of words. **Onomatopoeia** is the use of words that sound like what they describe.

In the play *Antony and Cleopatra*, Enobarbus's description of Mark Antony's first meeting with Cleopatra illustrates Shakespeare's use of sound very effectively:

> The barge she sat in, like a burnished throne
> Burn'd on the water: the poop was beaten gold;
> Purple the sails, and so perfumed that the winds were love-sick with them; the oars were silver
> Which to the tune of flutes kept stroke, and made
> The water which they beat to follow faster
> As amorous of their strokes.

The alliterated words 'barge', 'burnished', 'burn'd' and 'beaten' all focus attention on the magnificence of the vessel. The word 'burn'd' is stressed – normally an iambic line begins with an unstressed syllable or word. All the alliterated syllables are stressed, giving a rhythm that echoes the stroke of the oars. The consonance of the repeated 's' sounds helps to create an atmosphere of sensuality. The consonant 's' is often used in this way and the term **sibilance** is applied to this.

Read the extract below, which is taken from Act 3, Scene 3 of *Othello*. It deals with the same theme – reputation – which we considered in the earlier extract. It also looks at the theme of jealousy and provides further insights into Iago's character. This time, however, Iago is given verse.

Key terms

Alliteration: the repetition of an initial consonant sound.

Assonance: repeated vowel sounds.

Consonance: repeated patterns of consonants.

Onomatopoeia: the use of words that sound like what they mean, e.g. quack, hiss.

Sibilance: repeated use of the consonant 's'.

> ***Iago***:   I do beseech you,
> Though I perchance am vicious in my guess –
> As I confess it is my nature's plague
> To spy into abuses, and oft my jealousy
> Shapes faults that are not – that your wisdom,
> From one that so imperfectly conceits,
> Would take no notice, nor build yourself a trouble
> Out of his scattering and unsure observance.
> It were not for your quiet nor your good,
> Nor for my manhood, honesty, wisdom,
> To let you know my thoughts.
>
> ***Othello***:   What dost thou mean?
>
> ***Iago***: Good name in man and woman, dear my lord
> Is the immediate jewel of their souls.
> Who steals my purse, steals trash; 'tis something, nothing;
> 'Twas mine, 'tis his, and has been slave to thousands;
> But he that filches from me my good name
> Robs me of that which not enriches him,
> And makes me poor indeed.
>
> ***Othello***:   By heaven, I'll know thy thoughts.
>
> ***Iago***: You cannot, if my heart were in your hand,
> Nor shall not, whilst 'tis in my custody.
>
> ***Othello***: Ha!
>
> ***Iago***: O beware my lord of jealousy;
> It is the green-eyed monster which doth mock
> The meat it feeds on. That cuckold lives in bliss
> Who certain of his fate loves not his wronger,
> But O, what damned minutes tells he o'er
> Who dotes, yet doubts, suspects, yet fondly loves.
>
> ***Othello***: O misery!

Commentary

Iago dominates the dialogue much as he did in the earlier exchange with Cassio and Othello can only react. Iago is pretending to be reluctant to talk of his suspicions about Desdemona and Cassio where really he is inventing them for his own ends and therefore needs to encourage Othello to listen. The show of reluctance will make Othello more inclined to believe him. Iago's speech is in verse and it is very convoluted. It begins simply 'I do beseech you', which could easily be a natural speech utterance but moves on into a self-deprecating acknowledgement of his own interest in spying (with a **subtext** that he is good at it). His suggestion that Othello should take no notice of him is highly ironic. The second part of this speech contains a trio of repeated negative phrases and clauses and is followed by a second: 'manhood, honesty, wisdom'.

> It were not for your quiet nor your good,
> Nor for my manhood, honesty, wisdom,
> To let you know my thoughts.

Key terms

Subtext: the meaning beneath the surface of the spoken or written dialogue.

These work persuasively, as in a prepared speech, to reinforce the idea of Iago's reluctance where ironically he seeks the opposite of what he says.

Not surprisingly, Othello is confused by this speech and his question 'What dost thou mean?' is no different from one that might occur in spontaneous speech. Iago's answer is firmly on the theme of reputation. A number of rhetorical techniques are used to show the enormous value he claims to place on a good reputation. This contrasts sharply with the views he expressed to Cassio in the earlier extract we looked at. He uses the metaphor of the jewel to show the worth of reputation and demeans the value of money by speaking metaphorically of his purse as 'slave to thousands'. Antithesis is used to compare the loss of a purse, which is trivial, to the loss of reputation, which is truly impoverishing. The stress on the word 'Robs', which breaks the iambic pattern, emphasises the value Iago claims to put on reputation. Indeed, the guiltless loss of her reputation costs Desdemona her life.

The exchanges that follow are more similar to spontaneous speech:

> *Othello*:   By heaven, I'll know thy thoughts.
>
> *Iago*: You cannot, if my heart were in your hand,
> Nor shall not, whilst 'tis in my custody.
>
> *Othello*: Ha!

Turn-taking is suggested by the shared lines. Nevertheless, the alliteration of 'heart' and 'hand' gives Iago's words an intensity that would be unlikely in natural speech. However, Shakespeare maintains the illusion of natural conversation in these exchanges in verse. Othello's exclamation 'Ha!' suggests how exasperated and suspicious he is becoming.

In Iago's next speech, he ironically warns Othello to beware of jealousy, famously described with the metaphor of the 'green-eyed monster'. He goes on to contrast the contentment of the ignorant cuckold with the suffering of one who is aware of his wife's betrayal. A pattern of contrasts is used to show the plight of the latter:

> Who dotes, yet doubts, suspects, yet fondly loves.

Of course, the audience is aware that Iago's intention is to destroy Desdemona's reputation and to inflame Othello into a destructive fit of jealousy in order to gain his revenge. Shakespeare uses dramatic irony to very good effect in these exchanges, further developing the audience's awareness of Iago's clever, manipulative, devious and vindictive character.

💡 Other dramatic techniques

Structure

In the examination you are required to select an episode to use, in conjunction with an extract printed on the examination paper, to explore the central aspect of the question. This might, for example, focus on a theme or the development of a character. If you select this episode from a different stage of the play to the printed extract, you will be able to discuss how the structure of the play contributes to the playwright's exploration of this aspect.

Conflict

The extracts you are given and the episodes you might choose are likely to show conflict or tensions between the characters or perhaps the resolution of these. This is an essential part of the dramatic process. In the dialogue, just as in spontaneous speech, you may see patterns of dominance arising.

Suspense

For an audience, a significant factor in maintaining interest is the creation of suspense. The audience does not know, for example, what will happen to Aston and Davies in *The Caretaker*, or whether Godot will ever arrive in *Waiting for Godot*, or why Alan blinded six horses in *Equus*. Dramatic irony is often used to increase suspense; for example, in *Othello* the audience's awareness of Iago's plotting creates great suspense about what will happen to Desdemona.

Monologues, soliloquies and asides

In Chapter 3 on character in Unit 1, we looked at how monologues, soliloquies and asides can reveal character. These devices enable the dramatist to reveal the views actually held by the speaker and are therefore powerful tools in both the characterisation and the development of themes. Choosing an episode that includes an example of one of these features could offer you an opportunity to explore a different way of dramatising the area you are discussing.

Mood and atmosphere

The words spoken by the characters, whether as part of a dialogue or alone, contribute to the creation of a **mood** or **atmosphere**. In *Waiting for Godot*, the prevailing mood is of powerlessness. In *Othello*, after Desdemona's death, a mood of intense anger in the exchange between Emilia and Othello changes to remorse when he realises that he has killed his innocent wife.

Plot

The plot is also a key element of any drama. Whether it contains events such as murder and suicide or deals with less extreme events, the plot is of central interest to the audience. However, when you are discussing contributions to the plot you must be careful to avoid merely retelling the story. For example, Iago's deliberate destruction of Desdemona's reputation leads to Othello's jealous rage and, ultimately, to Desdemona's death so you might include some reference to the plot in a discussion of the theme of reputation but you must not simply retell the story.

Stage directions

In many of the modern texts you have looked at, stage directions are detailed and include very specific descriptions of the setting and of the actions the actors should make. In your discussion of the topic specified in the examination you will be able to explore the dramatic contribution which is intended to be made by the stage directions.

The works of Shakespeare and other dramatists of his time were often not published before they were performed. There are few stage directions in Shakespeare's plays and *Othello* is no exception. Nevertheless, the text itself contains indications of how the words should be spoken and can paint a picture of the setting.

▪ Link

Remind yourself of the chapter on dramatic structure on p26.

▪ Link

Remind yourself of the chapter on character on p15.

💡 Key terms

Mood: 1. (grammar) the function expressed by the verb form to create indicative sentences (for example, 'He is speaking'), imperative sentences ('Tell us what you think'), interrogative sentences ('What is your opinion?') and exclamatory sentences ('Be quiet!'). 2. used interchangeably with the term 'atmosphere' to describe the characteristic feeling conveyed by a literary work, as created by the author's choice of setting, action, characterisation and language.

Atmosphere: the characteristic mood or feeling conveyed by a literary work, as created by the author's choices of setting, action, characterisation and language.

▪ Link

Look again at the comments on stage directions on p54.

Preparing for the examination

For the Unit 2 set text question in the examination, the question 'will focus on speech representation and stylistic and linguistic issues within the set text, with a short section of the text printed to provide a basis for close analysis'.

This question is worth 30 out of the 75 marks available in the examination, split between Assessment Objectives 1 and 2.

▓ For AO1, you will need to show your ability to choose relevant linguistic and literary concepts and terminology to help you analyse and write about your chosen text. The accuracy of your own written expression will also be assessed. *(15 marks)*

▓ For AO2, you will need to show in detail that you understand and can analyse the ways in which structure, form and language shape your chosen writer's meaning. *(15 marks)*

You are advised to spend approximately 40 minutes on this question. This is not much time for the task so you need to be well organised and take care not to overrun on the time you spend on Section A.

In answering this question you will be using the knowledge and terminology you have acquired during the whole of your study of AS-level English Language and Literature. To be successful you need to remember the following:

▓ Make sure you have a really thorough knowledge of your set text. You are not allowed to take your text into the examination with you so you need to know it well enough to be able to select a relevant extract quickly and to quote from it to illustrate the points you want to make. These quotations do not need to be lengthy.

▓ Use the extract that is printed on the page to make a close analysis of the ways dialogue is used and refer in detail to the other episode you have chosen from your set text.

▓ Include specific examples from both extracts to illustrate your points.

▓ Revise the terminology you have learned for all the parts of your AS-level English course so that you can use it comfortably in your analysis. Remember to discuss what effects are created by the use of this terminology and to avoid simply 'feature spotting'.

▓ Avoid the temptation to start writing straight away. Allow yourself a few minutes to think and plan. Do not forget to mark the key words in the question.

▓ For this question, you are required to select an episode from the set text to use in conjunction with the extract printed on the examination paper. You need to choose your extract carefully so that it is appropriate to the requirements of the question. More guidance on this is given below.

▓ Think carefully about the approach you are going to take in answering the question. Some advice on this is given below.

▓ **Link**

Look at the glossary at the end of this book. This can provide a useful list of key terminology to revise.

The examination question

The kinds of question you will be asked will follow a pattern. Look at the specimen questions that are available on the AQA website and you will find that they all have a similar structure. There are also some sample questions on pp154–60 of this book.

The questions for both genres are similar. In each case, you are required to look at how the author uses dialogue to achieve a particular aim, such as exploring character, relationships, themes or other issues. For the novel, you are asked to consider how other stylistic effects contribute to fulfilling this aim whereas if your set text is a play, you have to discuss the dramatic techniques. The second part of the question asks you to look at the printed extract and **one** other episode.

Selecting an appropriate episode

For this question, you will be asked to discuss the extract from your set text which is printed on the examination paper and an episode of your own choice. You should select this episode carefully, ensuring that it will help you to answer the question.

When you read the printed extract, it is useful to place it in its context in the novel or play. If, for example, you are given an extract from early in the set text, it might be useful to choose a later episode so that you can show how the particular aspect you are exploring develops.

To enable you to choose a suitable episode, you need to know your text thoroughly. When you are studying it you will learn about the themes, characters, relationships and other issues with which it is concerned and you should make a note of any extracts that would be particularly useful in discussing each of these as you progress through the text. In your revision, you can then focus on these extracts and learn some short quotations from each of them.

You will find it helpful if you can identify before the examination some episodes that you could use to discuss several different aspects of the text. For example, the extracts you have already looked at from *Othello* could be used to discuss both the theme of reputation and Iago's character.

If you were given the first of these extracts in the examination paper and you were asked to explore the treatment of the theme of reputation, the second extract would be a very good one to use as not only is it concerned with the theme but it is also in verse, in contrast to the first episode, giving you a chance to discuss a wider range of techniques. If your set text is a novel and, for example, you are asked to explore how a character is revealed, you could choose an extract in which understanding of the character is developed through narrative rather than dialogue.

Structuring your answer

The first thing to remember when you are planning your answer is that you are being asked to write about the extract printed on the examination paper and **one** other episode. You must give equal weight to both of these in your answer.

AQA Examiner's tip

Candidates often disadvantage themselves by failing to carry out the instructions given in the question. If you focus almost exclusively on the printed text you will seriously limit the success of your answer, as you will if you neglect the given extract and only discuss the episode of your choice. It is also surprising how many candidates choose to write about more than the material that is specified in the question.

Link

It is useful to look at the marking grid provided for examiners, which is available on the AQA website.

Practical activity

Look again at the two extracts from *Othello* which are concerned with the theme of reputation. You will find them on pp141–2 and p147. This will help you to see that selecting a verse extract as your choice of episode for this question would give you the opportunity to comment on the representation of speech in verse as well as prose.

Practical activity

List the main themes, characters, relationships and other issues from your set text. Identify suitable episodes that you could use to illustrate them. Learn some appropriate quotations and test yourself on them.

AQA Examiner's tip

All too often candidates write about the printed extract and only remember to add on a bit about the other episode at the end of their answers. Some candidates do the opposite and virtually ignore the printed extract. Each of these approaches will mean that you cannot achieve high marks.

The printed extract is there to 'provide a basis for close analysis'. You should use it to comment in detail on the dialogue and any other relevant features, illustrating your answer with suitable quotations. These should be no longer than is necessary to support your points. Your comments on the second extract should bring out clearly how it too contributes to the development of the aspect of the text specified in the question. If you can quote from it to substantiate your points, you will make your writing more authoritative.

There are two main ways in which you might structure your answer. The first is to analyse the printed extract and then to move on to a discussion of your chosen episode. If you do this, you must ensure that both parts of your answer address the question clearly. It is important to give equal weight to both sections; one of the dangers with this approach is overrunning on your commentary on the printed extract leaving you too little time to write about the other episode.

A more sophisticated way of structuring your answer is to write about both pieces of text together using material from each of them to illustrate your points. The best candidates are likely to use this approach as it allows comparisons and contrasts to be made, avoids repetition and helps to ensure an even weighting of the two episodes is maintained.

A suggested framework for comparing the extracts

1   As with all examination questions, you should highlight the key words in the question. As all of the questions for this section of the examination follow a common structure and focus on the use of dialogue and other stylistic or dramatic techniques, you are only really looking for the aspect of the text you are being asked to explore. The key words in the question below have been highlighted for you as an example.

   Othello: **William Shakespeare**

   How does Shakespeare use dialogue and other dramatic techniques to explore the theme of reputation?

   In your answer you should refer closely to the extract printed below and to *one* other episode in the play.

2   Read the printed extract carefully and consider what points you can illustrate using it. Choose an episode that you think will expand or complement the points you want to make. You might find it useful to use a pattern note to plan your answer as you can easily note down your points quickly as you think of them and then go on to organise them. Placing the main topic in a central circle will help to keep your mind focused on it. This question focuses on the two episodes discussed on pp141–2 and p147, taking the verse extract as an example of an episode of your own choice. This extract could be used to answer questions on a number of different aspects so you need to be careful to remain focused on 'reputation'.

   Decide whether you are going to discuss the extract first followed by the episode you have chosen or whether you are going to take an integrated approach.

3   Discuss the use of dialogue, bringing out clearly how it contributes to the exploration of the aspect of the text you have been asked to explore. It is important to remember that you must not simply 'feature spot' (for example, 'Pinter uses a filler here' or 'Shakespeare uses a metaphor') without further comment. Instead, you must explore the significance of relevant features that you decide to comment on. What do the fillers suggest about the speaker? What

Given extract (Iago with Cassio)

Spontaneous speech features
Yes
- Adjacency pairs
- Direct address – 'What man'
- Same topic
No
- Fillers
- Complete sentences
- Careful structure

Prepared speech features
- Triplets
- Repetition
- Metaphors
- Dramatic irony
- Assertions

Other dramatic aspects
- Dominance
- Tensions
- Suspense
- Mood
- Stage action implied – Iago apparently solicitous

Reputation
- Value of reputation
- Effect on Cassio
- Effect on Othello
- Importance to the plot

Own episode (Iago with Othello)

Spontaneous speech features
Yes
- Turn-taking
- Exclamations
No
- Fillers, hesitations
- In verse

Prepared speech features
- Triplets
- Repetition

Verse features
- Metaphors
- Antithesis
- Metrical effects

Other dramatic techniques
- Dominance
- Tensions
- Suspense
- Mood
- Little indication of stage action

Fig. 1 *Comparing the extracts*

effects does Shakespeare achieve by using this metaphor or this sequence of metaphors? If you are using an integrated approach, you will need to take examples from both texts.

4 Discuss the other stylistic or dramatic techniques used. Again, you must relate your comments firmly to the central issue that you are discussing.

5 Provide a brief conclusion summing up your argument. If you run short of time, do not worry if you need to leave out this conclusion; you will gain most credit for the points you make in the main body of your answer.

☑ Sample questions and answers

Here are examples of the sorts of questions you will find in the examination. Other specimen questions for all the set texts are available on the AQA website.

Read Questions 1 and 2 below and the sample responses and examiner's comments that follow. Try writing a complete answer to the question on your set text.

Note that the extracts for Questions 3 to 8 have not been included here owing to space restrictions, although page and chapter references are given to help you locate the appropriate extracts. However, in the examination the extract will be included in the examination paper, as you will not have your copy of the text with you.

1   *Enduring Love*: Ian McEwan

How does McEwan use dialogue and other stylistic techniques to explore the theme of love?

In your answer you should refer closely to the extract printed below and to **one** other episode in the novel.

'You're very cruel,' he said. 'But you've got all the power.' He inhaled deeply through his nose again, as though preparing himself for some difficult circus feat. He managed to look at me as he said simply, 'You love me. You love me, and there's nothing I can do but return your love.'

I said nothing. Parry drew another deep breath. 'I don't know why you've chosen me. All I know is that I love you too now, and that there's a reason for it, a purpose.'

An ambulance with a whooping siren went by and we had to wait. I was wondering how to respond, and whether a show of anger might see him off, but in the few seconds that it took for the din to recede I decided to be firm and reasonable. 'Look, Mr Parry … '

'Jed,' he said urgently. 'It's Jed.' His interrogative style had deserted him.

I said, 'I don't know you, I don't know where you live, or what you do, or who you are. I don't particularly want to know either. I've met you once before and I can tell you now that I have no feelings for you either way … '

Parry was speaking over me in a series of gasps. He was pushing his hands out before him, as though to repel my words. 'Please don't do this … It doesn't have to be this way, honestly. You don't have to do this to me.'

We both paused suddenly. I wondered whether to leave him now and walk up the road to find a taxi. Perhaps talking was making matters worse.

Parry crossed his arms and adopted a worldly, man-to-man tone. I thought perhaps I was being parodied. 'Look. You don't have to go about it like this. You could save us both so much misery.'

I said, 'You were following me yesterday, weren't you?'

He looked away and said nothing which I took as confirmation.

'What possible reason would you have for thinking I love you?' I tried to make the question sound sincere, and not merely rhetorical. I was quite interested to know, although I also wanted to get away.

'Don't,' Parry said through a whisper. 'Please don't.' His lower lip was trembling.

Sample response

This extract shows us the strange one-sided love affair between Jed Parry and the narrator, Joe. Ian McEwan uses dialogue and a variety of stylistic techniques to explore the theme of love effectively in this extract, as well as in the part of the book when Clarissa returns home after spending the evening with her brother and Joe has been at home worrying about Jed Parry.

One of the features of spontaneous speech in the extract is that Jed interrupts Joe; for example, when Joe says 'Look, Mr Parry ... ' Jed was 'speaking over' Joe. These interruptions show how passionate Jed is about Joe. Jed also pauses in his speech, shown with the ellipsis in 'Please don't do this ... ', showing that he is upset and pausing to control his emotions and think about what to say next. In terms of adjacency pairs, both Jed and Joe refuse to respond to each other in places. Joe asks questions like 'You were following me yesterday, weren't you?' to try to take control of the conversation and change the subject a bit. Jed just speaks in statements such as 'All I know is that I love you too now, and that there's a reason for it, a purpose', leaving it open for Joe to respond.

In his language choices Jed often uses clichés to do with love, such as 'It doesn't have to be this way'. His behaviour is typical of someone in love, such as finding it difficult to look at Joe, whispering, speaking urgently and 'his lower lip was trembling'. This maybe shows that Jed is acting a part. Joe's utterances are the opposite of Jed's – he speaks in a formal register such as calling him 'Mr Parry' and 'What possible reason would you have for thinking I love you?' This shows that he does not love Jed at all and is confused by what is happening. Both Jed and Joe use repetition in their speech. Jed repeats 'You love me, you love me' to really emphasise what he is saying. Joe repeats 'I don't know you, I don't know where you live, or what you do, or who you are' to try to emphasise how he does not have any feelings for Jed.

One of the stylistic techniques Ian McEwan uses is he includes similes. For example, he describes Jed breathing 'as though preparing himself for some difficult circus feat'. Another interesting image is the ambulance with a 'whooping siren' going by. This adds to the impression that this is a dramatic moment and a crisis point. It also might suggest that there is something unhealthy about what is going on, as ambulances take away people who are sick. Perhaps it is suggesting that Jed is sick as he is imagining that Joe loves him.

The other episode I am going to look at is the scene when Clarissa returns home to find Joe worrying about Jed. Clarissa has been out to dinner with her brother who is getting divorced, which is a contrast to how much Joe and Clarissa love each other. The genuine love between Joe and Clarissa is in complete contrast to the weird fantasy relationship that Jed thinks he is having with Joe. In the scene I have chosen, Clarissa tells Joe how much she loves him. Although this is a bit similar to Jed telling Joe how much he loves him, it is much more genuine as Clarissa and Joe have been together for years. Clarissa and Joe finish off each other's sentences, showing how close they are. They stand in Joe's study kissing, which is an image of their intimacy and love.

In conclusion, Ian McEwan explores love in different ways, contrasting the genuine loving relationship between Joe and Clarissa compared to Jed's feelings for Joe, which cannot be genuine as they have sprung up only after the brief encounter between them in Chapter 1 when they both try to rescue the boy in the balloon.

Examiner's comments

This response has mixed success. The essay is clearly structured and organised using a relevant framework. The introduction, however, does little more than repeat the question, and although the candidate's choice of second episode is identified, no real connection is made at this point. The candidate focuses quite closely on the extract given but comments only briefly on the second episode, giving broad general comments. The choice of episode is relevant and a connection to the printed extract is eventually made. However, both extracts come from the early chapters of the novel, meaning that the candidate reveals only limited knowledge of the text.

For AO1, the candidate describes some significant features and uses a reasonable range of terms, referring both to features of dialogue and a couple of other stylistic techniques. There is clearly some engagement with the text printed in the examination paper and some explanation of features. However, this response is also underdeveloped in places; for example, a simile is identified but no analysis is offered. The essay is written in a clear and appropriate, if relatively unsophisticated, style.

For AO2, the candidate responds with some confidence and comments on some distinguishing features. However, they have concentrated on one text at the expense of the second episode.

2   *Othello*: **William Shakespeare**

How does Shakespeare use dialogue and other dramatic techniques to present the relationship between Othello and Iago?

In your answer you should refer closely to the extract printed below and to **one** other episode in the play.

Othello: How shall I murder him, Iago?

Iago: Did you perceive how he laughed at his vice?

Othello: O Iago!

Iago: And did you see the handkerchief?

Othello: Was that mine?

Iago: Yours, by this hand: and to see how he prizes the foolish woman your wife! She gave it to him and he hath given it his whore.

Othello: I would have him nine years a-killing. A fine woman, a fair woman, a sweet woman.

Iago: Nay, you must forget that.

Othello: Ay, let her rot and perish and be damned tonight, for she shall not live. No, my heart is turned to stone: I strike it and it hurts my hand. O, the world hath not a sweeter creature: she might lie by an emperor's side and command him tasks.

Iago: Nay, that's not your way.

Othello: Hang her, I do but say what she is: so delicate with her needle, an admirable musician. O, she will sing the savageness out of a bear! Of so high and plenteous wit and invention!

Iago: She's the worse for all this.

Othello: O, a thousand, a thousand times: and then of so gentle a condition.

> *Iago*: ... Ay, too gentle.
>
> *Othello*: Nay, that's certain. But yet the pity of it, Iago – O, Iago, the pity of it, Iago!
>
> *Iago*: If you are so fond over her iniquity, give her patent to offend, for if it touch not you it comes near nobody.
>
> *Othello*: I will chop her into messes! Cuckold me!
>
> *Iago*: O, 'tis foul in her.
>
> *Othello*: ... With mine officer!
>
> *Iago*: That's fouler.
>
> *Othello*: Get me some poison, Iago, this night. I'll not expostulate with her, lest her body and beauty unprovide my mind again. This night, Iago.
>
> *Iago*: Do it not with poison, strangle her in her bed – even the bed she hath contaminated.

Sample response

Shakespeare presents the relationship between Othello and Iago in the play as a complex one. Othello is an exceptionally capable general who, perhaps because of the racial slurs he has to endure, is easily manipulated by Iago. Iago seeks an appalling revenge, both for being overlooked for promotion and for the mere possibility that Othello has cuckolded him. In addition to the printed extract, I am going to look at the last part of Iago's exchanges with Roderigo at the end of Act 1, including Iago's soliloquy which is spoken immediately after Roderigo's exit.

Dramatic irony is a major tool in Shakespeare's presentation of the relationship. The audience is aware of Iago's resentment towards Othello from the beginning of the play and of how he disguises it. In the extract, Iago reminds Othello about the handkerchief, which was originally Othello's gift to his wife, to infuriate him. The audience, and Othello, have just witnessed Iago's stage management of an incident in which Cassio appears to have been given this handkerchief by Desdemona. Iago manipulates the dialogue with particular skill to systematically increase Othello's anger. In the dialogue with Roderigo, and in his soliloquy from Act 1, Iago reveals his feelings towards Othello and one of his motives for revenge, with a clarity which the audience cannot miss:

> I hate the Moor,
>
> And it is thought abroad that twixt my sheets
>
> He's done my office.

In the printed extract, Iago dominates the dialogue even though Othello generally has the longer utterances. The way in which Iago has gained dominance in the relationship is shown when Othello asks for instructions: 'How shall I murder him, Iago?' and again at the end of the extract when his plan to poison Desdemona is overruled by Iago's imperative 'Do it not with poison'. In the episode with Roderigo, Iago overwhelms him with lists of insistent imperative clauses such as 'Put money in thy purse'.

Throughout the extract, there is a tension between Othello's love for his wife and his jealous anger which Iago continually reinforces. Iago only needs to make short suggestions to change the tack of Othello's thoughts. For example, when Othello begins to think of his wife's attributes – 'A fine woman, a fair woman, a sweet woman' – Iago counters immediately, bringing Othello back to thoughts of murder. 'Ay, let her rot and perish and be damned tonight, for she shall not live.' This pattern is followed throughout the dialogue with Othello softening and Iago bringing him back with short utterances. The pattern of antithetical triplets that Shakespeare uses in the examples above shows these rapid mood shifts very clearly.

In the exchanges with Roderigo, Iago dominates by sheer volume of words so that the episode only falls into a typical conversational pattern as he is about to leave. Iago seeks to make money out of his dupe, Roderigo, so the outcome he desires ('Put money in thy purse') is repeated frequently, as are references to 'the Moor' which bring out a racial aspect to his feelings about Othello.

In the extract, Iago answers Othello's first question with a second, breaking the usual pattern of adjacency pairs. However, as the dialogue continues, Iago's comments always relate closely to Othello's words in a stylised version of the adjacency pairs that would be found in spontaneous speech. There are no overlaps or interruptions: Iago waits for Othello to complete each thought before either reinforcing it, if it suits his murderous purpose, or contradicting it.

The dialogue in the extract is entirely in prose, unusual for a character of Othello's rank and therefore indicating his loss of self-command. In contrast, Iago's soliloquy is in measured verse and it brings out the clarity with which he works out the precise track his revenge will take. He shows a clear understanding of Othello's nature, viewing his admirable qualities only in terms of the ways in which they will make him easy to deceive:

> The Moor is of a free and open nature
>
> And thinks men honest that but seem to be so
>
> And will as tenderly be led by the nose
>
> As asses are.

The simple simile of the 'asses' brings out Iago's obvious contempt for Othello. In contrast, although Othello speaks in prose, the sustained metaphor, 'My heart is turned to stone: I strike it and it hurts my hand', reveals his terrible tension. The vivid image of striking the heart with the hand suggests the extremity of his emotion. The contrasting lexis when he describes Desdemona shows how she matches the ideal of womanly virtue: 'delicate, admirable musician, gentle'. The semantic field of death that begins this speech expresses Othello's desire that Desdemona should be both physically destroyed and damned, bringing out the extent to which Iago's manipulations have caused obsessive jealousy to cloud his reason.

In comparison to the powerful images contained in Othello's prose extracts, Iago's soliloquy, though in blank verse, is generally very plain with the exception of the culminating rhyming couplet that sums up Iago's self satisfaction and evil intentions:

> I have't. It is engendered. Hell and night
>
> Must bring this monstrous birth to the world's light.

The pauses, the sinister metaphor of the monstrous birth with 'Hell and night' as midwives and the antithesis of the rhymed 'night' and 'light' all serve to show the depths of Iago's evil purposes towards Othello.

So, from the beginning of the play, Shakespeare presents us with a relationship based on deception. For all his fine qualities Othello is easily deceived and Iago, for motives that do not entirely seem to match the extremity of his revenge, finds it easy to take advantage of him. For the audience, the prevailing use of dramatic irony leads to a painful awareness of the ways in which Iago leads Othello 'by the nose', thus heightening and maintaining the dramatic tension throughout the play.

Examiner's comments

This is a very successful response. The candidate has structured the essay carefully using an integrated approach with close reference to both the printed extract and the chosen episode. The episode is well selected, allowing the candidate to comment both on Iago's designs and on their effects. Contrasting styles of dialogue are made available for comment by this choice. The candidate uses both the extract and the episode to make some detailed points about the dialogue and makes well-substantiated comments about a range of dramatic techniques. The extracts are well contextualised and the candidate shows a strong grasp of the play as a whole.

For AO1, the candidate shows a clear overview of the text and engages closely with its meaning. The writing is fluent and cohesive. A range of significant features is explored with appropriate illustration from both the extract and the episode. Terminology is used accurately and effectively showing close engagement with meaning.

For AO2, the candidate shows a strong sense of overview, being able to integrate comments on extracts from two widely separated extracts from the text with considerable success. There is a close focus on detail with a very evident grasp of the text. A clear awareness of textual structure is shown. The candidate shows a good understanding of features of speech.

Sample questions from other texts

1 *Great Expectations:* **Charles Dickens**

   How does Dickens use dialogue and other stylistic techniques to present class differences between his characters?

   In your answer you should refer closely to the extract printed below and to **one** other episode in the novel.

   (For the extract, refer to pages 202–3 in the Penguin Popular Classics edition. The extract begins 'Joe, how are you, Joe?' and ends 'Still more, when his mourning 'at is unfortunately made so small as that the weight of the black feathers brings it off, try to keep it on how you may.')

2 *The Lovely Bones:* **Alice Sebold**

   How does Sebold use dialogue and other stylistic techniques to present the relationship between Susie and Ray?

   In your answer you should refer closely to the extract printed below and to **one** other episode in the novel.

   (For the extract, refer to page 74 in the Picador paperback edition. The extract begins 'I hesitated' and ends 'You mean Sir Laurence Olivier.')

3 *Eden Close:* **Anita Shreve**

   How does Shreve use dialogue and other stylistic techniques to explore ideas about family?

   In your answer you should refer closely to the extract printed below and to **one** other episode in the novel.

   (For the extract, refer to pages 110–11 in the Abacus paperback edition. The extract begins ' "I've been calling all afternoon," Martha says at once' and ends 'There is a silence.')

4 *Waiting for Godot*: **Samuel Beckett**

How does Beckett use dialogue and other dramatic techniques to explore Vladimir and Estragon's feelings about Pozzo and Lucky?

In your answer you should refer closely to the extract printed below and to **one** other episode in the play.

(For the extract, refer to pages 30–1 in the Faber paperback edition. The extract begins '*Estragon* (*timidly*): Please Sir' and ends *Estragon* (*not to be outdone*): A disgrace. He resumes his gnawing.')

5 *Equus*: **Peter Shaffer**

How does Shaffer use dialogue and other dramatic techniques to explore Alan's relationships with his parents?

In your answer you should refer closely to the extract printed below and to **one** other episode in the play.

(For the extract, refer to pages 27–8 in the Penguin Modern Classics edition. The extract begins '*Alan* (*jumping up*): Dad!' and ends '*Alan*: I'm sorry old chum.')

6 *The Caretaker*: **Harold Pinter**

How does Pinter use dialogue and other dramatic techniques to explore the battle for dominance in the relationship between Aston and Davies?

In your answer you should refer closely to the extract printed below and to **one** other episode in the play.

For the extract, refer to page 23 in the Samuel French hardback edition. The extract begins '*Davies* (*after a pause*): Eh, look here, I been thinking' and ends '*Davies*. Bells? (*He moves down LC*)'

Learning outcomes for this section:

Knowledge, understanding and skills

Now that you have completed Section B of this unit, you should be able to:

- explain how speech is represented in dialogue in both novels and plays
- show an understanding of the ways in which stylistic and dramatic techniques are used in texts
- use relevant linguistic and literary concepts and terminology in your analysis of texts
- integrate the knowledge you have gained both in Unit 1 and in your study of speech in Section A of this unit with the new material covered in Section B
- apply your knowledge and understanding appropriately in selecting and commenting on extracts from your set text in the examination.

Transferable skills

Your study of this unit and Unit 1 has provided you with a framework of terminology and concepts that you will be able to use in your A2 studies. The skills you have acquired should include the ability to:

- use appropriate terminology in support of your analyses
- compare different types of text
- create a piece of your own work based on a set text
- write fluently and coherently.

Revising for the examinations

The most important prerequisite for achieving the highest possible marks is to enter the examination room thoroughly well prepared for what you need to do. This includes knowing your set texts thoroughly, understanding which assessment objectives apply to each question and understanding how to apply relevant techniques so that you put all of your knowledge and skills to their most effective use. Revision for the examinations is important but must be seen as the culmination of many months of consistent hard work. A couple of weeks' intensive revision can never be an adequate substitute for consistent application throughout the whole course of study.

Re-reading the relevant sections of this book will highlight what you need to do in the examination for each unit but there is some general advice that can be applied to all of the examinations you will face in English subjects.

Know the rules

Make sure that you know the following:

- How long is the examination?
- How many sections does the examination contain?
- How many questions do you need to tackle, and from which sections?
- How many marks are available for each question?
- How long should be spent on each question?
- Is it an open book or a closed book examination (that is, are you allowed to refer to an unmarked copy of a set book during the examination or must you memorise quotations and rely on memory only for making references to the book during the examination)?
- Which Assessment Objectives apply to the examination?

Mind the GAP

Some of the examination papers require you to write in a creative/imaginative/transformative mode. For such questions you need to plan very carefully to ensure that the writing you produce is appropriate to the task which is presented to you. The three key considerations are:

Genre

Audience

Purpose

Genre

The task may require you to write a letter, a report, an extract from a novel or short story, a newspaper report or a magazine article, for example. Make sure that you produce writing that matches the specified genre. Your own reading should be sufficiently wide to enable you to be familiar with a wide range of genres and sub-genres so that you are able to make informed decisions in the examination about what genre conventions you need to incorporate into your writing to make it as authentic as possible.

Audience

The task will also specify (directly or by implication) the target readership for your answer. You may be required, for example, to write for a general adult audience if your task is to produce a serious report for a national daily newspaper such as *The Times* or *The Guardian*. Your approach would need to be modified if you were asked to write for *The Mirror* or *The Sun*, to reflect the different audiences and the distinctive approaches of tabloid newspapers.

Purpose

The task specified on the examination paper will also identify a purpose for your writing, and you need to be quite sure that you reflect that purpose accurately in what you produce. You may, for example, be asked to analyse a problem; it would be a serious mistake to interpret that as a request for a persuasive piece which embraces a particular solution and tries to influence readers to accept that solution to the exclusion of all others.

As with your judgements about genre and audience, your interpretation of the purpose of the task should be firmly rooted in the wording of the task. Examination questions are worded carefully to make them as clear as possible, NOT to try to catch you out. Candidates' misjudgements about genre, audience and purpose invariably arise from a failure to read the question carefully or a wilful insistence on answering a different question from the one set.

The Triple T Test

For all questions it's also helpful to apply the Triple T Test: have you understood the:

- task
- timing
- techniques required for success?

Task

Any examination is a test of what you *know*, what you *understand* and what you *can do*. Knowing the texts you have studied is vital, but in itself is not enough to guarantee that you will do well in the examinations. On one level, knowing the text may simply mean that you know the plot well and can recount it faithfully in fine detail. However, your examination question will definitely NOT ask you simply to re-tell the story of a novel, a play or a poem. If that is what you do in your answer you will severely limit the credit which an examiner will be able to give your work. Knowing the text well at AS level means knowing the plot well but also knowing about the writer's distinctive uses of language and structure in his or her exploration of themes and ideas.

Make sure that you understand exactly what the questions or task require you to do. The first and the most obvious step – but one neglected by a significant number of candidates – is to read the question closely and analyse it in terms of what you, the candidate, need to do in order to produce a relevant and effective response.

Timing

You need to know exactly how much time you can afford to spend planning and writing each answer. In examinations that consist of two or more sections, it is vital that you relate the time you devote to each question to the number of marks available. Depending on the nature of the question or task, you will need to spend time planning your response. In the case of questions on unseen texts, it is vital that you allocate enough time to read and annotate the text thoroughly. Refer carefully to the advice given earlier in this book about the techniques that need to be applied to particular questions in the examination.

Technique

When you write about a set text or a text encountered for the first time in an examination paper, you need to demonstrate your understanding of those aspects of the text that are relevant to the question or task. The essential strategy is to be able to identify relevant aspects of the text, to select relevant evidence to illustrate those aspects, and finally to write about your chosen evidence in such a way as to fulfil the requirements of the question. This process is shown in the flowchart below:

Point ⟶ Evidence ⟶ Explanation

If you approach your examinations with a firm grasp of this approach, you will make the best possible use of your knowledge and understanding and have the confidence that you will achieve a grade that reflects your abilities.

Further reading

Margaret Atwood, *Negotiating with the Dead: A Writer on Writing*, Virago, 2003

Robert Eaglestone, *Doing English: a guide for literature students*, Routledge, 2000

Stephen Fry, *The Ode Less Travelled: Unlocking the Poet Within*, Arrow Books, 2007

Sidney Greenbaum, *The Oxford English Grammar*, OUP, 1996

Ron Norman, *English Language and Literature: An Integrated Approach*, Nelson Thornes, 1998

Andrew Taylor, *A Plum in Your Mouth: Why the Way We Talk Speaks Volumes About Us*, HarperCollins, 2006

Glossary

A

Abstract noun: the name given to a thought, feeling, idea or concept; for example, happiness, imagination, destiny.

Accent: the characteristic pronunciation features and speech rhythms of a speaker, usually related to regional or social influences.

Adjacency pair: a pattern of speech in which one utterance is followed by an appropriate linked response.

Alliteration: the repetition of an initial consonant sound.

Allusion: a reference to another work of literature or other source by a writer. The writer may well assume that the reader has some knowledge of the work referred to and will understand the allusion.

Antagonist: a character who is in opposition to the protagonist, who creates conflict with the main character.

Antihero: the main character of text who lacks the conventional heroic qualities.

Antithesis: the juxtaposition of contrasting words or phrases to create a sense of balance or opposition between conflicting ideas.

Antonym: a word or phrase which is opposite in meaning to another, for example, *hot and cold, fat and thin.*

Aside: a brief line or speech spoken by a character to the audience, and unheard by the other characters on stage, in which the speaker reveals inner thoughts and intentions.

Assonance: repeated vowel sounds.

Asyndetic list: a form of list, in which there is no conjunction (such as 'and' or 'but') separating the final two items. This can give an open-ended feel to the list, perhaps suggesting there is more that could be added. The opposite to this is a syndetic list, such as 'At the market I bought apples, oranges, pears *and* bananas'.

Atmosphere: the characteristic mood or feeling conveyed by a literary work, as created by the author's choices of setting, action, characterisation and language.

B

Bathos: a sudden descent from elevated language or subject matter to the ordinary or the commonplace. Often used for comic effect.

Byline: the name of the writer shown at the top of a newspaper report or article.

C

Caesura: a pause in the middle of a line of verse, usually indicated by a punctuation mark.

Caricature: a portrayal of a character in which certain features are exaggerated, usually for comic effect.

Chaining: the linking of a series of adjacency pairs to build up a conversation.

Chronological order: the sequencing of events in the order in which they occur in time.

Clause: a construction which contains, as a minimum, both a subject and a verb. It can stand alone as a sentence, as in 'I bought a book' (main or independent clause) but may be part or a larger construction, as in 'when I went out' (subordinate or dependent clause).

Climax: the most decisive moment of a play or other literary work, also referred to as the crisis.

Closed book examination: an examination in which you are not allowed to take your set text into the examination room.

Closed question: a question phrased in a way that offers the respondent only a limited choice of possible answers, usually with yes or no, or a one word answer; for example, 'Do you like cheese?'

Coherence: the continuity of organisation and meaning that unifies a spoken or unwritten text.

Cohesion: the grammatical and lexical devices, such as repetition and the use of pronouns and ellipsis, that link the parts of a written or spoken text.

Comedy: a play or other work intended to entertain and amuse the audience, in which the problems encountered by the characters are resolved happily.

Comic relief: a humorous episode included in a tragedy to relieve the emotional tension of the drama, which may also heighten the tension through the shock of the contrast.

Complex sentence: a sentence with two or more clauses linked by subordinating conjunctions.

Complication: the problems, dilemmas and conflict encountered by the characters in a play during the rising action of the plot.

Compound sentence: a sentence with two or more clauses linked by co-ordinating conjunctions.

Concrete noun: the name given to a physical object or thing; for example, car, book, sausage.

Conflict: the struggle or tension central to a drama, and leads to the development of the action.

Connotation: the associations and feelings we attach to words in addition to their core meanings;

for example, although 'smile' and 'grin' refer to similar facial expressions, the word 'smile' has connotations of warmth and friendship, whereas the word 'grin' may have connotations of falseness, malice or stupidity about it.

Consonance: repeated patterns of consonants.

Context: the social situation, including audience and purpose, in which language is used; this situation is an important influence of the language choices made by speakers and writers.

Continuum: an imaginary line running from one extreme to another showing a range of other possibilities in between. In discussing speech texts, a transcript of a casual conversation would be towards one end of the continuum and a formal legal declaration, such as the words of the wedding service or taking an oath in court, at the other.

Contractions: words abbreviated using an apostrophe, e.g. *we're* for *we are* and *can't* for *cannot*. Note that the apostrophe goes in the place of the missing letter or letters.

Co-ordinating conjunction: words such as 'and', 'but' and 'or' which are used to link together independent clauses; for example, in the sentence 'He likes swimming but he hates shopping' each clause could stand independently.

Crisis: the climax or most dramatic moment of a play.

D

Denouement: the final resolution of the plot in a play or novel.

Dialect: a variety of a particular language, characterised by distinctive features of accent, grammar and vocabulary, used by people from a particular geographical area or social group.

Dialogue: conversation between two or more characters represented in writing.

Direct speech: the use of actual words spoken, without modification, as part of a narrative, description or explanation.

Discourse markers: words or phrases that give structure to speech or writing, enabling a writer or speaker to develop ideas, relate points to each other or move from one idea to the next, e.g. however, likewise, in addition, in contrast, nevertheless, furthermore, therefore.

Dramatic irony: a situation in a drama where the audience is aware of something that some of the characters on stage do not know about.

Dynamic verbs: verbs that describe physical actions, such as 'jump'.

E

Elision: the running together of words or the omission of parts of words, such as 'gonna' for 'going to' or 'y'know' for 'you know'.

Ellipsis: the omission of part of a sentence. 'Hope you get well soon' is an example of ellipsis, as the pronoun 'I' has been left out. Ellipsis can also be represented by three dots (…) to indicate the missing part of the sentence.

End-stopped line: a line of verse with a punctuation mark at the end of the line to indicate a pause.

Enjambement: continuity of the sense and rhythm from one line of verse to the next without end-stopping.

Eponymous hero: a central character who gives his or her name to the title of a novel, play or poem, e.g. Othello, Charlotte Gray, David Copperfield.

Euphemism: the use of inoffensive or indirect words or phrases instead of word or phrases that might cause hurt or offence; for example, a euphemism for dying is 'to pass away'.

Exposition: opening part of a play or novel that introduces the main characters and explains the background to the story.

F

Falling action: the part of the plot of a play that follows on from the climax, leading to the close of the play.

Feet: units of rhythm consisting of particular patterns of stressed and unstressed syllables (see iamb).

Figurative language: language that draws an imaginative comparison between what is described and something else, resulting in an image that cannot literally be true, but which may enable us to perceive something more vividly or allow us greater insight into the story or character. See simile, metaphor and personification.

Fillers: sounds such as 'erm', 'um' and 'er' that speakers use to fill pauses in speech. Many speakers also use expressions such as 'y'know' and 'like' as verbal fillers.

First person narrative: a story that is narrated by a character from within the story itself, using the pronoun 'I'.

First person pronoun: the first person pronouns are I, me, myself. We use these words to stand in place of our name.

Flashback: the technique of shifting from the present to a scene in the past in order to show something of significance that has happened previously.

Free direct speech: direct speech presented without, or with minimal, reporting clauses such as 'he said'. Some writers also omit the speech punctuation in free direct speech.

Free indirect speech: a form of indirect speech that reports the words of a character, but omits the reporting clause such as 'he said that…'.

G

Genre: a class or category of text, with its particular conventions or language, form and structure; for example, short story, science fiction novel, Shakespearean comedy.

H

Hedge: a word or phrase such as 'maybe', 'perhaps' or 'sort of', used to soften the impact of what is said, or to make speech sound more polite.

High frequency words: words that are commonly encountered in written and spoken texts and are therefore likely to be to audiences.

Hyperbole: deliberate exaggeration, often used for comic effect.

I

Iamb: a metrical foot (or unit) with the rhythm: unstressed/stressed (x /).

Iambic pentameter: a line of verse with five iambic feet.

Idiolect: a combination of habitual language choices which is unique to an individual speaker, seen in such features as pronunciation, choices of vocabulary, phrasing and grammatical patterns.

Idioms: characteristic expressions used by speakers from particular groups. Formed from groups of words whose meaning is known through common usage rather than by their literal meaning, e.g. 'you're driving me up the wall'.

Imagery: in literary terms imagery refers to the pictures created by a writer's choice of language, for example, their use of metaphor or personification.

Inciting moment: an event that occurs early on in a play and triggers the rest of the action.

Indirect speech: also called **reported speech**. Speakers' words are referred to but not quoted verbatim and are usually preceded or followed by verbs such as *said* or *reported*. Speakers' words are transformed into a past tense account

Interruption: when a speaker begins to talk before the previous speaker has finished, in an attempt to take over the conversation and gain control.

Intrusive narrator: an author who inserts his or her own opinions into the story.

Irony: a mismatch or discrepancy between what is written or said and what is actually meant.

J

Juxtapose: to place side by side; in texts, writers may juxtapose ideas to create interesting or surprising effects.

L

Lexical choices: the vocabulary selected by a writer to create a specific tone or effect.

Literal language: language which conveys meaning according to the explicit, non-figurative sense of words or phrases.

Low frequency words: words that are not commonly encountered in written and spoken texts and therefore may not be familiar to audiences.

M

Main clause: a part of a sentence that is grammatically independent and may exist alone or alongside a subordinate clause.

Metaphor: a direct comparison drawn between two different things as if the subject really is the thing it is being compared to; for example, 'Her hands were ice-blocks' or 'He was a bear of a man'.

Micropause: a very short pause in a spoken text.

Middle-market newspapers: newspapers aimed at a readership expecting comprehensive news coverage but with a lighter touch than that of the quality papers.

Mode: the medium of communication used, usually speech or writing.

Modifier: a word or phrase which, when used in conjunction with another word, provides readers or listeners with additional detail or greater precision about the sense of that word.

Monologue: an extended speech delivered by a single character.

Monosyllabic words: words with only one syllable.

Mood: 1. (grammar) the function expressed by the verb form to create indicative sentences (e.g. he is speaking), imperative sentences (e.g. tell us what you think), interrogative sentences (e.g. What is you opinion?) and exclamatory sentences (e.g. be quiet!).

2. used interchangeably with the term 'atmosphere' to describe the characteristic mood or feeling conveyed by a literary work as created by the author's choice of setting, action, characterisation and language.

N

Narrative viewpoint: the perspective or point of view adopted by a writer in order to tell a story.

Narrative voice: the tone or style of a narrator's speech, which gives us an impression of the narrator's character.

O

Omniscient narrator: an omniscient narrator has a complete overview of the story, and can move freely between different characters and scenes, with full knowledge of everything that happens.

Onomatopoeia: the use of words that sound like what they mean, e.g. quack, hiss.

Open book examination: an examination in which you are allowed to take unmarked copies of the books you have studied into the examination room and refer to them if you wish as you write your answers.

Open question: a question that is phrased in an open-ended way so that the respondent can answer in a wide range of ways; for example, 'what sort of food do you like?'

Overlap: when a speaker begins to talk before the previous speaker has finished, perhaps because of their enthusiasm to join in the discussion or to show support for the speaker; an overlap is generally more cooperative and supportive, and less competitive than an interruption.

Oxymoron: apparently contradictory terms are placed together, for example bittersweet.

P

Paradox: an idea that seems to contradict itself, such as 'ignorance is bliss'.

Paragraph: a subsection of a written text, usually devoted to one main idea or stage in a narrative, comprising at least one sentence.

Paralinguistic features: non-verbal aspects of communication such as intonation or pausing, which work alongside language to help speakers to convey meaning effectively.

Parallelism: the repetition of the structure of a phrase or sentence, often for rhetorical effect; for example, 'that's one small step for man, one giant leap for mankind'.

Participle: parts of verbs which indicate present or past progressive forms (-ing) such as 'she is running/she was running' and past perfect forms (-ed), such as 'he shouted/he was shouted at'.

Pathetic fallacy: the literary technique of representing internal human states and emotions through the description of external details such as landscape and weather. In this sense 'pathetic' means arousing sympathy; in other words, the term 'pathetic' suggests that the landscape is in *sympathy* with a character's feelings. The word 'fallacy' reminds us that this supposed relationship is a deception: inanimate landscapes and weather systems cannot truly echo the feelings and emotion of people, even though writers might have us believe otherwise.

Pause: a short break in a spoken text, the duration of which is recorded in seconds, for example (2.0).

Pentameter: a line of verse containing five feet.

Personification: a form of metaphor where something that is not human is endowed with human characteristics; for example, 'the windows stared blankly'.

Phatic utterance: words spoken to establish social contact and express friendly intentions towards another person rather than to convey significant information (e.g. 'nice day today').

Phonetic spelling: the spelling of words to represent how they are pronounced (e.g. …'elp me orf this 'orse).

Phrase: in the hierarchy of grammatical units, the phrase comes between word and clause. There are five types of phrase:

Noun phrase (e.g. *the red dress*)

Verb phrase (e.g. *will be running*)

Adjective phrase (e.g. *nice hot sweet*)

Adverb phrase (e.g. *quite inexcusably*)

Prepositional phrase (e.g. *wherever* and *whenever*).

Polysyllabic words: words with more than one syllable.

Popular press: newspapers aimed at a readership expecting light entertainment as well as news.

Proper nouns: names of particular persons and places, e.g. London, Adam Smith.

Protagonist: the central character in a play.

Q

Quality press: newspapers aimed at a readership expecting serious and detailed news coverage.

R

Realism: a style of writing in which life is portrayed in an accurate, realistic manner.

Register: a type of language defined in terms of its appropriateness for the type of activity or context in which the language is used,

including the purpose, audience and situation of a piece of speech or writing.

Repair: a self-correction in spontaneous speech.

Repetition and replacement: a text pattern in which some words or phrases are repeated and others replaced, for example, 'We must plan for a strong economy, we must plan for full employment, and we must plan for a healthy nation.'

Reporting clause: a phrase such as *he said* or *she replied*, that accompanies spoken language and indicates who is speaking.

Resolution: the point in a play in which the complications of the plot are worked out and a conclusion reached.

Restricted narrator: a restricted narrator has only a limited view of the story, usually focusing on the experiences of a single character.

Rhetoric: the technique of using language persuasively in order to influence the opinions and behaviour of an audience.

Rhetorical question: a question that implies its own answer and is not used to elicit information but to achieve a persuasive effect (eg. 'Are we to stand idly by while our rights are trampled on by a dictator?').

Rhyming couplet: two lines of verse in which the words at the ends of each line rhyme.

Rising action: the part of the plot of a play in which the action develops towards the climax of the drama.

S

Second person pronoun: *you, your, yourself,* (or in older and in biblical texts *thou, thy, thyself*) in place of a name.

Semantic field: a group of words within a text relating to the same topic; for example, tyre, brake pedal, starter motor and exhaust are all from the semantic field of cars.

Semantics: the study of the meanings of words.

Sibilance: repeated use of the consonant 's'.

Side sequence: a sequence of utterances inserted into a conversation, which causes the main topic of the conversation to be temporarily suspended.

Simile: an imaginative comparison drawn between two different things, linked with the words 'like' or 'as'; for example, 'her hands were as cold as ice' or 'the man was like a bear'.

Simple sentence: a sentence with only one clause.

Soliloquy: a speech delivered by a character who is alone on stage, in which inner thoughts and feelings are revealed aloud to the audience.

Stative verbs: verbs that describe states of being and thought processes, such as 'to be', 'to think' or 'to seem'.

Stock character: a one-dimensional stereotypical character, often included to make a point or represent an idea rather than as a realistic portrayal of a person.

Style: the particular way in which a writer or speaker conveys his or her ideas.

Subordinate clause: this depends on the main clause; for example, in the sentence 'I went to a salesroom where I saw a great sports car.' The clause 'where I saw a great sports car' cannot stand alone.

Subordinating conjunction: words such as 'although', 'because' or 'unless', which are used to link a main clause to a subsidiary or dependent one; for example, in the sentence 'Although it was raining, the party was a success', the phrase 'although it was raining' is secondary in importance to the main point of the sentence – 'the party was a success'.

Subplot: a set of events that is secondary to the main story of a play, but which may enhance our understanding of the main plot, for example by mirroring or contrasting with the main events.

Subtext: the meaning beneath the surface of the spoken or written dialogue.

Symbolism: a writer's deliberate use of an object or action to represent an idea or concept beyond its basic meaning. For example, a white dove is just a bird on a literal level, but is often used to signify the idea of peace.

Synonym: a word that has the same or similar meaning to another word; for example, 'smile' and 'grin' are synonyms, as they mean more or less the same thing, but carry different connotations.

Syntax: the study of the way words are combined to form sentences.

T

Tag question: a phrase tagged on to the end of a statement to turn it into a question; for example, 'we're going to the zoo today, *aren't we?*' Words such as 'right', 'yeah' or 'OK' can also be used with the same function; for example, 'see you at sevenish, yeah?'

Text: the term used to refer to any piece of written or spoken communication; in this book, text may refer both to complete texts and to extracts.

Third person narrative: a story told from a less personal point of view than a first person narrative, such as from the author's own perspective.

Third person pronouns: the third person pronouns are he/him, she/her and it in the singular form, and they/them in the plural. They stand in place of nouns and names. They are referred to as

third person, as they follow the first person I/we, and the second person you.

Tone: the mood or feeling of a text.

Tragedy: a serious play, often portraying the fortunes and misfortunes of the main character. The central character, or tragic hero, is often of high status; his or her downfall results from a particular character flaw, such as Othello's jealousy or Macbeth's ambition.

Transcript: an exact written representation of speech.

Triplet: a pattern of three repeated words or phrases.

Turn-taking: the pattern of spontaneous interactive speech in which participants cooperate or compete for the roles of listener/speaker.

U

Understatement: the deliberate adoption of restrained language, often to achieve an ironic or humorous effect (e.g. 'It isn't very serious. I have this tiny little tumour on the brain.' J.D. Salinger, *The Catcher in the Rye*.

Utterance: a unit of spoken language, the end of which is indicated by a pause or a change of speaker. This term is often used to describe a 'spoken sentence', as an utterance may not follow the expectations and grammatical conventions of a written sentence.

V

Verbs: words which describe actions, such as 'to run' or 'to walk'.

Voice: the distinctive manner of expression that is characteristic of a particular writer or speaker, or of a created literary character.

Index

Acknowledgements

The authors and publishers wish to thank the following for permission to use copyright material:

British Broadcasting Company for an extract from the Gobstopper Show broadcast on BBC Tees; Bloomsbury Publishing Plc for extracts from Khaled Hosseini, *The Kite Runner*, Bloomsbury, 2003; Georges Borchardt, Inc. on behalf of the Estate of Tennessee Williams for extracts from Tennessee Williams, *A Streetcar named Desire*. Copyright © 1947 by The University of the South; The Conservative Party for an extract from a speech by David Cameron at the Conservative Party Conference, October 2005; Crown copyright © material is reproduced under Class Licence No. CO1 W 0000195 with the permission of the Controller of HMSO and the Queen's Printer for Scotland; Faber and Faber Ltd for extracts froam David Hare, *Murmuring Judges*, Faber and Faber, 1991; and Harold Pinter, *The Caretaker*, Samuel French, 1960; and Samuel Beckett, *Waiting for God*, Samuel French, 1965; Guardian News & Media Ltd for an extract from Ros Taylor, 'Inquest hears girl was 'probably strangled or smothered', *Guardian.co.uk*, 8.1.08. Copyright © Guardian News & Media Ltd 2008; Little, Brown Book Group for extracts from Valerie Martin, *Property*, Abacus, 2003; and Anita Shreve, *Eden Close*, Abacus, 1989; Lloyds TSB Bank plc for an extract from a Direct Marketing letter, September 2007; Palgrave Macmillan for an extract from Dennis Freeborn, *Varieties of English*, Macmillan, 1993; Private Eye Magazine, Pressdram Ltd, for an extract from 'Glenda Slagg "José M-m-m-m-Mourinho!?!!..."' *Private Eye* issue 1194, p16; The Random House Group Ltd. for extracts from Ian McEwan, *Enduring Love*, Jonathan Cape, 1997.

Every effort has been made to contact the copyright holders and we apologise if any have been overlooked. Should copyright have been unwittingly infringed in this book, the owners should contact the publishers, who will make corrections at reprint.